# Riding the Wind

Praise for other books by Peter Marshall

### Nature's Web: Rethinking Our Place on Earth

'For all its learning, this book is earthy and approachable, and I think essential.'

Walter Schwarz, Guardian

'An extraordinary book, of great learning and intellectual insight ... written at a cracking pace.'

Jonathon Porritt, Resurgence

'It should be read by everyone who cares for the planet.'

Philip Ball, editor of Nature

'Deserves to be a standard work.'

Edward Goldsmith, Ecologist

### Demanding the Impossible: A History of Anarchism

'Interest in anarchy as a legitimate political tradition was reawakened by the publication of Peter Marshall's massively comprehensive *Demanding the Impossible*, a brick-sized history that received rave reviews.'

Peter Beaumont, Observer

'Indispensable.'

Richard Boston, Guardian

'This very big book ... will be the standard work of reference until well into the 21st century.'

Colin Ward, New Statesman and Society

'Stimulating and funny and sad. What more can you ask of a book?'

Isabel Colegate, The Times

### William Godwin

'Marshall steers his course with unfailing sensitivity and skill. It is hard to see how the task could have been better done.'

Chosen as 'Book of the Year', Michael Foot, Observer

'The best biography for more than a century.'

Spectator

'Handsome and substantial, ... authoritative and up-to-date, comprehensive and scholarly.'

Times Literary Supplement

'A labour of love, a magnificent scholarly undertaking which must long remain the standard work on the subject.'

Historical Journal

# Riding the Wind

## A New Philosophy for a New Era

*'He could ride the wind, and travel wherever he wished ...*
*Among mortals who attain happiness, such a person is rare.'*
*Chuang Tzu, c.350 BC*

## Peter Marshall

CASSELL
London and New York

By the Same Author

*William Godwin*
*Journey through Tanzania*
*Into Cuba*
*Cuba Libre: Breaking the Chains?*
*William Blake: Visionary Anarchist*
*Demanding the Impossible: A History of Anarchism*
*Nature's Web: Rethinking our Place on Earth*
*Journey through Maldives*
*Around Africa:*
*From the Pillars of Hercules to the Strait of Gibralta*
*Celtic Gold: A Voyage Around Ireland*

Cassell
Wellington House, 125 Strand, London WC2R 0BB

370 Lexington Avenue, New York, NY 10017-6550

First published 1998

**British Library Cataloguing in Publication Data**
A catalogue record for this book is available from the British Library.
ISBN 0–304–33425–1 Hardback

Typeset by BookEns Ltd, Royston, Herts.
Printed and bound in Great Britain by CPD Wales, Ebbw Vale

# Contents

Contents

*For Elizabeth*

# Acknowledgements

This work was written by the sea in North Wales and by the river Tamar in Cornwall. I would like to thank my family, who have all inspired and challenged me in different ways: my mother Vera, my brother Michael, my son Dylan and my daughter Emily. Special thanks to Jenny Zobel, Colette Dubois, and my nieces Julie and Sylvie. Conversations and shared experiences with my close friends Jeremy Gane, Graham Hancock, Dei Hughes, Emily Gwynne-Jones, David Lea, Jonathan Lumby, John Schlapobersky and Peter Tutt have all left their affectionate fingerprints on the book. I am particularly indebted to Elizabeth Ashton Hill, John Clark and Richard Feesey for reading and commenting on different versions of the manuscript. Elizabeth has also given me warm encouragement throughout. Fellow riders of the wind, thank you!

I would like to thank my editors at Cassell: Steve Cook, who took on the work; Jane Greenwood, who encouraged me during its early stages; and Janet Joyce, who brought it to publication. The copy editor Philip Hillyer did a fine job. Bill Hamilton has remained as efficient and insightful as ever.

Peter Marshall
Bromebyd
Easter 1998

# Preface

One day in the desert, a girl found a strange object which she had never seen before. It was hard, transparent and elongated at one end. She could make out the signs 'c' and 'o' on it, but did not understand what they meant. She took it back to the encampment of her people who lived in the desert and had never made contact with the outside world.

The members of her clan were astonished to see the object. Truly, it had magical qualities. It could pound nuts better than wood. It could carry water much better than ostrich eggs. It could make things larger if you looked through it. If it was held to the sun it could make leaves catch fire. Truly, it was a wondrous object.

But then the disputes began. Everybody wanted to use it. Neighbours who had lived peacefully together for years started fighting with each other. A group got together and kept it for themselves, forcibly preventing others from seeing it. They said it gave them special powers to tell them what to do. In the meantime, the hunting and gathering of food was neglected. The clan was heading for disaster as the dry season approached and they had not collected enough water to survive in the desert.

It was then that the elders intervened. They called a special meeting of the whole clan and asked whether they really needed this object which had brought such dissension and hard times on them. There were some very good arguments for and against, and at one stage the group who held it threatened to wreak vengeance on them all. But eventually, a young man with great powers of eloquence, who took the side of the elders, persuaded the others that they should get rid of the object and return to their old ways.

He was assigned to carry it to the country where the sun rose and where legend had it that there was a vast lake of water as far as the eye could see. He set off on a long journey. During many days, he crossed the burning plain, climbed over cold mountains, and eventually came to the shore of the great lake. He met many animals and birds on the way but no human beings. It was true that the water went as far as the eye could see. From the top of a high cliff against which the waves crashed, the young man took the strange object and threw it with all his might far out into the sea. The waves opened with a small splash and then it was gone.

He returned to his clan and when he arrived exhausted after many weeks' walking he found that they had returned to their old ways. Neighbours got on well with each other. They had enough water for the dry season. All their needs would be met.

They had been saved. But only for the time being ...

# INTRODUCTION

There is a growing sense of unease and confusion at the beginning of the twenty-first century. The winds of change are increasing in strength. We are deep in a transitional period, on the threshold of something new which is not yet fully defined. The prevailing mechanical and materialist world-view is crumbling but no new coherent model has yet emerged. We are aware of how we are destroying the planet, and yet somehow we are unable to change direction. We know that we cannot continue to maintain the present system for long but we are addicted to the good things it provides.

*Riding the Wind* offers a way out of the apparent impasse, a new philosophy for a new era. It openly questions and challenges many of the fundamental assumptions and practices of Western society. Combining ancient wisdom with modern insights, it proposes nothing less than a major shift in human consciousness and a new direction for Western civilization, a move away from mechanical thinking and mindless consumerism, away from endless growth and ruthless exploitation of the earth, towards a sustainable society and a vibrant culture in harmony with nature.

*Riding the Wind* develops the new philosophy of liberation ecology. Liberation ecology is holistic, deep, social and libertarian. It is holistic in approaching things from the perspective of the whole. It is deep in asking profound questions and going to the roots of things. It is social in tracing the ecological crisis to the presence of hierarchy and domination in society. And it is libertarian in seeking to free humanity, society and nature from their present burdens so that they can all unfurl and realize their full potential.

By developing a coherent philosophy of nature, *Riding the*

1

*Wind* offers firm ground on which to develop our moral values and social actions. It considers our limits as human beings as well as our possibilities. It explores those ideas and values which are essential if we are to ride the winds of change and to live well in the third millennium. Above all, it presents an imaginative and exciting way of healing ourselves, regenerating society and renewing the earth.

*Riding the Wind* invites you to go on a mental and spiritual journey, a quest to understand the world, our place within it, and our purpose in life. All it asks in return is for you is to have an open heart and an enquiring spirit and to leave your habitual perceptions and fixed ideas in the outer harbour of your mind as we set sail across the ocean of philosophy.

The following is offered not as a system but as a suggestion. It is only one possible formulation. Similar conclusions may be made from different beginnings. There are many tracks to the top of the mountain, and many ways through the forest. I invite you to accompany me on a less-travelled path. You may notice that others have gone before me; others will certainly follow. Yet on their journey, they may not see the same things or linger at the same spot. They may talk where I remain silent.

I do not see myself as anything more than a bridge, a stepping-stone, or a rope. Wise travellers will use them on their way but will leave them behind. I am no more than a ferryman to be forgotten as you continue your own journey.

# 1

# The Love of Wisdom

One day a young Greek philosopher travelling in
southern India came across some men sitting naked in
a circle on a rock in the noonday sun. The nearby
villagers had told him that there were wise men called
Brahmins to be found sitting on the rock. They sat in
silence, meditating. The traveller stood in the shade of
the rock for some time, fearful of disturbing them. They
ignored his presence as they ignored the fierce rays of the
sun. He waited. The sun gradually moved down in the
cloudless sky. The shadows on the ground lengthened
but still the Brahmins sat in the circle in silence. At last
the traveller, worried that he might not find shelter for
the night, plucked up enough courage to interrupt their
meditations and to ask a question.

'Excuse me, sirs', he said. 'I have come a long way
from a country in the West. I have come all this way to
ask you about the nature of the universe. Will you
discuss the subject with me?'

There was a long silence. At last one of the men, the
one with the whitest hair, opened his eyes and turned
slowly to the intruder. His thin lips broke into a broad
smile. His brow was calm, his glance serene, his eyes
steady.

'Of course', he said, beaming. 'As soon as you take off
your clothes and join us on this rock.'

Riding the Wind is a work of philosophy in the widest sense. By
philosophy I do not mean the nit-picking of pedants or the will to
power of academics. I look to the original meaning in the Greek

3

word *philosophos*, 'love of wisdom'. Philosophy in this sense is an activity concerned with the nature of the universe, our place within it, and how we should act. It is concerned with general principles and fundamental questions, the assumptions behind all the other branches of knowledge, first and last things.

And the Brahmins were right: to do philosophy well, it does not just involve the head but the whole of our being – mind, body and spirit.

The first woman on the savannah to raise her head to the sun and wonder what was its source, or to look at the new-born babe between her legs and ask where it came from, was the first philosopher. Philosophy further developed when people asked each other what was beyond the ridge, beyond the mountain, beyond the seas, beyond the sky, beyond death. It was triggered off by puzzlement and continued through curiosity.

On the canvas of one of his great Tahitian paintings, Gauguin asks, 'Where do we come from? What are we? Where are we going?'

In recent times it has become fashionable to dismiss such questions as unanswerable, insoluble. They are just so many bees buzzing in a bottle and it is the task of the philosopher to let them out and fly away. Yet these imponderables have an uncanny tendency to keep on posing themselves. As the third millennium begins, people are asking them with more frequency and more urgency than ever before.

Millions upon millions of us are seeking the answers to the big questions: we want to understand the riddle of the universe and the enigma of life on earth. We want to know whether the universe has any plan or purpose, or whether it is just an arbitrary combination of atoms. We want to know whether consciousness is a permanent feature of the universe or whether it is the result of random evolution on a tiny planet spinning in space. We want to know whether good and evil are inherent in the universe or just human creations. We want to know whether we will be able to survive the next catastrophe or whether life on earth is doomed. We want to know whether it is possible to live well on earth or whether we will forever be wracked with doubt, anxiety and confusion.

*Riding the Wind* does not claim to offer one easy answer to these questions, but it tackles them directly and aims to encourage the process of self-enquiry and personal growth. It is intended to awaken people from the slumber of materialism, of consumerism, of despair. To attain this we need to develop our reason, our intuition and our imagination. The sleep of reason breeds monsters, said Goya, but naked reason alone can lead to the cold, analytical planning of the destruction of the world. The heart must be bold enough to reassert its influence and reason sensitive enough to recognize its rightful claim. We need reason fired by feeling, informed by intuition and fuelled by imagination. We need to acknowledge the intelligence of the heart. We need a form of enlightened romanticism, a synthesis of reason and feeling, science and poetry, form and meaning, all within the shaping power of the creative imagination.

We therefore value the oldest tradition of philosophy which aims to release us from the cage of prejudices and dogma, from the habitual beliefs of our age or country. Its ultimate aim is to liberate us from our mind-forged manacles and to make us calm, wise and free. Such a philosophical approach unavoidably questions authority and encourages people to think and imagine for themselves. This is not always easy, as our traditional beliefs form part of our personality and we open ourselves up to censure and ridicule if we act out of part. But once the quest for knowledge has begun it must follow its course, whatever the temptations, tests and obstacles on the way.

By its very nature, an enquiry of this sort is bound to be subversive. It comes as no surprise that Lao Tzu went into exile or that Socrates was condemned to death. *Riding the Wind* questions the fundamental assumptions of Western civilization with its belief in inevitable progress through science and technology and its goal of material comfort. In the process it will also undermine the crumbling paradigm which asserts that evolution is blind, that Lord Chance rules, and that we are nothing more than naked apes or sophisticated biological computers. It will also refine and develop the new holistic and ecological world-view – already emerging everywhere – which discerns an implicit order behind the apparent chaos of the universe, pulsating life swimming against the stream of entropy, a living organism emerging from the shell of the megamachine.

Philosophy is primarily an activity, a process of thinking. Some make a shallow distinction between thought and action, as if they are two separate activities. To act without thinking, they say, is to make meaningless gestures; to think without acting is

5

shadow-play with spooks. But the distinction is false, for acting and thinking are inextricably connected as mind and body in the whole being. To think is to act, and thought is action. We reveal how we think in our actions, and how we act in our thinking. Thoughts are soaked in blood. The person meditating in his cave can influence the world as much as the person on the barricades. Whatever Marx might say, to interpret the world is to change it. By altering our consciousness, we change our being in the world.

Philosophy is also a way of life for those who take it seriously, not just a game of chess. Like a tree on a mountain side, it is rooted in the earth and reaches for the heavens, and the deeper it goes, the higher it reaches. It not only enables us to live well on earth but to prepare for death. Living is dying as much as dying is living. Through its careful practice, we can make contact with the ground of being, we can dive into the ocean of reality.

Just as we are all poets, so we are philosophers. As soon as we ask where we come from, what are we, and where are we going, we are asking philosophical questions and are being philosophers. You need no preparation for philosophy. Philosophizing is like swimming. The only way to swim is to get into the water. Sometimes it helps to dive into the deep end.

My own approach to philosophy is holistic. It is holistic in asserting that the whole is greater than the parts. It recognizes that everything is interrelated and interwoven in nature's web and that individual parts can only be fully comprehended in relation to each other and from the point of view of the whole. The various parts of nature are so interdependent that they cannot be isolated and abstracted without altering their identity and the organic unity of the whole. It is not possible to discover the essence of a complex thing by analysing it into its parts, nor can complex wholes be reduced to the simple properties of their parts. Beings and things are not isolated entities but form sets of relationships and their identity can only be understood with reference to each other. This is obviously true of an ecosystem but it is also true of the universe as a whole.

At the same time, holistic thinking does not deny the rich diversity of things and beings; indeed, it celebrates and honours them. It asserts that human beings are social beings who benefit from co-operation and mutual aid, yet equally recognizes the uniqueness of each individual and his or her autonomy. We are all products of our environment, all interrelated, but because of our consciousness and foresight we can change our circumstances and in the process change ourselves. Therein lies our freedom. We are part of the whole, in a metaphysical, social and moral sense, but we are also unique, autonomous, self-directing individuals. No one is an island; we are part of the main; but also we cannot relinquish our irreducible individuality. Indeed, the more social we become, the more we can realize ourselves as individuals.

Holistic thinking is dialectical in seeing that change takes place through the dynamic interplay of opposites. 'Without contraries, there is no progression' wrote William Blake. The opposing forces are not binary and separate, but two aspects of the whole. They are complementary and flow into each other. They can come together into a higher state of being through a process of preservation and transcendence. In logical terms, thesis and antithesis may be subsumed into a higher synthesis which contains them both. In biological terms, father and mother may be said to be united in their children. We can see this dialectical movement of change at work throughout nature. Without the interpenetration of opposites and their resolution, the world would remain in a static condition of rigid immobility.

Holistic thinking goes beyond mere description of the world to reveal it as it is. It identifies with the object of thought. To understand the formation of a glacier it makes sense to lie on a glacier and to imagine what it must be like to be millions of tons of ice inching imperceptibly down a valley and scouring its bed. Not content with geology and history of rocks, holistic thinking tries to think the being of the rock. To understand the behaviour of wolves, it can help to run with wolves in the imagination if not in the wild.

Holistic thinking involves contemplation and meditation. In the stillness of the world, in silence, it penetrates to the heart of matter and to the core of existence. In this process of contemplating a mountain, the mountain ceases to be a mountain before it becomes a mountain again more fully comprehended.

Holistic thinking is a form of reverential listening which tunes into the voice of the earth and the music of the spheres. It goes beyond analysis and unfurls in open receptivity. In stillness, it hears the heartbeat of Being. It involves letting go, floating with the living stream of life, riding the wind. The wise open their souls to the oncoming wave; they are surf-riders of the infinite.

Holistic thinking is organic in understanding the universe as a

7

living organism, more like an animal or a plant than a machine. It asserts the organic unity of the whole and denies the distinction between the inorganic and organic, the animate and the inanimate. Land, sea and sky are not just the dead backdrop or setting for life. Life is all-pervasive, in a child's cry, in a falling leaf, in a rain drop. A stone is 'alive' as a new-born baby is alive, but in a different way.

Holistic thinking goes beyond the dualism of mind and body, consciousness and matter. All that exists has a potential for consciousness and subjectivity. Mind is not just a Ghost in the Machine, as some modern philosophers would have us believe. We dwell in a world infused with life and consciousness. The computer in front me, the flower on my desk, the tree through the window, the cloud in the sky, my lover at my side are all alive and part of a living organism. The life force is an invisible current flowing through all things and beings, rising and falling, diverging and uniting, but ever present and always creative.

Ultimately, holistic thinking recognizes that all things come from the One and proceed to the One. All is One and One is All. There is unity in diversity throughout the universe; indeed, the greater the diversity, the more overall the harmony. It comes as no surprise that the Greek word *kosmos* originally meant both the universe and harmony: they are synonymous.

# 2

# The Way of the Universe

They had been there a long time. They were cramped and constrained. Their food was not fresh and the water was dirty. The air was stale and seemed to be getting worse. Their waste smelt bad and was building up. It was dark. They slept long hours. Some said, 'Go on'; others said, 'We can't go on.'

The only diversion was to watch the flickering world in front of them: the people there seemed to move and breathe more freely; they had fine clothes and ate good food; they copulated and fought each other.

Then it happened. The fighting people of the world disappeared and some new persons came, both women and men. They were dressed simply in white robes although their faces were of many hues. They had calm brows and steady gazes and walked gracefully. They came to them and undid their chains and turned them around and showed them the fires which had thrown the shadows of the fighting people on to the wall of the cave in front of them.

Many rubbed their eyes; they could not believe it. The figures they had taken to be real on the wall were just shadows thrown up by the fires behind them.

There was a dim ray of light shining into the dark cave. The newcomers held out their hands and offered to lead them to the light. Many of the people were confused and some rushed back to their seats opposite the wall and tried to put on their chains again. Others began fighting and copulating like the shadows had done. But a few took the

9

*hands of the newcomers and walked towards the light. It was difficult at first, for they were so used to the dark. But they grew in confidence as they moved up the passageway towards the light which shone brighter and brighter at every step. At last they came out of the cave and found themselves on the side of a great snow-capped mountain. Below them a sparkling river ran between trees in a green valley under the deep blue sky.*

*Some grew angry and looked up at the noonday sun and were blinded and stumbled back into the cave. Others remained quiet and sat down and gradually became accustomed to the light.*

*So this was the real world. They had awakened.*

Many modern Western philosophers have been keen to draw the limits of possible knowledge, to show that the limits of our mind and our language leave us in a conceptual and linguistic cave in which we cannot know the sky above or the earth below as they really are.

It may well be that the structure of our minds – the way it imposes categories of time and space and causality on to the external world – makes it impossible for us to know the ultimate nature of things in themselves. Through our mental processes we may only know appearances and not the reality of objects around us: things as they appear, not as they are. What is the inner being of the red rose in the thin glass vase beside me on my desk?

But this does not mean we cannot know the nature of reality.

Our language – and its grammar and logic too – limit our knowledge. The limits of our language limit our world. 'What we cannot speak about we must pass over in silence', said Wittgenstein. By learning a new language we learn a new way of perceiving and experiencing the world. I do not know all the words by which the Inuit know 'snow'; I am all the poorer. I do not know all the conditional cases that the Australian aborigines have in their language; my sense of the future is different.

The logic of my first language, English – like all European languages – is based on a binary logic which states that there is an excluded middle: something is or is not. Since this is the case I cannot express clearly the shades of affirmation and negation between 'Yes' or 'No' which, for instance, the Japanese can in their language.

My language also suffers from being based on a subject-predicate form which encourages me to think in terms of subject and object, person and the world, as if they are separate and opposed to each other. 'I' am not 'the world', it implies; the 'other' is not 'me'. It denies the ineradicable nature of our 'being-in-the-world' and undermines a sense of relationship with all things. By contrast, Chinese does not have a rigid subject-predicate form and does not require the personal pronoun attached to a verb: 'am' stands for 'I am'. Perhaps this helps explain the greater sense of relationship in Chinese thought.

We may dwell in the house of language, but light shines through the windows from afar and we can see another world beyond the walls.

Ultimately things escape words. Because a baby has no word for the breast it does not mean that it does not seek it out. To name a thing is to limit it. We try and control the world by classifying and naming things but they will always escape us. To know the nature of things it is not enough to know the names for things. We must leave words behind and experience things directly. The purpose of a spade is to dig a hole. When the hole is dug the spade is forgotten. In the same way, the purpose of words is to communicate ideas and feelings. When the ideas and feelings are well said and easily grasped, the words may be forgotten.

If the mind and language can only offer a limited view of the world, then perhaps sensory experience is a surer guide. Yet our senses are notoriously unreliable. In the desert, we think that we can see an oasis, but it is a mirage. In a storm at sea, we may see green light shining at the masthead, but it is St Elmo's fire, an effect of electricity in the air. We might see the sun disappear at noon and think that it is the end of the world, but it is only an eclipse as the moon temporarily obscures it from us.

Experience is not always a reliable guide, even of causality. Because something has happened before, it does not mean that it will happen again. Human experience tells us that the sun will always rise in the east. The chicken sees the sun rise in the east and a hand comes down with grain. One day the sun rises and the hand comes down but this time to wring its neck.

But this does not mean we cannot know the nature of reality.

If we dwell on external form, we can easily be misled by appearances. A philosopher once saw a sign in a shop window which said 'Trousers Pressed Here'. He returned home to fetch

**11**

his trousers, but when he went into the shop with them, he found out that only the sign was for sale.

What is real and what is imagined can often be very confusing. In my twenties, when I was living in London, I heard a knocking on the door of our shared house at dawn. Thinking it was the milkman, I went down bleary-eyed in my dressing gown in order to pay him. On opening the door I was thrown against the wall by armed men. They searched the house and were particularly interested in one man who was a teacher at a local school. It turned out that when my friend had taken his trousers to be pressed at a local laundry, the woman thought that he looked like an IRA terrorist. She had mistaken his identity. The armed men said they were from the Anti-Terrorist Squad. After they had left as rudely as they had arrived, without apology or explanation, I rang up the local police station. They said they had no record of the Anti-Terrorist Squad visiting the area. There was no way of checking. Had the incident really taken place?

But this does not mean we cannot know the nature of reality.

Those analytical philosophers who are eager to draw the limits of knowledge create for themselves their own conceptual and linguistic caves in which the imagination languishes and intuition grows mouldy. Analysis is not enough. To dissect is to murder.

To know something in depth you have to identify with it. You cannot know what a horse is like unless you have galloped across an open plain or along a beach; it is not enough to cut it up in a laboratory. The same is true of the external world or nature. We can only know it well if we live within it, dwell in its embrace, see ourselves as a thread in its intricate web. We can only understand a mountain if we climb a mountain and be like a mountain. We can only get to know the sea if we live by the sea, swim in the sea, and drift with its currents and feel the pull of its tides. Yet even this offers only a partial view of reality.

There are many different understandings. Logical positivists early in the twentieth century claimed that only empirical and logical statements made any sense because they are open to proof. A logical statement is true or false according to whether it follows the laws of logic; its truth will depend on its internal coherence. An empirical statement can be true or false depending on whether it corresponds to the observable world; its effects can be tested and disproved. Metaphysical and moral statements, on the other hand, are strictly speaking senseless because they cannot be shown to be true or false. As such, they are no better than expressions of feeling; they are best passed over in silence.

But this does not mean that we cannot know the nature of reality.

Metaphysical and moral beliefs are the foundation of our being in the world and what most inspire our thoughts and actions. Analytical reasoning and sensory experience certainly have their place in the search for knowledge and meaning, but first principles in metaphysics and ethics are based on intuition, and intuition can be a profound and reliable guide. The heart has its reasons that reason cannot comprehend. We have to learn to listen to our hearts, to feel the heart's rhythms, to understand its language, and to appreciate its intelligences. We should acknowledge the true promptings of our inner voice of intuition. The ancient Chinese appreciated this when they said that the organ of thinking is not the head but the heart.

It is often in moments of peak experience, epiphany or ecstasy, that we suddenly have an insight into the nature of things, into the heart of reality. We can prepare ourselves for the moment, but cannot predict when it will come. After many years of careful preparation, the moment of enlightenment, the point of seeing into the nature of reality, might be triggered off by a tiny and insignificant event: the song of a bird, the falling of an autumn leaf, the curve of a wave. If it is a real and lasting insight, it will be translated into our everyday life.

Certain experiences can shape our whole mental and spiritual lives. They can be good or bad in the sense that they can be negative or uplifting; either way they help us on our path to understanding.

In my mid-twenties, as a deliberate philosophical experiment I took LSD for the first and last time in my life with two friends in the country. Lying on the grass in a tent, I had at first the impression that I was not talking to my friend but to his father, then his grandfather, and then his great-grandfather and so on until I was conversing with his remotest ancestors. I had gone back in time; next, I began to travel in space.

The roof of the tent burst into thousands of sparkling gems, full of wondrous colours and refracted light, each gem reflecting all the others. They were like drops of dew in a spider's bespangled web. I was no longer in a tent but in a Hindu temple. I

13

left the shelter of the temple and went out into the starry night and lay down in the grass to look up at the sky. The stars whirled round and round as in a Van Gogh painting. For a while I felt protected by the presence of ancient oak trees around me. But it was not for long. I suddenly felt a great energy pulling me up to the heavens. I tried desperately to remain in my body, to be grounded on earth, fearful that if I let go I would never return. The pull of space became irresistible as if the laws of gravity were no longer operating on me. I repeated my address in London to myself like a mantra, but I gradually forgot the words. My last contact with the earth was my telephone number; I saw it in great numbers in the sky, but they began to crack up and crumble, until they finally disappeared into dust.

As I left my body, I felt I was still attached to the earth by a thin purple silken cord but it snapped. I had no choice except to leave and whoosh through interstellar space where there was nothing living and nothing welcoming. I do not know how long I travelled out of my body but it seemed like aeons. The next thing I was conscious of was a feeling of hooks being dragged through all the veins of my body; the pain was excruciating. The hooks became broken glass. Then I came to. It was dawn. An orange-red sun was rising over a golden field of ripening wheat on a hill. I was lying in a ditch, entangled in brambles which were cutting into my skin. But it was only for a brief spell. I was off again into space. Then I returned. One moment, I was on earth, the next in space. Gradually the spells on earth grew longer. I was slowly returning to my body and the world. I was freezing cold and in great pain. I had experienced, I told myself, a bad trip.

But it was more than just a bad trip. The experience had a deep metaphysical significance for me. Although I had not slept all night, I found that I had manic energy which could only be exorcized by striding around the perimeter of a large field. As I walked, I kept telling myself in disbelief that the world is a pile of dry stones and there is no ultimate meaning. There is no God, no soul, no life after death. I felt terrible. I had had the opposite of a mystical experience, an experience of the world not as living spirit but as dead matter, as what Coleridge called 'an immense heap of *little* things'.

'I will not give myself up to despair', I told myself. Henceforth I would have to build the edifice of my life on a recognition that the world is nothing more than an accidental combination of atoms spinning in space. I would have to try and create meaning where there is none. In a world without values, I would forge my own. I would roll my stone up to the top of the mountain and know that it would always roll down before reaching the summit. I would accept stoically that there is no afterlife and I, my species and the solar system are doomed to extinction sooner or later. I would devote myself in the short time I had left on earth to changing society and to creating a better world.

I am no longer an existentialist. I am now certain that the universe is not a dead machine ruled by Lord Chance, but a living being evolving in a beneficent way, something one and indivisible. It has a soul or spirit. This became clear to me during certain experiences in the wilderness, in the West African rain-forest, far out at sea in the Atlantic, at the top of Mount Kilimanjaro, a hundred feet down off a coral reef in the Maldives. Sitting by a log fire in my cottage by the sea in North Wales, I am still sure. The realization brings me not despair but tranquillity and joy.

The creation is a living spirit; it forms a self-sustaining organic whole; it is very good and there is nothing to fear. The world is an *anima mundi*. It has a spirit and a language all can understand. This is not just wishful thinking on my part but a firm conviction. I now know that the vision at the beginning of my journey into space was the accurate one: the universe is a vast web of jewels in which each one reflects all the others and all are inseparable from each other. One is All and All is One.

Soul and spirit are often used interchangeably. In many ancient languages, the root meaning of 'soul' and 'spirit' is 'breath'. The word for 'spirit' in Hebrew (*ruah*), in Greek (*psyche*), and in Latin (*spiritus*) means breath. The same applies for the word for 'soul' in Sanskrit (*atman*), in Greek (*pneuma*) and in Latin (*anima*). The common intuition amongst the ancients was that soul or spirit was the breath of life. The ancients rightly saw the rational human mind as only one aspect of the soul or spirit, and they did not distinguish between the activity of consciousness and the process of life itself. The mind is not a thing but a living process.

The soul has generally come to mean that part of a person – the spirit of a person – which lives on after the death of the body. It is the essence of a person; we can relate to a person's soul, as we can to their body; we can become soul mates. Definition becomes even more confused because many cultures see spirit as a being born of the soul. The soul is deeper, more primordial. In many

15

stories, the spirit enters a body to gather news of the ways of the world and to carry them back to the world soul.

I sense that spirit is a kind of life force which animates the body of all living things. The words 'animal' and 'spirit' both find their roots in the Latin word *anima* for 'breath' which is associated with living from earliest times. When a person dies, their spirit leaves them. I have never personally experienced spirits floating about in the air, interfering with human affairs, but I have as in all things an open mind. To talk about the spirits of the woods and streams is for me a poetic way of saying that nature is animated by living forces. Spirit is intangible and incorporeal and its presence can only be felt by intuition rather than proved by science. But even people who claim to be materialists often talk as if a person does have a spirit: we can be in high spirits but we can also have our spirits broken.

In a wider sense, I sense spirit is something all pervasive in the universe, some invisible but palpable presence in all beings and things. The ancient Hindus described Brahman as spirit infused in all things, the medieval alchemists believed in an *anima mundi* (world spirit), while native Americans talk of the Great Spirit. It is close to a pantheistic view, which identifies God with the world, or an animist view, which sees immaterial force animating the universe – views which I find far more appealing and plausible than the idea of a transcendental God outside the creation. The universal presence of spirit inspires the sense of wonder and awe which I experience when faced with the mystery and grandeur of the universe and its unfolding potential for goodness, truth and beauty.

To talk of soul and spirit is to talk a very ancient language, to sing a very deep song. It recognizes that there are deep forces at work which are more than meet the eye; forces for life, vitality and creativity. To deny all existence of soul and spirit is to live in a flat, dry and impoverished world. If you think that nature is a dead machine it is a short step to treat it as such. Even a materialist and atheist has a sense of what it means to be soul mates or kindred spirits; it is the language of an ancient way of experiencing the world which is still relevant.

Some people have soul, some don't. Black Americans say they have soul music, eat soul food, and are soul sisters and brothers. Soul is linked to energy; someone can be the life and soul of a party or a movement. To have soul is to have something deep and intuitive, like natural rhythm or special insight. Some music and dance has more soul than others. Jazz has soul and so does flamenco, but not always. It depends on the musicians and the dancers and the situation. A mediocre performance can suddenly take off, as if new creative energy suddenly enters all those involved, both players and audience. Lorca called it in Spanish *duende*; he found it especially in the *cante jondo* – deep song – of flamenco singers, songs which like the blues are about life, death and love.

We have all experienced this deep song in ourselves and in others, especially in moments of creativity, when dancing, singing, painting, writing poetry, performing an experiment, making love, or even cooking a meal. Everything suddenly takes off and is performed with spontaneous ease. We enter a new plane of consciousness, a state of heightened perception. Whatever is done is done well. Everything seems to fall into place, without really trying. Life takes on a new intensity and meaning. One is inspired.

Some call it passing through the gate of power. The body takes over its own rhythm, like running down a steep hill and feeling that you are riding the wind as your feet choose their own path.

The Romantic poets described the experience as if a Muse had taken them over. Often when you first start writing, it feels like an uphill struggle, the words don't come, the ideas seem stale, the feelings flat, but then suddenly everything begins to flow – you feel inspired. You are in a state of animation.

It is difficult to define this *je ne sais quoi* which suddenly erupts; it is *duende*, it is soul. Those who have experienced it often describe it as if it were a creative energy which does not come from them but through them. It is as if some greater force is using you as a channel. You are no longer playing music; music is playing you. You are singing a deep song; you have soul.

The world for me is animated with spirit in that it is alive. Not only individual humans and other animals seem to have spirits, but even trees and rocks. Individuals also have souls. I suspect that the soul may well live on after the death of the body. I am looking forward to finding out.

But how can I know this? My deepest intuition tells me so. The inner voice, if you are quiet enough to hear it, is the surest guide. It can be heard in meditation, it can be heard whenever we are still, calm and open. It works when we are not consciously thinking. Like the voice of the earth, it has a clear and distinct timbre. Water becomes clear when it becomes still; so does the mind of the person who would be the mirror of the universe. By observing the processes of nature, by being still, it is possible to become vividly aware of what is.

How can I be sure that my inner voice is not the voice of a trickster? Because it is clear and carries its own conviction; because it is life-affirming; and because it enables me to settle into the deeper flow. And a sign of truth is that it makes one feel calm and free.

Although I aim to present sound reasoning and arguments for my beliefs in this book, I make no attempt to offer proofs. I am not a rationalist, but at the same time I am not a complete irrationalist. As we sail on the ocean of life, our passions and feelings might be the wind, but reason is our compass. Reason can free us from the bondage of our passions and can help us to understand and direct our feelings. But there is more under and beyond the sun than the eye can see and reason can comprehend. The last act of reason is to recognize its own inadequacy.

Logical and empirical statements can be demonstrated and proved according to the accepted rules of their disciplines. Two plus two equals four according to the conventions of mathematics. The daily setting of the sun can be demonstrated by appealing to observation and experience. Metaphysical and moral questions, like the nature of reality and right conduct, cannot be proved or demonstrated in a similar way. This does not mean they are just expressions of subjective feeling but it does mean that they require different treatment.

Rather than proving claims by disputation, it is better to see all things in the light of direct intuition. Intuition enables us to discover things when all else fails. There is an old Taoist story that one day a man went out for a walk along the seashore and lost a night-coloured pearl on his way home. He sent out Science to find it and got nothing. He sent Analysis to look for it and got nothing. He sent Logic to seek it out and got nothing. Then he asked Nothingness, and Nothingness had it.

But how can we distinguish between truth and falsehood? Modern Western philosophers maintain that a statement is true if it is internally coherent (that is, it follows the laws of logic and grammar); if it is self-evident (that is, clear and distinct or based on deep conviction); or if it corresponds to reality.

18

But truth and falsehood are not absolutes any more than right or wrong. Yes is Yes in the light of No is No. Happiness when pushed to the extreme can become disaster. Nothing but the truth can be false. Right turns into wrong, wrong turns into right. Clouds become rain and rain becomes clouds. The flow of life alters circumstances and thus things are altered in their turn.

Reality is obscured if we understand only one of a pair of opposites, or concentrate on a partial aspect. Opposites produce each other, depend on each other, complement each other. Yes is Yes in the light of No is No. Why oppose No against Yes, falsehood against truth?

Truth and falsehood are related to each other like the two ends of a pivoting arm. When the wise person grasps the pivot, he is in the centre of the circle and there he stands while Yes and No pursue each other around the circumference.

Truth is not only relative but it can also be subjective. What is true for me is not for you, and what is true today can be false tomorrow. Truth flows into falsehood as hot into cold and vice versa.

The truth is often paradoxical. It can be reached not only deductively, inferring from general principles to the particular, or inductively, from the particular to the general, but tangentially, from an angle. It can be neither this nor that.

What then is the nature of Ultimate Reality? It cannot be defined but it can be sensed. It cannot be put into words or comprehended as an idea but it can be felt. It follows that those who know do not speak of it, and those who speak of it do not know it. By speaking thus, I reveal my ignorance!

Can a part comprehend the whole? Can a frog in a well understand the ocean? Can you throw a net over the wind?

Ultimate Reality is the organic whole. It is immanent in all things, on earth as in heaven: in a blade of grass and in the North Star, in a cell of your body and in the Milky Way. Every centre is its circumference. If you say you understand it, you probably don't. But a child playing with a twig in a stream knows it instinctively; a bird flying in the sky follows it. It is what happens of itself.

Ultimate Reality is the groundless ground of Being and non-Being, the primordial continuum, the mother of all. It is prior to nature and the source of all energy and life. When and how it came about, I do not know. I can only observe its effects. I do not know its name. It cannot be conveyed by silence or noise. I will borrow the translation of the Chinese word *Tao* for it, because it seems closest to my understanding of the nature of reality. Tao nourishes and sustains all and gives it shape and life. It exists by and through itself. It is beyond words and concepts: 'The Tao which can be spoken is not the eternal Tao'. It is before heaven and earth, older than God and younger than a new-born babe. It does nothing but leaves nothing undone. It is the way of the universe, the grain in wood, the fibre in muscle, the pattern of a snowflake, the flow of water. Humans are born into the Tao like fish into water.

Ultimate Reality is the ground of Being and non-Being. They are different aspects of reality and one cannot exist without the other. In the West, we are trained from childhood to perceive Being rather than non-Being, what is rather than what is not. But non-Being is at the centre of our being. Life has no meaning without death, any more than light has without darkness. The ever-present possibility of our own death is the basis of our life. Living and dying are inextricably linked like a Celtic design of animals and plants.

In the West, we are brought up to see the solid objects in a field, not the space between them. In paintings, we skate over the blank areas. We do not like to read between the lines. We are impatient with silence. In the East, there is a greater appreciation of the space between objects, of Nothingness at the heart of Being. It is the hollow at the centre of a hub which enables the wheel to turn. Windows turn a prison into a dwelling. Usefulness comes from what is not there as much as from what is there.

Nothingness is not just a vacuum, any more than space is a neutral emptiness. It embraces all things; it is the heart of all things. 'To be' and 'not-to-be' arise mutually.

One day a man went into a shop and asked to see a jug. He examined it minutely. He then asked the owner to put his hand in the jug and feel the hole in it. The owner felt carefully all around the inside, and declared indignantly: 'You're just wasting my time. There's no hole in it!' As he left the shop, the stranger replied, chuckling: 'Your arm is inside the hole!' It is the hole in the jug which makes it useful, the Nothingness or non-Being at the heart of Being.

How does Ultimate Reality manifest itself in the universe? The universe is a constant process of transforming energy. This is a

20

world-view held by ancient sages, shamans and modern physicists. The exact origins of the universe remain a deep mystery, although there are many myths about its creation.

In Hindu myth, in the beginning was the primal person who divided into male and female and the two halves made love. The female then transformed herself into various kinds of animals, and out of the union with the male, they procreated all the different species. In the *Chandrogya Upanishad*, it is also said that the creation comes from a primal egg: 'In the beginning this world was merely non-being. It was existent. It developed. It turned into an egg. It lay for a period of a year. It was split asunder. One of the two egg shell parts became silver, one gold. That which was silver was the earth. That which was of gold was the sky.'

The Jews and Christians have the account in Genesis. Modern scientists have the myth of the Big Bang – the primal orgasm – which took place some 15 thousand million years ago. But the origins of the universe remain obscure. Why did it happen? What came before the creation? Looking at it in a linear way, searching for a beginning, one always comes up against a deep mystery. If there was a primal man, an original egg, a Creator, a Big Bang, who or what created them?

This causal, linear way of thinking always ends up with the paradox of the unmoved mover. The pursuit is pointless, like a cat chasing its tail. There is no need to go in search for the beginning and the end. The world is and we are. Why seek unnecessary complications?

What we do know is that change is a permanent feature of the universe. As the Greek philosopher Heraclitus observed: 'You cannot step twice in the same river, for fresh waters are ever flowing upon you.'

How does change occur? Change occurs through the dynamic interplay of opposites. The ancient Taoists called the complementary forces *yin* and *yang* which together constitute *ch'i* (matter-energy) of which all beings and phenomena are formed. The Chinese ideograms of *yin* and *yang* originally referred to the sunless and sunny sides of a mountain. *Yin* is the supreme feminine force, characterized by darkness, coldness, passivity and associated with the moon. *Yang* is the masculine counterpart linked with brightness, warmth, activity and the sun. They are further associated with the yielding and firm, weak and strong,

21

dark and light, falling and rising, after and before, short and long, earth and heaven. But these apparent opposites are not in a state of war, but complementary – more like lovers embracing than warriors fighting. They are also in all things and beings – including ourselves – and are responsible for the endless diversity of life within the overall unity.

In the famous Taoist symbol of an S in an O, the objective (white) emanates from the subjective (black) just as the subjective emanates from the objective. They constantly wax and wane like the moon. Both are fundamentally interrelated and flow into each other: black contains white and white contains black. They seem like black and white dolphins, forever playing together. Yet each polarity is contained in the other and one cannot exist without the other. The apparent contraries of subject and object, beauty and ugliness, good and bad, dark and light therefore spring from subjective individuality and limited vision; from the perspective of the whole, all such distinctions are transcended.

Energy flows between *yin* and *yang*, the negative and positive, the female and male. I have my female side and my lover has her male side. We complement each other, flow in and out of each other and ourselves.

This is a dialectical way of looking at the world. It is a simple rhythm to dance, a rhythm which reveals the world as it is. The whole evolves through the reconciliation of opposites. What went before is taken up by what comes after. In metaphysical terms, non-Being arises with Being which is united in Becoming. In nature, an oak produces an acorn and out of the acorn grows a new tree which eventually replaces the old tree. The process is vital to the life of the forest. In a similar way, two squirrels produce offspring who take up their different characteristics and take their place after their death. And so life continues and everything is taken up. Life is a process of creative self-realization through the dialectical interplay of complementary forces.

From the standpoint of the whole, opposites are two aspects of the same thing, like the sunny and shaded sides of a mountain, two profiles of a face, two faces of a coin. Since all opposites are polar they are united: the way up and the way down is one and the same. Being and non-Being, light and dark, life and death, negative and positive, north and south are not in conflict but integral aspects of a larger whole.

The universe forms an organic whole. The Chinese called the whole, the Tao. Tao existed before humans made distinctions between things and beings and named them. How it works is not clear. It operates mysteriously and secretly. It has no fixed shape and follows no definite laws. It is unfathomable. 'Tao produces both renewal and decay', wrote Chuang Tzu, 'but is neither renewal or decay. It causes being and non-being but is neither being or non-being. Tao assembles and destroys but is neither the Totality or the Void.'

Everything is interrelated in the whole. Of this we are certain. When the British soldier plunged his bayonet into the stomach of an Indian monk who was meditating, the holy man raised his dying eyes and said: '*Tat tvam asi*'. The translation of the ancient Sanskrit is 'That art thou'.

Not one thing is better or worse from the standpoint of the whole. On the scale of being, higher is not better than lower. From a moral point of view, good and ill are one. When we look at things in the light of the Tao, nothing is best, nothing worst. Each thing, seen in its own light, stands out in its own way. It can be seen to be 'better' than something compared to it on its own terms, but when seen in terms of the whole no one thing stands out as 'better'. Tao is great and complete in all things.

If we cannot know the origins of the universe, can we be sure that it exists? How can I be sure my study exists when I am not in it to perceive it? Certainly things are not always as they appear. What appears to be a snake at first sight in the shade of ignorance, is recognized in the full light of knowledge to be a piece of rope. Common sense can lead us to common folly. But although I can sometimes be mistaken by appearances, I am certain that the external world does exist. The world is out there. I do not have to hit a tree with my boot to realize it. It is not just an illusion. All fixed forms and categories – things, events, ideas – are impermanent and transitory, but the world exists; it stands out of nothingness. That is a certainty on which I build the dwelling of my life and thought. And like all first principles in mathematics, logic, metaphysics and ethics it is based on direct intuition.

My mind constructs the world to a degree; it brings it forth in a particular light. If I had a different perceptual and conceptual apparatus, it would not appear the same. The world does not appear to me as it does to a fly with a thousand-sided eyes. As a person is, so he sees. If he sees nature as a dead machine, it follows that as an inextricable part of nature he must see himself as a dead machine.

In the act of perception, the human mind and the external world both play an interrelated part. This might be called a process of 'mutual arising': as the universe produces our consciousness, so our consciousness evokes the universe. 'To be' and 'not to be' arise mutually. The sun would not be light without eyes, nor the universe exist without consciousness. There is therefore a mutual fitness between me and the world, between the microcosm and the macrocosm, the person and the planet. The mind is exquisitely fitted to the external world just as the external world is fitted to the mind. Our relationship is one of mutual interdependence. I am the world and the world is me: we are part of each other. Thou art that; that art thou, *tat tvam asi*.

I am a being-in-the-world, not separate from it. I am not a passive observer, but an active participant, an involved subject. There is a unity between subject and object, perceiver and perceived. My relationship with the world is also one of care. I care for the world as I care for myself. If the world is sick, then it affects me. If I am sick, the world can cure me. It is not a relationship of 'I–it', the human subject and the external object. It is a relationship of 'I–thou', the lover and the loved, a relationship which can become a 'we' and an 'us'. We are both threads in the seamless web of nature.

# 3

# Nature's Web

*Within the seeds of things there are germs. When they find water they develop in successive stages. Reaching water on the edge of land, they become a scum. Breeding on the bank, they become the plantain. When the plantain reaches dung, it becomes the crowfoot. The root of the crowfoot becomes woodlice, the leaves become butterflies. The butterfly suddenly changes into an insect which breeds under the stove and looks as though it has shed its skin ... Combining with an old bamboo which has not put forth shoots ... This begets the leopard, which begets the horse, which begets man. Man in due course returns to the germs. All the myriad things come out of germs and go back to germs.*

Lieh Tzu

Modern science confirms ancient wisdom that the universe is a dynamic web of relationships, vibrating with life. We sail on a vast, multidimensional ocean of cosmic energy out of which has evolved life and consciousness. The old reductionist, mechanistic paradigm still prevails in the way we think and talk about everyday matters, partly because of the inescapable presence and profound influence machines and technology have in our lives. People still talk of the mind as a computer, the body as a machine, and farming as a chemical process. But many are beginning to wake up to a much more exciting and unpredictable world.

The new paradigm has been evolving since the nineteenth century, with process philosophers like Hegel and Whitehead and evolutionary theorists like Darwin. Science in the twentieth century has had an even greater influence, with relativity theory, quantum physics, systems thinking, biology, ecology and, more recently, chaos theory. The fresh model for the universe which is emerging is not the dead machine of the old physics, but the living organism of the new life sciences. We have moved from the mechanistic world view of Descartes and Newton to a holistic and ecological one. The result has been a fundamental shift in our thinking and perception. We are witnessing nothing less than the rebirth of nature.

The word 'nature' can be confusing. It has at least three main meanings. It can denote the essence or character of something (as in human nature or the nature of wood). It can mean the inherent force which influences the world (as in Mother Nature). Or it can refer to the entire world itself, the given, the creation, nature as a whole. The latter can be taken to include or exclude human beings, as the phrase 'man and nature' implies. In one sense everything that exists is natural, including whatever humans do, but it makes sense to contrast the 'natural' – what is given – with the 'artificial' – what humans create from the natural with their artifice. Humans in the West have gone far in leaving the natural world and their natural desires behind them, creating an artificial world of artificial desires. In the process they have depraved their natures and injured nature as whole. To 'return to nature' is therefore a return to health and to the harmony of the natural world before it was distorted by humans.

Rather than being a machine governed by universal laws, the most accurate and suggestive metaphor for nature is that of a web. Nature (as a whole) not only consists of an invisible web of forces but the entire universe is a collection of animated fields. It is a constant process of transforming energy. Being and non-Being combine to form Becoming. The smallest particles of matter, according to quantum mechanics, are not separate entities, hard packets of atoms, but vibrating waves of energy (quanta). Moreover, nature is not just an accidental combination of atoms but has an underlying pattern and shows signs of self-organization and self-regulation. Nature has a spontaneous order.

Newton depicted the universe as a machine governed by the eternal and immutable laws of time and space. Certainly we impose a grid of time and space on the world in order to make dates and places: without them, I could not meet you outside a railway station at a particular time. But since Einstein's relativity theory, time and space are no longer considered separate and unchanging co-ordinates; indeed, they form a kind of continuum which is curved in the presence of dancing matter. They are dynamic qualities in an interrelated universe: the curvature of space and time not only affects but is affected by everything that occurs in the universe. Time is relative and space is not the container, but a constituent of the material universe.

Far from being universal and unchanging, the so-called laws of nature may best be described as regularities observed by humans in one corner of the universe. The smoothness and uniformity we discern in the universe may be simply a result of the way we see it. The pattern observed here in our solar system might not apply elsewhere. A different intelligence might well organize the universe into more than three dimensions and discern different regularities at work. Other worlds may have followed different laws. A scientific theory is therefore nothing more than a model of the universe, or a particular part of it, and the laws of nature a set of rules which relate observed quantities in the model to our understanding. When talking about the laws of nature, we are therefore really talking about ourselves.

We should be clear that we are talking about probabilities, not certainties; about perceived rhythms, not iron laws. Indeed, a natural law in this sense is best understood as a tendency or even a trend, as something which on the basis of past experience and observation is likely to continue for the foreseeable future but which may not always do so. And the laws themselves are evolving as the universe itself evolves. The scientists' dream of discovering all the laws of a totally predictable universe is a fantasy of the wildest imagination, comparable to trying to know the mind of God.

Although science offers an interpretation rather than an objective description of nature, it does not follow that the world is a mental construct and the laws of nature are figments of the human mind. The world as a harmonious whole is not just *maya*, an illusion, although it may be if we just dwell on its parts. The external world exists independently of the human mind, although its exact nature remains obscure. The laws used to describe it may not be eternal and immutable, but neither are they mere constructs of the disembodied mind. They are based on repeated observations and can be tested. They may be best understood as habitual trends in which the habits themselves are temporary and change within evolving nature.

Since the findings of relativity theory and quantum physics, we have become used to the idea that we live in a very dynamic and changing universe which it is impossible to predict with absolute confidence. The old goal of scientific determinism to predict everything once we knew the state of the universe at any one time is obsolete. All one can talk about sensibly is statistical probabilities. The old claim of scientists to be objective observers is a myth: the very process of observing nature changes what is being observed. The very act of measuring the position of a particle will change its velocity in an unpredictable way. Again, causation does not operate in a smooth way, with like causes regularly producing like effects. Jerky transitions take place from one form of energy to another through quantum leaps. Unpredictability thus lies at the heart of matter, spontaneity and creativity at the centre of nature.

After relativity theory and quantum physics has come chaos theory. Originally a concept developed in mathematics, it has been applied to all the disciplines of science. Many seemingly regular movements in nature, such as the swing of a pendulum, the beat of the heart, the drip of a tap, the collisions of atoms in a gas, on closer scrutiny appear random. Weather is notoriously difficult to forecast because of the number of variables involved – the old saws based on thousands of years' experience such as mackerel sky and mare's tails auguring bad weather are almost as reliable as the latest satellite pictures. There are many other movements in nature which cannot be easily predicted – the curve of a wave, the fall of a leaf in a waterfall, the form of a snowflake (every one is unique). Some ecologists have even suggested that chaos theory makes their efforts to discern a balance in nature impossible, whether applied to fluctuations of wildlife populations or the diversity of plant species within a habitat.

Chaos theory is a science of process rather than stability, of becoming rather than being. It confirms the ancient Taoist insight and the view of the Greek philosopher Heraclitus that nothing is permanent and that all is in flux. Nevertheless, even within chaos theory, an underlying pattern is observable in the way events seem to take place randomly. There may well be principles not yet discovered which influence the organization of complex systems. A general law of disorder, a kind of deterministic chaos, may emerge.

Einstein, rejecting the random implications which some philosophers and scientists drew from quantum physics, once said that God does not play dice with the universe. Chaos theory suggests that nature does play dice, but it may be with loaded dice. Perhaps a better analogy might be that nature plays poker with a pack of cards with a certain number of suits. The exact order of the cards cannot be predicted, but there are certain parameters and a limited number of possible combinations. And there may be some invisible jesters in the pack ....

At a deep level, modern science confirms the ancient belief that there is an underlying pattern in nature. Within what appears to be chaos may lie a more mysterious order. Moreover, chaos and order are not mutually exclusive within a larger whole. Indeed, like *yin* and *yang*, they are complementary principles which enable change to take place. Chaos and order, like the Greek gods Dionysus and Apollo, are both necessary for creation. The artist releases form from within the chaos of experience, just as the composer creates out of harmony and discord the overall beauty of music. In the Hindu tradition, it is understood that Brahma, the god of creation, Shiva, the god of disorder, and Vishnu, the god of preservation, are three essential elements in the process of birth, life and death in the earthly cycle.

Nature, any more than the universe, is not random. It has a spontaneous order. It has no fixed symmetry and is unique – like the crystals in a snowflake or the ripples of sand at low tide – but it follows a certain organic pattern which is to human eyes invariably graceful and beautiful. The pattern is more like a supple process than a rigid law. It is not fixed and static, like the Ten Commandments carved in stone, but like billowing clouds in the sky or flowing water in a river.

There is indeed a pattern in the grain of wood, the fibres of muscle, the constellation of the stars, the matrix of the universe. Within the unbroken wholeness of the totality of things, there is an implicit order. We can therefore be confident that for all the surface turbulence there is at a deeper level within nature a discernible pattern and order, like the slow-moving currents of the oceans below the storm-tossed waves.

But what about entropy? Is not the universe losing energy and becoming more disordered? Will not the universe, created in a Big Bang 15 thousand million years ago, be heading for a 'heat death' in five thousand million years time? This is the scenario which some scientists infer from the second law of thermodynamics, known as entropy, which states that there is a loss of energy during changes in a closed system which leads to increasing disorder. As a result, the universe is inexorably running down and will eventually succumb to a 'heat death' in which there is no more energy to do work. If this is the case, the universe is destined to eternal darkness. The prophets of gloom are vindicated.

There is, however, something which swims against the current of chaos. It is the life force, the deeply mysterious *élan vital*, which counteracts the tendency towards entropy in a discernible way. Life in its broadest sense may be defined as a process which increases the complexity of forms by converting energy. When an organism can no longer grow or maintain itself it dies. The inevitable death of some organisms enables others to live. As Erwin Schrödinger, pioneer of quantum physics, argued: 'A living organism has the astonishing gift of concentrating a "stream of disorder" on itself and thus escaping the decay into atomic chaos.' The apparent chaos of nature thus provides a basis for evolutionary creativity.

Individuals can experience this sudden burst of creative energy when they feel an overflowing abundance of life. In such a state, they feel capable of doing anything, and indeed often achieve apparently 'superhuman' tasks. If this happens to humans, who are nature rendered self-conscious, then it must happen to the rest of nature. And since they are microcosms of the universe, it must happen to the macrocosm of the universe.

The modern life science which has most changed the way we think about nature is ecology. It developed out of the new 'systems' way of thinking which sees things in terms of relationships, contexts, networks and webs. It is a form of process thinking which looks for interactions and connections. It is the very opposite of Descartes' method of analytical thinking, fundamental to earlier science, which breaks down wholes into parts. The systems approach is holistic and integrated, holding that the properties of parts can only be properly understood from their relationships in the organization of the whole. Rather than taking something apart to understand it, it puts it into the larger context. It is interested not so much in the basic building blocks but in the fundamental principles of organization.

This way of thinking comes through not only in quantum physics but above all in ecology. In its broadest sense it is the study of the *oikos* (Greek for household) of the earth. Ernst Haeckel, the German biologist who coined the word in 1866, defined it as 'the science of relations between the organism and the surrounding outer world'. It has come to mean the study of the relationships between all members of the Earth Household. An ecosystem is a community of organisms interacting with their physical environment as an ecological whole. It is concerned with the totality of a community and its environment. An ecosystem can be centred on a single plant, a wood, or the entire earth. Most organisms are complex ecosystems themselves. The term 'web' rightly gives a sense of the interdependent and interwoven nature of all life.

Nature is therefore a complex system of interacting processes, a vibrating web of energy and life. One event does not occur at a time, nor do events operate in sequence. Each system which is part of the whole can survive only if it continues to react with its surrounding systems, giving and taking. A flame, for instance, requires combustible material and takes oxygen from the air; it gives in return ashes and heat and gases.

To see nature as a web of interwoven and mutually dependent organisms goes beyond the old idea of the Chain of Being. This depicted nature as rising in hierarchical fashion from the lowliest creature to the highest, from earthworms to lions, from plants to animals, humans to angels. Living systems, it is now clear, do not form hierarchies but rather networks at different levels. An ecosystem is a network of organisms, in which each organism forms a node, with each node itself a network of organs and so on. In the past, applying their hierarchical ideas of society to nature, scientists placed the 'higher' systems above the 'lower' ones like a pyramid. But in nature's web there are no hierarchies, only networks nesting within networks, rather like Russian dolls. There is no 'above' nor 'below', let alone 'superior' and 'inferior' species. Any 'level' looked at in a system is really the level of the observer's attention. The most important organisms for the continuance and flourishing of life on earth are not the mammals but bacteria.

Nature forms a vital, spontaneous order. The ancient Chinese phrase for 'nature', *tzu-jan*, may be literally translated as 'of-itself-so'. It may also be translated as 'spontaneity'. Modern science confirms this ancient view that nature is spontaneous, self-generating, self-organizing, self-regulating, self-sustaining and self-renewing. It exists by and through itself, without beginning and end. There is no need to postulate a Creator or an ultimate goal. All parts of the single organism regulate themselves spontaneously.

Out of the flow of nature emerges a spontaneous order. Because of the mutual interdependence of all beings, if left alone, nature will find its own equilibrium, its own unity in diversity, its own stability in change. If not forced into conformity, all beings will harmonize their interests. This is true in nature as well as society. Without external compulsion, harmony will prevail. We humans can oppose the spontaneous order of nature by trying to impose our own pattern. We can try and conquer and redirect it to our narrow ends. But nature will always have the last word and reassert its course, just like the water from a stream will eventually break through a dam built by a child.

The new science of physics, the life sciences, and above all ecology, confirm the ancient wisdom that the universe is a dynamic network of relationships vibrating with life. It may not be governed by eternal and immutable laws, but it has an underlying pattern. Its surface chaos gives way to deeper order. In its evolving field of energy, there is ample room for freedom, spontaneity and creativity; indeed, it thrives on it. In the language of ancient wisdom, the universe has a world soul; in the language of modern physics, it is a field of animated forces. The dead machine of the Scientific Revolution has been resurrected as nature's web.

# 4

# Creative Evolution

*At the beginning of all things Mother Earth – Gaia – emerged from Chaos and bore her son Uranus as she slept. Gazing down fondly at her from the mountains, he showered fertile rain upon her secret clefts, and she bore grass, flowers, and trees, and with the beasts and birds proper to fill each. This same rain made the rivers flow and filled the hollow places with water, so that lakes and seas came into being.*

*Along then came Father Time, Chronus. Uranus fathered the Titans upon Mother Earth but she persuaded them to attack their father after he had banished his other rebellious sons, the Cyclopes, to the Underworld. Led by Chronus, they surprised the sleeping Uranus and Chronus castrated him with a sickle and gave him to his mother. The Titans then released the Cyclopes and gave dominion of the earth to Chronus, Father Time – with his sickle.*

Time is a central part of our being-in-the-world. The ancient Chinese and Greeks saw it as for ever moving in a circle, but in the West we have adopted the Judaeo-Christian view of time as moving in one linear direction – an arrow of time, from past, present to future. The world has a beginning and will have an end.

In the universe all is flux. There is no complete or given form of subject or substance, but a universal process of substance-becoming-subject. Everything evolves, the seasons come and go, the moon waxes and wanes, and we are born, grow old and die. We measure the passing of the seasons by a year, the rising and falling of the sun by a day. We mark the passage of time during

33

the day by reference to the steady rhythm of a clock. The resulting calendar time is a grid we impose on nature, a grid which is not entirely exact, hence the need for a leap year. This objective, calendar clock time is measured as a succession of discrete moments – years, days, hours, minutes, seconds. It depicts time in spatial terms, as a sequence of events. It runs in a linear way, from A to B, from one millennium to the next. What goes before is the past, what is happening now is the present, and what is to come is the future.

Yet experienced subjectively, time is a constant state of flux, expanding and contracting according to our mood. We have all had the experience of an hour lasting a minute, and a day lasting an age. The truth of the paradox 'time stood still' is known to us all. Time here is experienced by intuition as a flow which is not measurable in relation to a standard. It coincides with our subjective experience of life as an indivisible continuum and not as a series of separate states or events. This experience of time as continuous duration is more real than clock time. The symbol of the clock in which time is measured spatially should not be confused with the reality of time as flux, any more than the map should be mistaken for the territory.

Time, as Einstein observed, is relative to our position in space. Indeed, as we have seen, the universe really forms a continuum of time and space. Commonsense notions of before and after, of past, present and future become hazy. An event on earth would appear to take place at a different time observed from Mars. A clock, because of the pull of gravity, ticks slower in a mine than at the top of a mountain.

We no longer live in a predictable universe in which all is given. The world is not the causal and determined machine of the Newtonian paradigm. The future is not predetermined by the past. The doors of the future are open to creative and spontaneous change brought about by the self-generating activity of nature itself. The laws of nature are not eternal and immutable, but observed regularities which hold for the present. The laws themselves are evolving and existing laws may be replaced by new laws as nature continues to evolve.

It is not clear whether time moves in circles, spirals, or in a straight line; indeed it would seem to be misleading to think of it in spatial terms. What is clear is that all things are in a state of flux, and that nature itself evolves. The events which take place in the world are irreversible: you cannot put your foot in the same river twice. Ever since Darwin, we have come to accept that the earth is thousands of millions of years old and that the geological record shows that land masses and seas have risen and fallen and different species have come and gone. Over 99 per cent of all species that ever existed have become extinct. Our species was very late to evolve and may become extinct early.

For Aristotle, it was clear that nature has a design and purpose (*telos*). The universe is a vast complex of organisms with each one striving to attain the end assigned to it. He explained the nature of an organism in terms of its potential and function. Every organism has a function of its own, and its pleasure is derived from the exercise of that function. The end of man is to use his reason which distinguishes him from the other animals. The end of nature is the pleasure of man.

Darwin on the other hand depicts nature as blind. Lord Chance rules. Evolution occurs through natural selection and the survival of the fittest, the 'fit' being defined as the best adapted to their environment. But it is the combination of chance mutations from a particular generation which make it more likely that its offspring will survive and breed. In modern genetic terms, the fittest will depend on the random shuffling of the genes of the two parents which determines what characteristics will be passed on.

The teleological approach of Aristotle is too deterministic and the evolutionary approach of Darwin too random. Aristotle does not allow for creative evolution, while Darwin denies all purpose. Yet it seems that there is an underlying order on which natural selection operates. Evolution is neither random nor predetermined, but there is a discernible tendency towards growing diversity, complexity, consciousness and subjectivity. Although it may not have an overall design or fixed purpose, living nature does appear to be mindful.

Evolution is a holistic process and not merely a mechanism of adaptation and can only be understood adequately by examining the interaction and interdependence between species, ecosystems and the earth as a whole. At the heart of evolution, there is also a creative urge. An intrinsic quality of all living systems is the creative unfolding of life. The life force manifests itself in all the numerous varieties of living forms. This, more than chance, might well be the cause of variations which are passed down from generation to generation and eventually form new species. It

35

operates like an invisible current, first emerging at an unknown time in prehistory, diverging and intensifying, expanding consciousness and subjectivity. All beings and things partake of the life force, but it manifests itself to the greatest degree in the most conscious animals such as humans and whales.

There may even be 'morphogenetic' fields within and around organisms which contain a kind of collective memory on which a member of the species draws and to which it in turn contributes – the biological equivalent of the collective unconscious. In this way, the biologist Rubert Sheldrake has argued, the habits of species are built up, maintained and inherited. The evolutionary process therefore evolves both habit and creativity. Without creativity, no new habit would emerge; without the influence of habits, creativity would lead to a chaotic process of change. Through evolutionary creativity, new patterns of organization come into being and through repetition the patterns become habitual if favoured by natural selection.

Living organisms would therefore seem to inherit not only genes but also morphic fields responsible for their habitual patterns of behaviour. A developing organism might be able to tune into the morphic field of its species, drawing on a collective memory. The existence of such fields may explain the behaviour of schools of fish or flocks of birds which seem to act as a single organism. The exact nature of these fields cannot be described, but they do have observable and testable effects.

At the same time, evolution is not just a case of organisms adapting to their environment. The environment itself is shaped by the web of living systems. The evolution of living organisms and the evolution of their environment form a single evolutionary process: they are partners in co-evolution.

From this perspective, the future is not predetermined by the past in a totally predictable world. The doors of the future are open to creative and spontaneous change. There is no inherent purpose or final cause; the observed laws of nature are merely the shapes which nature temporarily takes. They may be replaced by new laws as nature continues to evolve. But there is a tendency towards greater consciousness, diversity and complexity which, as the most powerful species on earth, humans can either encourage or check. They are now jeopardizing their own existence by reducing biological diversity and spoiling their own dwelling-place on earth.

Life on Earth began around 3500 million years ago and humans first emerged in East Africa about 3.5 million years ago – 5 seconds before midnight in a 24-hour day. At some stage in prehistory as tool-using animals, they developed their consciousness to such an extent that they were no longer attached by biological specialization to a particular niche. As conscious, unspecialized creatures, they were able to live and flourish in different habitats and climates on earth. Since then they have colonized planet earth and seek to colonize other planets.

From the first nature of natural evolution, they passed into the second nature of cultural evolution. They have now developed their powers and control over nature to such a degree that they are capable of directing the future course of evolution, whether it be through genetic engineering or the destruction of habitats and species. Through consciousness we can escape the chains of necessity, but we can also impose new manacles on ourselves and the rest of the creation.

But how does this process of evolution take place? Darwin argued that evolution occurred through the natural selection of the fittest in a struggle for existence in the natural world. Although Darwin carefully defined the 'fittest' as the species most adapted to its environment, his notion of the survival of the fittest was misapplied to society by many Social Darwinists who argued that certain nations, classes, races, or individuals were 'fitter' to flourish and rule than others. Furthermore, his depiction of the struggle for existence not only led many to see nature as 'red in tooth and claw' which needed taming by man, but was also used as a natural justification for competition in society.

Darwin made clear, however, that he used his term 'struggle for existence' in 'a large and metaphorical sense, including dependence of one being on another, and including (which is more important) not only the life of the individual, but success in leaving progeny'. He was also careful to use the terms 'higher' and 'lower' not in a moral sense, but in the neutral way as a geologist describes different strata of fossils. He was also struck by the overall harmony of nature and 'how plants and animals, most remote in the scale of nature, are bound together by a complex web of relations'. These caveats were overlooked by those who wanted to use his theory as a 'scientific' justification of their vision of the state of nature as nasty, brutish and short and of society as a war of all against all.

37

It has become increasingly clear that one of the most important factors, if not the most important factor, in evolution is mutual aid rather than competition. The most co-operative species seem to be the ones who are most successful in surviving and reproducing. Even the most insignificant organisms are important to the well-being of others. Sociability is therefore the greatest advantage in the natural and social world. The real struggle is not between individuals or species but against adverse circumstances.

Rather than organisms being merely gene-machines for selfish genes to reproduce themselves, it now seems that symbiosis plays a crucial role in evolution. The presence and influence of small cells living inside larger cells show that mutual dependence is a main avenue of evolution among all life forms. Ever since the emergence of nucleated cells over two thousand million years ago, life on earth has developed through increasingly intricate arrangements of co-operation and co-evolution.

Ecology, the study (*logos*) of the Earth Household (*oikos*), and ethology, the science of animal behaviour, have also shown countless examples of reciprocity and symbiosis within species and across species, from clown fish living amongst the tentacles of sea anemones, and hunting dogs who look after their elderly and infirm, to elephants who grieve for their dead. Left to themselves, trees flourish by their association in a forest, mutually assisting each other in preserving the conditions for survival. A forest is the triumph of the organization of mutually dependent species. Indeed, the whole of creation forms a Tree of Life which nurtures the soil and other species with its dead leaves only to be nurtured in its turn.

The Gaia hypothesis supports the insight of ancient wisdom and modern ecology that the earth is a living organism in which the whole is greater than the parts. It further confirms the view that the greater diversity of life on earth, the more overall harmony and stability there is. From this perspective, evolution is a process of change in which the earth as a living organism constantly seeks to create a diversity and a balance which are conducive to the continuance of life.

Gaia is not only evolving but is also a single living entity. The space shots of earth show that it is a marvellous green and blue globe, fragile and alone, spinning gently in infinite space. Its layer of life – the biosphere – converts energy from the sun to create all the myriad forms of living beings. To see it as a dead machine, or even as a sophisticated computer, is to be guilty of the most ostrich-like, flat-earth mentality. Even the geological crust is only a thin skin on a hot, molten ball with its own internal convection currents.

The very presence of life on earth makes the conditions appropriate and comfortable for its flourishing. The process of life itself, for instance, has made the right balance of gases in the atmosphere for it to continue. Long ago, there was virtually no oxygen and nitrogen on earth, but it has evolved to have a relatively constant ratio of 21 per cent oxygen to 78 per cent nitrogen, which is ideal for complex life forms. The life forms themselves now regulate and adjust the quantity of gases to maintain a climate which in turn fosters terrestrial life.

Gaia is not just an extremely complex system with regulatory properties, but a living organism. The physical and chemical world does not merely provide a backdrop or context for life, but is part of the life process. The old rigid divisions no longer hold between the physical and the biological, the inanimate and the animate, the inorganic and the organic. They are all inextricably interwoven. They not only interact with each other, but are integral parts of the larger living organism of Gaia. Gaia thus keeps the planet alive by regulating the chemical and physical environment. She also has an observable tendency to optimize the conditions for life on earth.

Human beings are the product of the long process of evolution of Gaia. They are amongst the most conscious and complex of life forms on earth. They are members of the community of life which infuses the whole planet and their society is a household within the Earth Household. We can perceive the world only because we are part of the sensible world we perceive. Gaia is perceiving herself through us.

As members of the earth community, we should act responsibly. Yet the activities of humans more than any other species affect adversely the conditions of life on earth and the future course of evolution. They interfere deeply with the course of evolution by making some life forms extinct, by destroying habitats, and by genetic engineering. They attack the vital organs of Gaia by releasing into the seas and the air compounds which upset the equilibrium and which undermine her restorative powers. They sap her vitality by killing off key species in her life-support system. Gaia is still robust but she is under strain.

We humans as a species are expendable. If we blow ourselves and our cities to smithereens with our nuclear bombs, Gaia will survive without us. In the past, she has experienced sudden catastrophes. The climate and chemical composition of the earth have remained stable for long periods until some internal contradiction or external force has caused a jump to a new state of homeostasis. She has recovered from ice ages and the impact of asteroids. Life on earth will continue, even if its forms are few and we are not there to witness them.

If we are not as a species to become guilty of attempted ecocide and matricide and kill ourselves in the process, we must recognize our place within Gaia as companions with other species, as members of a community of communities. We are not lords of the creation, with dominion over all that moves on the earth and in the air and the sea. We are not the highest links on earth in a Great Chain of Being. We do not have a God-given right to conquer and tame nature, nor does the moral progress of society depend on combating the way of nature. We do not have a unique role in injecting 'morality' into the evolutionary process.

Humans are only one small part in the whole creation, a thin thread in nature's web. On the other hand, we are not just lice on Gaia's back, a pest to be eradicated. Like all creatures on earth, we are an essential part of her diversity and beauty. Trouble arises when we multiply too much, oust other species and undermine the health of our host. If we have evolved special powers, they should therefore be used responsibly, in a life-affirming rather than a destructive direction. We may not be able to kill Gaia, but we have the ability to harm or heal, to hinder or foster the tendency in evolution towards greater diversity, complexity and consciousness. The choice is there.

Gaia is not only alive but also purposeful. Her purpose is reflected in the evolutionary process, a purpose which is not fixed and everlasting but which evolves and changes. The evolutionary tendency of Gaia is good-in-itself: it is life-enhancing, it is vital and it is beautiful. But the tendency can be reversed. It is not Providence at work within nature, or an immanent purpose to some preordained end. Gaia is not on a railroad of evolution going in one direction. We can check or redirect her potential just as we can place a slab of stone on a daffodil as it tries to grow towards the sun. We can temporarily block and distort the flow of evolving life on earth as we can dam a river and drown its valley.

40

We should not try and improve Gaia, let alone attempt to perfect her. We can try and limit their effects on us but we should accept that disease is part of health, catastrophe part of the overall harmony. Wolves and tarantulas in the wild, mice and slugs in the garden, colds and fevers in the body, are part of the diversity of Gaia. They are necessary for her long-term vitality as well as our own.

We can contribute to the well-being of Gaia by co-operating with natural evolution through our own self-development. The challenge is to work out how we can follow our own path as a human community while allowing the entire earth community to continue to unfurl and realize its potential. A key element in our own well-being is to honour and celebrate the goodness of the universe which is revealed in the richness, diversity, complexity and beauty of life on earth.

If humans have a role in the evolutionary process it is not in management. Given their past record, they are hardly capable of managing themselves, let alone becoming business managers of Gaia. Their role is not even as captains steering the boat of evolution, however steady their hand on the helm. It is not even as stewards, although stewardship is far better than dominion. If we do have a role it is as fellow-voyagers and companions with other species in the great odyssey of evolution, sailing across the oceans of time to an unknown land beyond the shimmering horizon, riding joyously the waves of life, without keeping slaves in the hold or shooting the albatross in the sky.

We are only beginning to understand the nature of Gaia. She may have an inherent memory, taking up the past as she develops towards the future. She may have an aura, a field of energy, invisible but powerful like electromagnetic or gravitational fields, responsible for her self-maintenance and regulation. Perhaps the periodic reversal of the magnetic pole or the sudden shift in the earth's crust result from some deep organization at work. She may be influenced by internal as well as external forces, resonating from within as well as vibrating in harmony with other planets.

For me Gaia is a living presence, keeping the world warm and comfortable and beautiful for us and our fellow beings. Animals, plants, rocks, water are all part of her pulsating body. Refined and subtle energies flow through her. Her steady breathing renews the air. Her gentle turning in space contributes to the music of the spheres.

I do not worship Gaia, any more than I worship any other god or human, but I revere her life forms and respect her moods. She has intrinsic value; she is valuable as an end in herself and not as a means to our ends. She gave birth to humankind and provides the conditions for our flourishing. By wounding her, we wound ourselves. Of this we are certain.

If there is something for us to do, it is to let go, to let Gaia take her beneficial course so that she can find her own harmony. Where we have disturbed her, we should withdraw and let the natural healing processes take place. Gaia can heal herself, if her atmosphere, land and sea are allowed to settle into their flow. Of this we are certain. Hands off the course of evolution! Let Gaia be!

# 5

# Being Human, Human Being

*There was a man who was so disturbed by the sight of his own shadow that he decided to discard it. The way he came up with was to run away from it. So he started to run, and run and run. The problem was that however hard he ran, his shadow kept up with him with effortless ease. He concluded that his failure was due to the fact that he was still not running fast enough, so he ran and ran and ran until one day he dropped dead. He did not realize that if he had only sat down and stayed still in the shade for a moment, his shadow would have vanished.*

Chuang Tzu

Humans create their own destiny, humans are perfectible, humans are godlike. This is the creed of the Enlightenment and it is a creed I share. We are unique and the most noble creatures in the world and our crowning glory is our intellect. This is the creed of the Renaissance. Of this I am not so sure.

At some stage in our development, the 'second nature' of consciousness, as Aristotle put it, evolved from the first nature of biological life and natural evolution gave way to cultural evolution. Our bodies may not have changed since the Stone Age, but our knowledge has multiplied. Accumulated knowledge was passed down orally until the invention of writing some 6000 years ago when the process of cultural evolution accelerated. Printing speeded up the process and now in the electronic age, communication is even faster. We are certainly *homo habilis* (skilful), but it is not so clear that we are yet *homo sapiens* (wise).

43

Given the observable trend in evolution towards greater consciousness, complexity and subjectivity, humans seem to be highly evolved. We do not know enough about whales to say that we are the most evolved. But at least in comparison with other forms of terrestrial life, humans are amongst the most consciously aware. They have a sense of self which distinguishes them from other selves. They have the imagination to envisage an alternative future to the present and the past. They are conscious of the influences at work on them and by changing them can change themselves. They can realize their potential.

At this stage in our evolution and development, we seem to have reached a peculiarly middle state. Our present condition is beset by contradictions and paradoxes. We long for immortality, but we are born astride the grave. We search for meaning and certainty, but flounder in a sea of confusion and doubt. We perceive an image of truth, but are unable to grasp it, equally incapable of absolute ignorance and certain knowledge. We will the best, but disaster follows. We try to create but often destroy.

We have free will, and yet become voluntary slaves. We have an idea of happiness and cannot attain it. Able to think and plan, we become the slaves of passion. Contemplating ourselves, we seem the noblest creature on earth; in contemplating the universe, we appear a grain of sand lost on a deserted shore.

We can split the atom and ride to the moon and yet we cannot avoid the natural catastrophes of floods and earthquakes. We have power over nature, but not over ourselves. Unable to hear the music of the spheres, the silence of infinite space fills us with dread. We turn away at night from the starry heavens, overwhelmed by its beauty, crushed by our own insignificance.

Refusing to ask fundamental questions, turning away from first and last things, trying to avoid pain and suffering, numbing the mind with superficial chatter, we moderns have become lost in the pursuit of illusionary security, material comfort and worldly power. We have confused being with having. Governed by inherited prejudice and acquired habits, our minds have grown cloudy and sleepy. The light of innate wisdom has lost its brilliance. We oscillate between boredom and fear, indifference and anxiety.

Being unable to avoid death and cure wretchedness, we have decided not to think about such things. In order to be diverted from thinking, to take our mind off our unhappy condition, we search for some agreeable pastime to while away the brief moment we have on earth. Unhappy in the present, we constantly look to the future. Thus we never actually live, but hope to live, and since we are always planning how to be happy it is inevitable that we should never be so.

This would seem to be our present condition. We are on a tightrope over an abyss, between ignorance and wisdom, sleep and awakening. But it need not be so. Many people are half awake when trying to sleep, and half asleep when awake. We can reach the other side. If we keep faith and have energy and vision, we need not fall.

If this is our condition and potential, what do we have to work with? The person is a living blend of body, mind and spirit. The body is not a machine, as some philosophers, biologists and doctors would have it, but a living organism. The mind is not a computer, however sophisticated. At one time the metaphor for the brain was hydraulics, and it was thought to work like a steam engine; now in this electronic age it has been reduced to wiring! The mind is not simply a collection of electrical and chemical reactions in the brain but a living process. Equally, the spirit is not just a ghost in the machine; indeed the mind may well be one aspect of the spirit. It is not certain that it lives on after death, but neither is it certain that it will not. My intuition tells me that my spirit might well continue; at least I am preparing for the coming journey and look forward to finding out what happens.

When I was a young man I rejected the muscular Christianity of my youth and became a convinced atheist, a humanist and an existentialist. Now in my middle age, I am not so sure. I have spent a lifetime thinking against myself and questioning authority. It now seems to me that pre-existence is as logical as an afterlife. If I am going to accept that my sense of self – my spirit or soul – does not end with the death of my body, then the doctrine of reincarnation seems more likely than ascent or descent into heaven or hell as in the Christian and Muslim scheme of things. At the same time, I totally reject the attempt to use the doctrine to justify the caste system in India where the higher ranks of society – the brahmins – are said to be more spiritually advanced than the poor who have only their past karma to blame for their lot.

Perhaps I should be wary, as Voltaire joked, that if I eat a chicken it could be my aunt. I had a sheep dog called Cai who seemed to understand and sympathize with human moods and feelings so well that I half suspected that he had been either a human in a previous life or is now one since he has died. I remain open to the idea, however absurd it might appear.

My deep intuition tells me that reincarnation is possible although I am by no means certain. My hunch is strong enough to make me prepare for the possibility of a voyage after death. I am ready to accept that the difficulties I have undergone are the result of my conduct in this life and possibly in previous ones. I accept responsibility for my past thoughts and actions and for my unmade future.

If I am not to be reborn on earth, then perhaps my spirit will transmigrate to another planet or another galaxy. There is ample evidence that there is life elsewhere in the universe. Perhaps I will travel in interstellar space for many lives before I become sufficiently enlightened to escape the arrow of time and the cycle of rebirth, *sansara*, and attain a state of nothingness or *nirvana*, the ultimate union with the cosmos. I await to see, without fear and trembling.

In the meantime, here on earth, my aim is to bring my body, mind and spirit into unison so that I may be able to realize my full potential as an all-rounded person. Within me, there are three treasures – vitality, energy and spirit. Vitality refers to sexuality, for the body is the house of life; energy refers to strength, and is the basis of life; and spirit refers to intelligence, the guide of life. If one is out of proportion, all three suffer. The alchemy of well-being is to bring together these aspects of the whole person, and to harmonize instinct, emotion and reason. Their care and cultivation are the basis of health, happiness and long life. Wise people nurture their spirit, keep their energy gentle, and their bodies healthy. They keep company with the evolution of all things and respond to the changes in all events. They ride the wind. I call this condition self-harmony.

What is the self? A person is born in Tao – the primordial ground of being – like a fish in water but gets lost as soon as he or she leaves the deep shadow of the pool. Initially a baby may not feel separate from its mother in the womb, but after birth it becomes increasingly aware of its own needs and desires as well as the Other – the limits and pressures of the external world – which thwarts or satisfies them. The ego begins to develop. The ego is that part of the self which experiences the 'I' as a separate individual, the 'I' in 'I exist'. But the influences of parents, of teachers, of widening society increasingly try to shape the ego into their desired image, so to differing degrees we develop a 'persona' which might be at odds with our self. The ego begins to act the roles it is expected to play in the game of growing up and can become disorientated when it confuses the masks of the acquired persona with the true self.

The ego is only the conscious part of the self. The persona is the mask which the ego adopts to deal with the pressures of surrounding society. But the self also has a conscious and an unconscious aspect. The latter often erupts into the former, especially in dreams when the conscious ego is relaxed. The personal unconscious contains repressed material – desires, memories, experiences, fantasies. At the same time the personal unconscious is part of a wider collective unconscious which all individuals can draw on. It is the receptacle of the accumulated experience of our families, our forebears and even our species, which often appears in archetypes and myth. It is part of our long memory and has a deep song.

This area of the unconscious is also the 'shadow'. It contains repressed experience and desires but is also the ground of creativity: without darkness, nothing comes to birth, just as without light nothing blossoms. The unconscious and the conscious, like dark and light, *yin* and *yang*, are complementary aspects of the mind. Growing in awareness involves acknowledging our shadow, accepting it for what it is, making it conscious. In the Babylonian version of the Flood, it is the black raven and not a white dove which brings the news of the recession of the waters; from the darkness comes new life.

In a condition of health, there is a natural flow between the conscious and unconscious so that fears and desires are not repressed but are made conscious and recognized for what they are. We can also draw on the ancient wisdom of the collective unconscious in the present and know the past without leaving our doorsteps.

Most people identify with their ego, which tries to satisfy both their own desires and instincts and the demands and pressures of society. One often inflames the other, creating artificial desires and spurious goals. We all experience the instinctive desires for food and sex. We all have the vital needs of food and shelter in order to live, and of loving relationships and a meaningful life to live well. The desire for food, sex and a good life are not so much the problem as our attachment or addiction to them. Our desires and needs often become inflated out of all proportion, especially in the West, and become uncontrollable drives for possessions, power and wealth.

In order to keep the wheels of profit turning, happiness is increasingly defined in terms of possession and consumption. Out of ignorance, we strive to satisfy our cravings, only to become more frustrated and unhappy in the process. The more we satisfy one set of desires, the more others emerge, like partridges out of the brambles. The only way out of this vicious circle is to realize that our craving inevitably leads to suffering and that all craving is folly. As long as a person remains attached to such craving, he will not only suffer in this world but will be chained to the cycle of *sansara*. The way out is to dissolve excessive desire, to become detached from material possessions, and to let go of the grasping ego.

Plato compared the soul to a charioteer directing two horses, one representing the instincts (appetite) and the other emotion. He believed that both needed to be kept firmly under control and act together. But anyone who has ridden a fiery horse knows that the more you pull on its reins, the more you build up its repressed energy until it can become a keg of dynamite. In the end the horse either submits and loses its fire, or else it bolts and throws off its rider. The best way to ride a fiery horse is with loose reins, a deep seat, and an empathy with the way it thinks and feels. Then you can gently direct its vitality, strength and energy and enjoy its headlong gallop, human and animal becoming one.

The same is true of sailing. Passion may be the wind, but if you hold the sails in too tight, the boat in a sudden gust will either capsize or the sails will tear. The wise sailor learns how to play the wind in the sails, not blocking but channelling its energy.

In the healthy and well-balanced person, harmony prevails between the mind, body and spirit (soul); between the head, belly and heart; between reason, instinct and emotion. One does not dominate the other, or the other deny the needs of one. This is the shamrock person, in which a trinity forms a complete whole. There is no need for Apollo to fight Eros. Desires need not be repressed but rather dissolved through greater understanding or redirected into more creative channels. In order to be an all-rounded person, to realize our full potential, we need to develop all aspects of our being.

Nature within us and without is not anti-rational. Our 'natural' instincts are something to act on and celebrate, not to crush or distort through repression. The person who talks about the need to tame 'the brute within' has a brutish mind. If you cannot trust nature, you cannot trust yourself.

In many ways the individual self is unique. Each of us has our own story, in this life and possibly in previous ones. No one can die our death for us. No one can share our karma. But every individual is also a set of relationships. There is no rigid distinction between the 'inner' or 'outer' self; it is just a question of emphasis or perspective. We are not isolated individuals, atoms floating in the ether, but social beings, members of a society. The self is not a separate entity, complete in itself, but an evolving, developing whole in a constant state of self-transformation in relation with other beings. Self-realization is therefore impossible without interaction with other people and the wider community.

Our being extends beyond the limits of the personal ego and the socially constructed self. We are ecological and cosmic beings as well as individuals and social beings. Before the self there is being, and before being there is the primordial ground of Being and non-Being. At the same time, we are members of a species and part of a widening community of beings. All living creatures are kindred souls. We are therefore trans-personal as well as personal beings. The self might be the centre, but it is part of an ever-widening web of relationships. To be fully ourselves, to find meaning in our lives, we need to go beyond the personal, beyond the narrow boundaries of our species and our planet to identify with the cosmos as a whole. It is not impossible. As below, so above: the microcosm of humanity mirrors the macrocosm of the universe. There are galaxies within our bodies as well as outside them. We humans are stardust, evolutionary marvels within the evolving universe.

To be complete the individual self must ultimately become part of the Universal Self, the self-in-the-Self, that is to say, to become part of the whole. In the Hindu tradition, this process is described as *atman* recognizing itself as part of *Brahma*; in the Taoist tradition, it means the self settling into the flow of the *Tao*; in the Hermetic tradition, the individual soul seeks to become part of the World Soul.

In this process of self-realization, the individual self identifies with the organic whole, unfolding beyond the ego to embrace the universe in its entirety. It goes beyond a personal identification with one's ego, family, clan, tribe, nation, race, species and planet to an ontological identification with Being as a whole. It brings an intuitive awareness that we and other entities are aspects of one single reality. Above all, it involves realizing that the appearance of separation and permanence in this measured and weighed world is strictly speaking *maya*, an illusion. The real world, of which one is a part, is the universal whole.

To realize our self-in-the-Self frees us from the chains of illusion and the mind-forged manacles which see beings and things as separate entities. Serene in the oneness of things, dualism vanishes of itself. It entails the joyful release from sufferings imposed on our grasping ego through ignorance. Once such unity is attained, death loses its sting and the mind becomes calm, joyous and free.

How can we know that we have moved from the conscious ego to realize our true self in the greater Self? You just do. It is easier to sense than to describe. You are no longer possessed by fears, by longings, by cravings, by anxieties. You feel 'at home' in the universe, in the wildest places, at one with all things. You experience awe in the face of the infinity of the heavens and an overriding sense of compassion for all living beings. Once you realize that One is All, and All is One, there is no longer any need to worry about being perfect or imperfect. You just are.

Most people have felt something like this at some time in their lives, when they have 'fallen in love' and the world around appears magical, or when they have had a peak experience in nature and they lose a sense of separateness. But it is usually fleeting and the 'falling out of love' or 'coming to' everyday reality only underlines the habitual divisions. Having once experienced the self-in-the-Self, a person knows intuitively that it is true and beautiful and that it can always be attained in the right conditions. It brings a sense of stillness, of centredness, in the Catherine wheel of life.

From this perspective, the personal self is not merely a series of fleeting selves or a fixed essence. It is an evolving self which comes from the primordial ground and can be reunited with it. As it becomes more aware, it is conscious of its connections with earth and heaven and realizes that to be whole it must identify with the universe. It means becoming truly human, a process in which the divine spark within us suddenly becomes a conflagration, and the ego is consumed in the fire of cosmic union.

But how can we reach this state? Is it up to us or is it predestined? Are we free or determined? If we are influenced by circumstances in this life, let alone in previous lives, to what extent are we able to shape our futures, to what degree are we free? There can be no doubt that the influence of our situation, of our time and space, of history and geography, is powerful. There also seems to be a cosmic law of cause and effect operating throughout the world.

In the Hindu and Buddhist tradition, this law of cause and effect is called karma. In Western philosophy, it is called determinism. Our lives and all existence are influenced by the endless chain of cause and effect, action and reaction. How this causality works is not clear, but it appears that every action we perform creates a force of energy that comes back to us rather like a boomerang. Eating too much makes us fat. Being cruel means that others will shun us. The more love we give, the more love we will receive. This seems to be a fact of experience – certainly of my own experience.

It seems our character to a large degree is the result of our previous thoughts and actions. Everything that is happening now – at this very moment – is a result of the choices you have made in the past. If you behave badly – selfishly or cruelly – it will come back to you and you will suffer as a result. On the other hand, if you are kind and generous, people will be good to you.

In terms of karma, we create good karma by our generous acts, bad karma by our cruel ones. Whatever happens, we have to pay for our unkind thoughts and deeds, our harming and causing harm to others. Many people talk of having to repay their 'karmic debts', but to talk of morality in this way sounds like a tax attorney or a government treasurer who weighs everything up in terms of profit and loss. A more organic and appropriate metaphor is to say that 'we reap what we sow'. To be more precise, we reap in the present what we have sowed in the past, and what we now sow we will reap in the future. It is part of the endless to and fro, the constant flow and transformation of energy in the universe.

But while there are undoubtedly causes which influence us, they are incomplete and open-ended. Such causes dispose but do not determine. They can tell us what will happen if they are acted

51

upon, but we did not have to follow them. In a similar way, it might be said that a horoscope predisposes a person to do certain things, but one does not have to do them. We are not totally predetermined. We are not foregone conclusions. We are not on a railroad track to the future from which we cannot deviate.

We may be to a large degree influenced by our circumstances, but we are also conscious and voluntary beings, capable of adapting to our circumstances but also of changing them. Our selves and our circumstances are intimately connected: we can change ourselves and thereby change our circumstances, or change our circumstances and thereby change ourselves. It is our consciousness which sets us free. Our mind is a link in the endless chain of causes and effects. To be completely determined, we could not have acted otherwise, but in all situations and as long as we live we always have an area of conscious choice. Therein lies our freedom. Even condemned prisoners in their cell are free in the attitude they take to their past life and their own imminent death. They can choose how they want to live out their last moments. In a sense we are all condemned prisoners in this world and cannot escape the ever-present possibility of our death.

Through our consciousness, we are capable of deliberate choice. We can choose those influences we want to check or develop, those motives we want to act on. Between ourselves and the world, there is a gap in which we can say 'no' to our conditioning. In this way, we are free.

Even many involuntary actions may be made voluntary. In meditation and yoga, we can regulate the beating of our heart and the breathing of our lungs. By observing our thoughts and feelings and the habits of our mind, we can change the way we think and therefore the way we act. By listening to our inner voice, we can become more in tune with our real needs. We can make our unconscious choices conscious. And we can act accordingly.

While the present is influenced by the past, the future is open and free. By my present thoughts and actions, I create my own future. By right thought and action, I can change myself and my life. I am free to work out my own destiny.

A direct corollary of freedom is responsibility. To be free is to be without excuse. You cannot say 'It was not my fault; I am not to blame'. Of course there are extenuating circumstances, of course conditioning plays an important role, but ultimately it is up to you whether you want to act on your conditioning or not.

You cannot avoid choosing. Even those who say, 'I have no choice' are choosing not to choose.

If I am free to choose different courses of action, then I must be responsible for my actions. For some an awareness of their responsibility is exhilarating, but for others it feels like a burden; it can even lead to anguish. There is such a fear of freedom, fear of taking responsibility, that many people prefer to be like billiard balls, moved only when moved, inert unless hit by something more energetic and purposeful. They see themselves as no more responsible for their actions than a dagger is for the murder it commits.

Being brought up to do what they are told in an authoritarian society, many people find it difficult to think and decide for themselves. They have been schooled into obedience and dependence. In some cases, the burden of responsibility is so great that they relinquish their freedom and become voluntary slaves, welcoming strong leaders and masters to tell them what to think and do. They are thus reduced to a state of voluntary servitude. They put up smoke-screens of wishful thinking or lose themselves in diversion to avoid confronting the prospect of their own freedom and responsibility.

There is no escaping the fact that within the self-created limits of our karma we are all born free. We come into life trailing clouds of glory but the shades of the prison house soon close in on us. In the garden of love, the deniers of life do their rounds with briars and pliers. If we let them, they bind us with the barbed wire of hypocrisy and conformity. They put a ball and chain around our necks and blinker our sight. They train us into obedience and dependence. But as soon as we realize that we can question authority and think for ourselves, as soon as we understand that whatever our past we can shape our future, as soon as we recognize that we are inherently free, then we can throw off our physical chains and liberate ourselves from our mind-forged manacles. By acting deliberately, by being aware of our motives and of the consequences of our actions, we widen the scope of our conscious choices. We become free. Freedom in this sense is a form of self-determination and is both negative and positive. It is freedom *from* external and internal restraints and freedom *to* realize our potential.

In every moment of our life, we are a field of possibilities. We have a vast number of possible choices. Some are made unconsciously and are involuntary; others are conscious and voluntary. In order to shape our future, we should become more aware of the choices we make in every moment, and thereby widen the range of our voluntary choices.

Most of us, as a result of our conditioning, react in a predictable way. We react automatically, responding like a trained circus horse to certain circumstances and people. If someone starts telling me what to do, I immediately resent it; if my daughter asks me for more expensive shoes while she is well-heeled, I grow hot under the collar; if someone shouts at me, I shout back. Much of this predictable behaviour is a result of habit, laziness, resentment or fear. But it is also the result of the choices we have made. We have chosen to be like that.

If we stand back and become spectators to what is happening, we can become aware of the causes and consequences of our actions and thoughts. We can ask: 'Why am I acting or thinking like this? 'What will be the consequences if I carry on like this?' In this way, we can become witnesses to our own bad faith and self-delusion. We become self-aware.

In our personal development, to make conscious and voluntary choices is a great advance. To be aware is the first great step towards liberation. It enables you to change your self, your life and your circumstances. The more you are conscious of your choices, the more you will be able to make the right ones. But this is only a transitional stage. The best state is being so aware that it is no longer necessary to make any conscious choices. You act spontaneously, making the right action at the right moment. You are no longer a calculator of causes and effects, motives and consequences, profit and loss; you just are, and without thought you aim straight.

If we want to create joy in our lives, we must learn how to sow the seeds of joy. But how can one be sure that one is performing the right action? The right action feels instinctively right. By listening to the inner voice, by being in tune with your heart, you just know whether an action is right or wrong. If it is the wrong action, you will feel congested in the chest, your brow will grow hot. If it is the right one, you will experience a sense of harmony between mind and body, head and heart. The spontaneous right action brings joy. It is also the most effective. With it the archer hits the bull's-eye, the sailor plays the wind perfectly in the sails, the child jumps across the stream without getting wet, and the poet finds the elusive word.

54

'But what can I do about my "bad karma"?', you might ask. 'What can I do about the past actions which have caused so much suffering?' Firstly, be prepared to accept without complaint the consequences of your thoughts and actions. Secondly, be ready to learn from the injury to yourself, to others and to the world which inevitably follows.

Becoming aware of one's own past wrongdoing provides a seed of opportunity for change and growth. It offers a challenge to face adversity and to transform it into something beneficial for oneself and one's fellow beings. In this way, the experience will make one stronger and wiser. 'But why must there be suffering and sorrow?', you might ask. Because that is the nature of life, the way of the world. You have to reap what you sow, just as you sow what you will reap. Learning from mistakes might be hard but it is worthwhile. You cannot climb a smooth rock face: you need the rough and the smooth to pull yourself up to the top.

By widening the sphere of our voluntary and conscious choices, we become effective actors in history and participants in the odyssey of evolution. We can perform good restoration work on ourselves and the world around us. We make spontaneously skilful choices. We aim well and achieve our end. We become calm and free, joyful and effective.

Ultimately there is no contradiction between free-will and determinism. Everyone is free within the limits of his or her self-created karma. We can free ourselves from the chains of illusion imposed on us by our circumstances and our ignorance. By right thought and action, we can change ourselves and shape our destiny.

To be authentic involves recognizing that we are free to choose, that we are responsible for our actions. We take up our past, acknowledge who we are, understand our limits and possibilities, and launch ourselves into the future. Because there is a series of causes and effects, we can act with the firm confidence that what we do now shapes what is to come. Our present actions create our future. In a sense, the future might be said logically to come before the present, for we act out our vision of the future in our present acts. We forge our destiny on the anvil of our imagination.

To become aware that we are responsible for our actions, that we are free to choose between life and death, between a good life or a poor one, can be supremely liberating. It means we need not always be stuck. We do not have to put up with deadening situations. We can change our lives and shape our future. We can realize our dreams.

# 6

# Playful Humanity

*Every day of their lives soon after dawn the women went to the deep well in the centre of their village to collect water for their households. One morning whilst awaiting their turn and chatting about the latest gossip, a fierce man rode up on a black horse. He demanded their jewellery. All the men in the village were already away working in the fields and there was no one to defend them. They had no alternative but to hand over their most precious possessions.*

*The fierce stranger demanded a shawl to wrap his booty in from one of the women which she used to tie her baby on her back. As she unwrapped it she stumbled in her alarm and her baby tottered on the side of the well. A great cry went up from all present. Seeing the tragedy unfurl before his eyes, the man grabbed the baby by its leg just as it was about to fall down into the dark interior of the deep well. In the rush, all his booty fell into the well. He did not cry out. His first concern was for the welfare of the baby. Afterwards, he said: 'Who would have acted otherwise?'*

If we are free to make our own destinies, does this mean that there is no such thing as human nature? Those who appeal to human nature usually do so for negative reasons, to show that there is a fundamental flaw in our make-up which acts as an insurmountable bar to any future improvement. 'Human nature is twisted', we hear. 'Humans are naturally aggressive and territorial and selfish. You cannot change human nature.' Such statements assert that human nature is not only flawed but imply that it is right that it should be so. An appeal to human nature in this way is usually in defence of the status quo or the imposition of even more draconian measures to keep humans along the 'straight and narrow'.

The view of traditional Christian moralists who asserted that we are born in original sin was given a pseudo-scientific gloss by Social Darwinists in the nineteenth century who claimed that life is a continuous fight in which the fittest – the strongest and most cunning – survive. In the twentieth century Freudian psycho-analysts further argued that we are in the grip of sexual drives which have to be repressed for society to function. In their attempt to reveal the biological roots of existing society, sociobiologists more recently have claimed that humans are little more than 'naked apes', naturally aggressive, driven by a 'territorial imperative' and governed by the 'selfish gene' which seeks to reproduce its kind. In other words, our natural state is not very different from the old vision of Hobbes in which there is a war of all against all and life is nasty, brutish and short.

The corollary is that a society of violent, property-owning egoists seeking power and wealth is natural and inevitable. A strong central authority in the form of the state is essential to curb human aggression, sexuality and selfishness. Human nature cannot be changed and any attempt to improve society is doomed to failure. The concept of 'human nature' in this scenario appears like a red-faced landowner with a loaded shotgun who prevents access to open rolling grassland and insists that we keep to the high-hedged road.

The trouble with appeals to 'human nature' is that it implies an unchanging and fixed nature which is the same in all times and places. Yet humans have evolved and behaved very differently at different stages of history and in different parts of the globe. Again, appeals to the 'state of nature' come up with very different conclusions. Far from Hobbes' nightmare, the natural world without the interference of humanity appears to be in a state of spontaneous order and overall harmony. Before the imposition of so-called civilization, the 'wilderness' without and within, in our nature and in the external world of nature, is fundamentally creative, positive and life-affirming. Like a daffodil bulb, given the right conditions, all life seeks to unfurl and realize its full potential.

If anything, it is closer to the truth to say that humans are fundamentally good rather than bad. This is not a modern Utopian belief but the teaching of ancient wisdom: the ancient Chinese and the ancient Greeks both asserted its truth. If a child is about to fall into a well, who would not give a warning to save it? This instinctive response of people shows their natural sympathy for others. Only someone whose nature had become depraved would find pleasure in the death of an innocent child.

'No man does wrong willingly', said Socrates. It is also my belief that people only harm others through lack of knowledge. Vice is the result of ignorance. If people were to realize that by doing harm, they were harming themselves they would probably not do it in the first place. It is only through ignorance that people go astray and become slaves of their egos and injure other beings. At the same time, everyone is capable of becoming enlightened and therefore good. Perfect wisdom is intrinsic in all people.

Since human beings as a species are evolving, and human societies have been so varied at different times and different places, it is misleading to talk of 'human nature' as if it were a fixed essence. Clearly there are some characteristics which are peculiarly human. We are a species which shares with other species the fundamental instincts of hunger and sex which have to be satisfied if the individual and the species are to survive and reproduce. But we are also *homo sapiens* – thinking beings – and at some stage in our development we have become capable of conceptual thought, symbolic communication and self-consciousness. We are the result of an evolutionary process which is going in the direction of increasing consciousness, complexity and individuality.

Beyond biological evolution, we have entered in the last million years a phase of cultural evolution, in which our accumulated experience is handed down from generation to generation, at first orally and more recently in words and images. We may even have a long memory in which the ancient experience of our species is not lost, as well as a short memory of our own lives. While we share biological needs with other animals, the manner in which they are expressed is influenced by our society and culture. And new needs have evolved within human society, such as the need for fulfilling work, loving relations, and a sense of meaning and purpose in the world. From our first biological nature has emerged a second 'human' nature which is conscious and purposeful.

While this human nature is not fixed and continues to evolve, it is possible to talk about a common human condition. We are born, we live, we die, and dying is an integral part of living. It is necessary to kill in order to live, whether it be plants or animals. Born in a particular time and place, within the context of a particular family, we have to work, mixing our labour with nature, in order to provide the means of sustenance. Everybody needs love and security and a sense of belonging. Each generation is obliged to search for meaning, truth, and happiness in their own way.

While there may not be human nature in the sense of an unchanging bedrock within us, we are born with a range of sensory, conceptual and linguistic abilities. Without these innate abilities, we would be unable to make sense of the world around us and act purposefully within it. Without them, we would not be able to think, to communicate or to create. They form the basis of our sense of personal identity and enable us to interpret and change the world around us.

These abilities are not fixed but open. They may be innate but they are shaped by experience. The old debate about the relative importance of heredity and environment, of nature and nurture, overlooks the fact that individually neither are constant variables and taken together they are extremely difficult to disentangle. From the moment a human being is conceived, heredity and environment interact on each other and later experience is always interpreted in the light of earlier experience. The experience in the womb and of birth is no doubt as influential in shaping a child's character as the first five years. And if the doctrine of reincarnation and karma is correct, we bring into this life the experience of previous lives.

The way our innate capacities are expressed will therefore depend to a large degree on the circumstances in which we are conceived and born and grow up. Our circumstances act as a series of limits and pressures on us. But our circumstances, like everything else in the universe, are in a state of flux. Moreover, since we are conscious and therefore voluntary beings we are not merely the passive products of our circumstances. We can change ourselves and thereby change our circumstances, and by changing our circumstances we change ourselves.

Like all animals, we are born with the drives for food and sex, without which the individual or the species would not survive and be able to reproduce. But how such drives are expressed depends mainly on the society and culture in which we live. The ancient Greeks, for instance, had a very different concept of love from that of modern Europeans, believing that in its noblest form it was only possible between men. Our modern view of love is based on a notion of relative equality between the sexes and is partly inspired by the romance of the courtly love tradition. At the same time, we can override the drives for sex and food. Some, such as monks or nuns, choose to deny their sexual drive by deliberately choosing celibacy. Others can fast even unto death.

In the nature-nurture, heredity-environment debate, few today would argue that you can tell a 'criminal type' by his or her physiognomy. But the dispute still rages about whether some races are innately more intelligent than others. We may not weigh brains any more to prove our point, but tests are used to measure IQ – intelligence quotient. If a particular racial group does better or worse, then the experts declare that they are more or less intelligent. But such tests only examine the existing definitions of intelligence in particular societies; in the West, this is narrowly defined by the ability to wield numbers, recognize shapes and understand language. Different societies value different kinds of intelligence and cultural influences play a crucial role in influencing the way people think and feel and imagine. Certain African ethnic groups do brilliantly in tests with shape but not with number and vice versa.

We are now told that there are genes for selfishness, genes for violence, genes for criminality, and even genes for homosexuality. The trouble with genetics – and molecular biology – is that it tries to isolate one element responsible for a particular type of behaviour and by doing so narrowly focuses on a part of the whole and misses the complexity of the system. The geneticists thus offer a new vision of original sin in the body and instead of tender love or spiritual enlightenment propose as a remedy the use of drugs: drugs to dampen down violence, criminality and sexuality. A drug against selfishness is not yet on offer. The geneticists' programme is the very opposite of a holistic or gestalt approach which sees the mind as an open system interacting with its own history and environment.

Another old chestnut is whether humans are fundamentally selfish or altruistic, doomed to self-interest or capable of benevolence. It has long been argued in the West that humans are fundamentally self-interested. This is said to be not only inevitable but beneficial: a hidden hand in society somehow transforms private self-interest into the general good. In certain situations, it might be good to help others but only if one helps oneself in the process. Some moralists have further urged 'enlightened self-interest' or 'cool self-love' which usually means using reason to maximize personal profit, deferring pleasure or undergoing short-term pain for long-term enjoyment.

Yet in many so-called 'uncivilized' societies, it would seem that many humans have an instinctive dislike of seeing others suffer. It is not their nature but the foundation of an unjust and unequal society which has corrupted and distorted natural instincts to make some people today self-interested and cruel. Indeed, it seems quite possible that humans can transcend narrow self-interest and practise universal benevolence, to go beyond the demands of family, class or nation and become impartial spectators of other people's needs. In certain circumstances, individuals have even given preference to the needs of a stranger over those of a member of their own family, clan or tribe. There have always been Good Samaritans.

It would appear that humans are equally capable of selfish and benevolent actions and it is the society and culture in which they grow up which decides which tendency is likely to prevail. Western society, based on the private ownership of property, tends to encourage an intense form of possessive individualism. It fosters competition and self-interest and the narrow doctrine of every man for himself and may the Devil take the hindmost. But there are many other societies, especially amongst hunter-gatherers and agriculturalists living close to the land, where mutual aid is the central virtue and 'thine and mine' is not recognized. There have also been many successful movements in history which have advocated and practised co-operation rather than competition as a means of attaining the general good and this, of course, is the principal difference between socialists and liberals.

In recent times, there has in the West been a renewed stress on the importance of self-love, especially in feminist and New Age writings. Many self-help books provide daily affirmations of self-love, such as 'I love and approve of myself. I am in the perfect place at the right time.' Members of therapy groups tell each other, 'I'm OK, you're OK.' Women's groups remind each other to pamper and indulge themselves. 'In the infinity of life where I am,' one is urged to repeat, 'all is perfect, whole and complete.'

At first sight this kind of self-love seems to be as egoistic and narcissistic as the old version. The goal of creating a comfortable home on a good salary and making a beautiful oasis for oneself in an ugly world seems like a selfish form of aesthetic materialism. Moreover, in many such self-help books, the status quo is usually taken for granted and the aim is not to change the world but to change one's own life for the better in the existing circumstances. They offer advice on how to get a better slice of the cake, not to question its ingredients or to imagine a different recipe.

In a society which places so much value on success, especially in terms of power and wealth and beauty, by definition the vast majority of people feel failures. If they have not 'made it to the top', they define themselves as 'losers'. So many people moreover grow up being told that they are not good enough, that they are hopeless, and that they will never learn, it is not surprising that they fulfil the prophecy. If you are constantly undermined, it is most likely that you will feel at best self-doubt and at worse self-hatred. In this context, the positive affirmation 'I love and approve of myself' is not self-love in the narrow sense of calculated self-interest but a celebration of self-worth and self-respect as the base for personal growth. We all need to love and be loved and feel ourselves loveable, especially in a world where hatred of self and others seems so prevalent. Again in a world where there is so much fear of change, fear of freedom, fear of the Other, where fundamental insecurity is the order of the day, it is inspiring to feel that there is an infinity of love in the world and that you are safe within the universe. In an ultimate sense, it is also true.

The women's movement has countered the organized love-lessness of the Western world by reminding each other that they should feel good about themselves, assert their worth, celebrate their own talents, and realize their potential. In this context, self-love need not mean narrow selfishness but a sense of self-worth; it need not mean looking after number one but seeing that it is in the higher interest of the self to become a creative part of the whole, of society, of nature and ultimately of the universe. This applies to men as much as to women. To realize that we are imaginative and creative beings, that we all have special talents and a unique individual worth, is an important step on the path of self-realization.

But true self-realization is only possible if we realize that while we are unique individuals we are also social beings, sets of relationships relying on each other in society. We are, moreover, members of the same species, with common needs and interests, as well as ecological beings, part of a community of communities and threads in nature's web. And ultimately we are cosmic beings, made from stardust and part of the infinite whole. Only when we realize this can we begin to realize our self-in-the-Self.

So far so good. There is no fixed essence of human nature, but an evolving self. We are capable of altruism as well as selfishness. But what about aggression? Isn't that a natural instinct? However much you try and improve society, won't aggression ensure that there will always be crime and wars?

But wait a minute! Aren't we mixing up different forms of violence? By definition, a crime is breaking a law, and about two-thirds of laws in the West are to protect private property which enshrines the appropriation of the common wealth into the hands of a few. From this perspective, property is a violent form of theft. With a fairer distribution of wealth and common ownership, there would be less occasion for crimes against property.

Again, wars are waged by states. A state, with its army and police, claims the legitimate monopoly of violence within a given territory. The violent nature of the state is most clearly shown when one state declares war on another. The justification for the coercive force of the army and police is that it prevents social violence, but in practice they tend to perpetuate the violence of the state. By enforcing the laws which protect the unjust distribution of wealth by the threat or use of violence they only aggravate social conflict. With the dissolution of the state and the decentralization of power, there would be less occasion for war.

Violence against others is always wrong. No doubt in a free and equal society without the state there would still be 'crimes of passion' as long as people were not enlightened. Individuals who commit such acts would have to be restrained by the minimum use of violence. But even such violence does not come from a primary drive of aggression but is largely the result of frustrated desire. Our society excites artificial desires for possessions and power to a point of madness, and then fails to satisfy them. It also celebrates success, power and privilege, but since only a tiny minority succeed the rest define themselves as failures and lack self-esteem. The result is a huge reservoir of frustration in society

64

which inevitably leads to aggression. And the more frustration, the more aggression and violence.

Modern Western society has developed a culture of violence. The clever dealers in the cultural market-place know the profits to be made from violence and provide a constant diet in the media. Young people see adults constantly being cruel and violent to each other in the media so it isn't surprising that they should think that it is normal. If you don't like someone, you hit them in the face or gun them down. If you are short of possessions, you just take someone else's. The more violence young people see, the more they will tolerate violence in the society around them. They learn to be innured to their own revulsion or fear of it. They also learn the excitement of violence and not the curbs.

Sexual aggression is often a result of frustrated sexual desire. Repressed people tend to want to repress others and the coercive institutions they create encourage coercive individuals. A certain degree of repression is inevitable – we cannot immediately gratify any passing whim – but the repression in Western society is far too excessive. While the dominant culture inflames sexual desire it then proceeds to prevent its satisfaction by a compulsive morality. The resulting repressed desire is transformed into aggression. The popular slogan 'Make love, not war' therefore has a deep psychological meaning. The more loving people are, the less likely they are to be violent to each other on a casual or on an organized scale.

Of course there need not be a direct relation between aggression and repressed sexuality. For many, celibacy can be a tranquil and positive state, and not only for monks and nuns. The sexual drive may atrophy through lack of stimulation. Repressed sexual energy – libido – can also be sublimated into creative work rather than be directly satisfied. Some writers, such as Balzac and Simenon, abstain from sex whilst writing, and some footballers sleep alone the night before a big match. But again there need not be a direct relation. Many artists are inspired by a good sex life, while many sportsmen and women do not feel their action on the field is related to their performance in bed. The Taoists and the practitioners of Tantric yoga avoid orgasm so that sexual energy can be transformed into spiritual energy and thereby increase their vitality.

In general, our vital energies, our emotional and sexual drives do not require the external restraints of a compulsive morality.

65

They regulate themselves spontaneously when not interfered with by artificial restrictions. There is no need for the mind to curb the body or for reason to repress sexual desire. The wise are not troubled by sexual desire; they either satisfy it directly, sublimate it into something else, dissolve it through meditation, or direct their attention to some other life-affirming activity.

Nearly all aggression is destructive, harmful to the perpetrator as well as the victim. In an enlightened society without the organized violence of the state, unjust property relations, and a compulsive morality, there would be much less occasion for aggression. What remains could be redirected into creative channels, such as exploration and adventure, sports and the arts. It is better to make love than fight, to climb a mountain than hunt a fox, and to play rugby than go to war.

But what about human perversity? Is that not a bar to any improvement? What of the perverse will which makes a guest deliberately spoil an otherwise harmonious dinner? What of the traveller on a train who has a sudden urge to push a fellow passenger out of the window on to the track? What of the person who wants to stick out his tongue just for the hell of it?

It could be argued that to act against one's own best interests is a giddy act of self-assertion; it might be against the utilitarian ethic but it brings a feeling of intense living. In an overly regimented and uniform society to raise fingers at authority could be a healthy sign of rebellion. Perhaps the vandalism of those living in high-rise estates or ghettos is a creative revolt of the human spirit against inhuman conditions.

Perhaps. But to react in such an egotistic and destructive way is a feeble alternative to trying changing the conditions themselves and developing a real sense of personal worth. Such *actes gratuits* – arbitrary acts without apparent rhyme or reason – take self-assertion to the point of absurdity. They are not the expression of personal freedom but a misuse of freedom and the denial of the freedom of others. Living in an absurd world, there is no need to be absurd.

Being perverse is not always negative. To be perverse is to deviate deliberately from what is regarded as normal, good or proper. By challenging the cultural and political status quo, I could be accused of being perverse. But it is not always clear that the statistically normal is good or proper. In a sick society, it is those who are well-adjusted who might be really off their rocker, while those who are considered mad are really sane since they refuse to conform to an insane situation. The abnormal in this case might be seen to be the most healthy and the normal to be sick.

The root of the word 'perversity' comes from the Latin *perversus* which means 'turned the wrong way'. If people or societies are going in a negative direction, then it might be right to turn the 'wrong way' in the circumstances. The philosophers who were considered perverse by the *ancien régime* in France are now recognized as great progressive revolutionaries. Yesterday's perverse subversives are today's accepted heroes.

Does this mean that there is no room for perversion in an enlightened society? Perversion is not the same as perversity. A perversion is usually defined as any 'abnormal' means of obtaining sexual satisfaction. But what is the normal or abnormal in sex? Is the normal the usual course of nature? If nature intends all acts of love to involve the possibility of conceiving, then contraception is against nature and therefore could be called a perversion. If the normal is defined as what most people do, then it could be argued that heterosexuality is natural and homosexuality is unnatural. Certainly Hitler thought homosexuals were 'against nature' and on those grounds should be eliminated. Yet the Nazis' policy of cold-blooded extermination was the most 'inhuman' and 'unnatural' of all.

If the normal is defined by what most people do, then in certain parts of California it might be abnormal to be heterosexual. But such statistical definitions of the normal are out of place. Indeed, the whole debate whether homosexuality is natural or unnatural, abnormal or normal, perverted or straight, would seem to be fruitless. To appeal to 'nature' in this way is always ambiguous unless the concept is carefully defined in a particular context. It could be argued that all acts committed by humans are 'natural' and therefore cannot be perverse. To love is undoubtedly natural, while the gender of the loved one is a question of choice.

In my view, individuals should be free to choose what relationships they wish to form, with three provisos. The first is that the relationship is based on consent and no one is being coerced. The second is that it does not involve an adult in any way exploiting a child or a vulnerable person. A vulnerable person is someone who can easily be hurt and taken advantage of. The third is that no one is harmed.

Harming others is always wrong. But what about sadism and masochism? Is finding pleasure in hurting others or being hurt admissible? Do the masochist and sadist form a happy couple? I would say not. Sadism and masochism are just an extreme form of domination and unequal power relations which cannot do anybody any good in the long run. It might be better to express such desires in sexual play between consenting adults rather than in wider society, but best of all is not to have the desires to dominate or be dominated in the first place.

But is it possible to have equal relationships, especially between the sexes? Do the differences in gender mean that there will always be differences in power and ability between men and women?

Because of their biological differences, it may well be that women and men have a different being-in-the-world. Women with their menstrual cycle would seem to be more in harmony with the rhythm of the moon than men. Men cannot experience the pain and joy of childbirth. Men seldom get breast cancer while women cannot appreciate the time-bomb of the prostate gland. Men cannot appreciate fully the experience of the female orgasm any more than women can experience the male orgasm. Women can enjoy sports as much as men but they may not be so strong in some areas.

But these biological differences do not mean that women are morally or intellectually inferior to men. Freud argued that since little girls are 'female eunuchs' they do not experience the threat of castration like little boys during the Oedipus Complex and as a result do not develop a strong super ego or moral sense. But Freud was simply giving a pseudo-scientific gloss to the old patriarchal image of woman as the 'weaker vessel' and as the temptress who pulls man down from his high moral ideals. The Oedipus Complex is far from being universal since it is narrowly based on the nuclear family and is not as crucial in human development as Freud imagined. In the end, he had to admit that female psychology remained a 'dark continent' for him. Anatomy is not destiny, nor does gender affect the moral sense. Animals share with humans a rudimentary moral sense, and many other factors are involved in developing a person's sense of morality whatever their sex. Women and men are equally capable of being cruel or kind, selfish or generous.

If there are no moral differences between the sexes are there grounds for intellectual inequality? It has long been argued that men think and women feel and that men are intellectually superior to women. Why are there so few great women scientists, painters, composers and philosophers? The reason is simple: in past history – his story – the contribution of women has been ignored and only now is beginning to be acknowledged. Women moreover have tended to be the carers and mothers in a patriarchal society while the men have been able to dedicate more time to creative work. There has long been a division not only between manual and physical labour but between so-called 'women's work' and 'men's work'. But the division does not always hold. In Africa, women do about 70 per cent of the work, including what is often considered men's work elsewhere such as trading or working in the fields. In the West, women have more opportunity to undertake intellectual and artistic work and men are beginning to appreciate the domestic arts. The old boundaries are breaking down.

Perhaps the women's movement in the West has had the greatest influence in seeking fundamental cultural change in recent times. In a violent and grasping society, it has brought to the forefront the importance of the traditionally 'feminine' values of caring, nurturing, relating, belonging and letting be. Such values are not biologically rooted in women and can be released within men, just as the historically 'male' values of discriminating, judging, dominating, fighting and bullying can develop within women.

Women in the West have long been considered closer and more connected to nature: the 'witches' of the Middle Ages knew its intimate rhythms, while the male scientists of the Scientific Revolution stood apart as impartial observers. It is not surprising that in patriarchal societies where men dominate nature, they subjugate their women; indeed, the domination of women by men may well have preceded the human domination of nature. In Western culture, men justified their domination by identifying women as being closer to nature than men: less rational and virtuous and more emotional, mysterious, moist, soft, rebellious and wild.

Although women through their sexual biology may be more aware of the cycles of birth and death than men, it does not necessarily make them any *closer* to nature. Both men and women are continuous with nature; both are nature rendered self-conscious.

Both would equally be enhanced by the ending of hierarchy and domination. The principles of diversity, interconnectedness, gentleness, co-operation, compassion, and tolerance, long associated with women, have no gender any more than supposedly the 'male' qualities of competition and rationality. All would benefit if both sexes recognized and honoured their common humanity as an integral part of nature's web.

It is society and culture, and not anatomy, which have fostered the traditional differences between the sexes. There is nothing in their nature which prevents women from excelling as much as men in the arts and sciences. In the past men and women may have channelled their creativity in different directions but they are both equally creative. All humans, whatever their sex, are inherently capable of reasoning and intuition, logic and poetry, mathematics and music.

The feminist movement has done much to redress the balance and to encourage women to realize their potential as intellectual, imaginative and creative beings. But by competing with Old Men with their macho ways some New Women have taken on their more negative attributes and become authoritarian and domineering. In order to be 'in control' of their lives, they end up wanting to control others. By practising assertiveness, they have become strident and aggressive.

A positive aspect of the men's movement, which developed largely in response to feminism, is that many men have developed the caring virtues traditionally associated with women, such as looking after children and the home. They deliberately eschew aggression and violence, and celebrate co-operation and peace. But just as some New Women have become too aggressive and assertive, so some New Men have become excessively meek and subservient. A few have become confused about their maleness and define their role as mainly supporting their women. Their women in turn take advantage of their meekness and exploit their caring sensibilities. In this role reversal, the New Woman has become the Old Man, and the New Man the Old Woman.

In the dialectics of race and gender, it may well be necessary to pass through a phase of conflict and confusion. Many oppressed ethnic groups feel the need to separate themselves off from their oppressors in order to define themselves more clearly and to appreciate their true worth: black power develops in relationship to the dominant white power which hitherto set the terms of the

70

relationship. In the same way, some women wish to separate themselves off from men in order to be clearer about themselves; they wish to oppose sisterhood to brotherhood. But to stay in this state of opposition is to freeze the dialectical movement forwards; it results in the paralysis of racism and sexism. After a period of opposition and even struggle, during which both sides become clearer about who they are, the next phase is the reconciliation of opposites in a higher synthesis in which individuals go beyond their divisive characteristics to recognize their common humanity. Being human ultimately transcends race and sex.

For women to become like traditionally dominating men, and for men to become like traditionally subservient women is no liberation for either sex. Matriarchy is just as bad as patriarchy. The aim should be to go beyond all 'archy' – rule – to create a society where men do not dominate women or vice versa and where there is no longer any domination or hierarchy, ruler or ruled. Such a society would celebrate the biological differences between the sexes as complementary and not make them grounds for discrimination. It would honour their common humanity and recognize that there are traditionally defined male and female qualities – *yang* and *yin* – the hard and yielding, the assertive and the caring, the thinking and the feeling, the logical and the intuitive, the adventurous and the retiring, to be found in both sexes.

The differences between groups of humans and between the sexes are something to celebrate, not to decry. A good society would not be reduced to a grey uniformity, but would have an equality of unequals, an equal opportunity for all to be their different selves. *Vive la différence!* The greater the diversity in society and nature, the more the overall harmony. But whatever the happy differences between humans, I do not believe that there are any innate checks to the physical, intellectual and moral equality of human beings, whatever their race or gender.

What is needed is a new society which does not define work on gender lines but transforms all work into meaningful play, play which fulfils rather than denies human creativity. *Homo faber*, working man, will thus be turned into *homo ludens*, playful man, or better still, playful humanity.

Does this mean that human beings are perfectible? The French historian and philosopher Condorcet thought so. He was so confident at the time of the French Revolution of the inevitable march of progress that he wrote while awaiting execution in a Jacobin prison that humanity would one day reach perfection. The German philosopher Hegel thought that the realizable goal of history is for humanity to become like God – all-conscious and self-causing. But there is no in-built, pre-determined plan of human perfectibility. We are not on a railroad track of history careering towards a particular terminus. Indeed, history shows that civilizations rise and fall and progress is not inevitable. One of the painful experiences of my own life is to see the economic, social and moral decline of large parts of the world. Yet while we may never reach perfection, we are still capable of continuous improvement. Whatever the mind of humanity can imagine, their hands can create. There is nothing in our make up which prevents us from improving, but equally nothing which guarantees it.

The future is of our own making; we can transform ourselves and our societies. It is up to us. In our lives, and in our history, we can remain like caterpillars. Crawling can be fun, close to the earth, wiggling our feet without conscious thought. But it is also good to enter a chrysalis stage of meditating on the nature of being human and on the nature of the world, a period of stillness and transformation. At this stage, something extraordinary can happen. We can break out and discard our former selves. We unfurl our butterfly potential. We stretch our new wings and fly.

# 7

# Reverence for Being

*There was a man living by the sea-shore who loved seagulls. Every morning he went down to the sea to roam with the seagulls, and more birds came to him than you could count in hundreds. One day his father said to him: 'I hear the seagulls all come roaming with you. Bring me some to play with.'*

*Next day, when he went down to the sea, the seagulls danced above him and would not come down.*

Lieh Tzu

When professors of ethics appear and start talking about the meaning of justice, you can be sure that people are no longer spontaneously just. If rulers insist on the duty of helping one's neighbour, you can be sure they do not practise it. Morality arises only when society has deviated from nature, lost its natural roots in Tao. Elephants do not discuss co-operation, they just co-operate. When goodness is lost, there is justice. When justice is lost, there is ritual. Since we have reached the stage of empty ritual at the dawn of a new age, it is unfortunately necessary to work out a new morality for a new society, a morality which places humans within the unified field of nature's web.

The three great qualities of morality are intuition, imagination and sensibility. Intuition is the only guide to first principles, enabling us to decide what the object of morality should be. Without imagination, we would be locked up in our own egos and our own minds. The imagination is the most important faculty of morality because it enables us to go out of ourselves and consider the interests of others and of the whole from the perspective of a concerned and sympathetic observer. It enables us to imagine the pain and pleasure of others, even if it is by analogy to our own. It helps us to imagine what it is like for a woman to see her family die from starvation, what it is like to be a calf unable to move in a crate, or what it is like to be a puppy with a broken paw.

The third essential quality of morality is sensibility. Vivisectionists might have the imagination to realize the predicament of a chimpanzee with artificially induced AIDS in a small cage, but unless they have a degree of moral sensibility they will not wish to prevent its suffering and stop their research. Without sensibility, we are unable to empathize with the pains and pleasures of others; without sensibility, we would not try to save a child who has fallen into a well, or release a wild goat caught in briars.

Ethics are not just expressions of feeling, verbal equivalents of 'I approve' or 'I disapprove'. Moral principles express feelings, but they can also be developed by sound reasoning and supported by strong evidence. At the same time, some systems of ethics are clearly relative to different cultures; indeed, they often appear to be part of the will to power of a people, embodying those values which they aspire to and find most difficult to attain.

The Ten Commandments derive from the experience of the Jews in the Middle East some three thousand years ago; they are based on the possessive ownership of private property and enshrine a view of the rightful relationship between men and women as monogamous marriage. Clearly neither institution is universal – Muslim men marry several wives, while many ethnic groups have no sense of 'mine' and 'thine'. It is therefore difficult to argue that the ten commandments are universal moral principles. Indeed, William Blake liked to point out that Jesus Christ broke all the ten commandments sometime during his life.

To find one single overarching moral theory – a single set of guidelines and priorities – is as elusive as the grand unified theory in physics. Different moral theories have their merits in different circumstances and areas. Theories of rights are often at odds with utilitarian ethics, since numbers and consequences have no sway over the right to life of an individual. While theories of rights engender respect for individual organisms, they are vague about larger systems and collections, like valleys, lakes, and nature as a whole which require a more holistic approach. Ethics, like every branch of human understanding, evolves and any moral concept

74

is best considered provisional as it may develop with further enquiry.

Some theories are more appropriate than others when dealing with certain dilemmas and situations. It is not only a form of ethical colonialism but unecological to assert that moral principles are universal, regardless of circumstances. I am a vegetarian, but I cannot expect the Inuit living on polar ice to be vegetarian without them abandoning their traditional ways. If we adopt a general moral principle, it should always be adapted to the light of the particular circumstances. Indeed, circumstances might lead to the abandonment of a particular moral principle and the recognition that the case in question is a law unto itself. There never is a rule without an exception. Circumstances vary so much that it is impossible to bring them all under the same moral umbrella.

At the same time, this does not mean that we drown as moral beings in a sea of relativity. There are, I would argue, some universal values, such as the sacredness of life and the principle of doing minimum harm. Nature can also offer an objective ground for our moral beliefs. The way things are is relevant to how they should be.

It has long been fashionable for relativists to argue that nature can teach us nothing and all values are human creations. Because something 'is', they argue, it does not follow that it 'ought' to be. Of course this so-called 'naturalistic fallacy' holds in many cases: because there is struggle in nature, it does not follow that there ought to be struggle in society. Because something exists in the natural world, such as viruses, earthquakes and drought, it does not follow that it is 'good'. The idea that whatever is, is right, is deeply conservative. Nature is not always the consoling mother of the Romantics nor the cruel taskmaster of the so-called Realists: if anything, it is indifferent to human purposes. The weather is never miserable; it is people who interpret it to be so.

But there is no rigid distinction between 'is' and 'ought'. Whatever exists is always a potentiality; it has been something and is in the process of becoming something else. We can evaluate 'what is' in terms of its unrealized potential. 'What is' in this sense contains 'what should be': a daffodil bulb, if it is to unfurl its potential and to realize its nature, 'should' become a yellow flower with long green leaves.

Nature is not just a lump of matter, a dead collection of resources, but a complex web of life with an evolving pattern. Nature is infused with meaning and purpose. As we have seen, nature has the ability to organize and maintain itself and is evolving towards greater consciousness, complexity and subjectivity. Its purpose is not predetermined but it has a potential which seeks to unfold and realize itself as a bulb seeks to become a flower and blossom.

With consciousness comes a moral sense, but it is not restricted to humans. Our seeking the good is only one part of the vast process of value emerging in nature, a process in which all beings seek to attain their own good. The good of the earth realizes itself through the attainment of the good of all the beings of the earth. Not only humans but all complex mammals, especially elephants, apes, dolphins and whales, appear to have a moral sense and pursue what they consider to be their good.

Any consideration about human conduct inevitably involves their natural setting and evolutionary potential. The fact that the universe works in a particular way, and that humans have a particular place within it, is relevant to their moral considerations. We can decide to go with the grain of things or against it; either way, the direction of the grain has a bearing on our decisions. Ethics thus has a natural history and nature is the ground for ethics and is a rich source of values and ideals. Indeed, all values are rooted and grow from nature since humanity is a form of nature's self-expression.

There has undoubtedly been a great advance in environmental ethics in recent times by extending the notion of natural rights from humans to animals, and from animals to plants, and from plants to embrace all organisms. Elephants and trees as well as humans have moral standing. At the time of the first Universal Declaration of Rights during the French Revolution, rights were only applicable to white, property-owning males. Only in the twentieth century were they extended in the West to women and non-white peoples. But now it is common to defend not only human rights but animal rights, the rights of plants, and even the rights of microbes and bacteria to life, liberty and the pursuit of happiness. The move has undoubtedly had a revolutionary and liberating effect.

The problem with applying the principle of rights in order to defend Gaia and its myriad of life forms is that it narrowly focuses on individuals. What about groups of individuals, ecosystems, biotic communities, the biosphere, the planet itself? Do they all have rights? What if their rights clash?

The principle of rights is based on a notion of possessive individualism. The individual is presented as possessing certain natural rights – the right to life, liberty and property – which are seen as extensions of the self. To assert one's right also presupposes a state of conflict with other owners of rights and if they are to be enforced then some coercive authority like the state is deemed necessary.

Since this is the case, the principle of utility might at first sight seem to be more relevant to a sound environmental ethics. A utilitarian approach has as its objective the good of the community as a whole. In the past, considerations of general good were restricted to human society, which was largely achieved by the conquest of nature and the enslavement of animals. But the notion of the 'good of the whole' can be extended to embrace animals as well as humans, the good not only of the land, but of the sea, of the air, and of the ecosphere itself. It need not stop there and can embrace the cosmos.

The immediate problem with this approach is the definition of the 'general good'. The early utilitarian philosopher Jeremy Bentham defined it as 'the greatest happiness of the greatest number'. But this implies that it is still based on a notion of ethical individualism, with the general good defined as a sum of individual goods. Bentham further went on to interpret happiness as 'pleasure' and sought to minimize pain and maximize pleasure. But are all pleasures of equal value? Is the pleasure of skittles as important as the pleasure of poetry? Are intellectual pleasures superior to physical pleasures and is the pleasure of virtue superior to both? Is it better to be a satisfied pig or an unhappy philosopher?

The question is a crucial one, one which has profoundly influenced my own life. In my view the pursuit of truth, which may be pleasurable or painful, is more important than the pursuit of happiness. During the existential phase of my life in my twenties and thirties, I found the 'truth' about the universe to be painful: there is no God and the universe is without ultimate meaning. Then in my forties, I was not so sure and now I suspect that the truth about the universe may be joyful: the creation is good and our purpose is in following its way. My own experience further tells me that the more you seek happiness, the less you are likely to find it. It sneaks up on you when you are pursuing the right path. One day you wake up and say 'Hey, I'm happy! Life is great!'

There are other problems with the notion of the 'greatest happiness of the greatest number'. What about the minority? Is their happiness to be sacrificed for the good of the majority? Again, how do you decide between the competing claims to happiness of different groups? Does the happiness of foxes trump that of fox-hunters?

If, as the utilitarians do, we define happiness in terms of pleasure, how do we calculate the pleasures of other beings? By analogy with ourselves as warm-blooded mammals, it is comparatively easy to imagine the pleasure in the case of foxes, bears and lions, but not so easy with insects, jellyfish and barnacles because they are so different from us. Is it possible to talk of the happiness of ecosystems like woods and rivers and mountain ranges? It is virtually impossible to calculate the happiness across a mixed group within an ecosystem.

In the circumstances, I suggest that it is better to replace the utilitarian notion of happiness as pleasure with that of well-being, the well-being not only of humans and animals but of nature as a whole. This offers a more holistic approach which gives value to the parts as well as the whole, to individual entities and groups. It recognizes that a part is a unique expression of the whole and the good of a part cannot be reduced simply to its function in contributing to the good of the whole. Neither the part nor the whole comes first; indeed, each part is a relative whole in relation to its own parts.

Going beyond the old debates about utility and rights, I propose a system of ethics for our dealings with each other and the rest of nature which I call liberation ecology. It combines ancient wisdom with modern insights. It has four fundamental moral principles based on deep intuition:

(1)   The first is that nature has value in itself. It is not simply a means to our ends, but an-end-in-itself. And since it has intrinsic value, it deserves our unconditional respect. We should treat it well.

(2)   The second moral principle is that all life is sacred. All life forms are intrinsically valuable. The life of plants and animals are as sacred as the life of humans. And since all life is sacred, it deserves our reverence. We should treat it well.

(3)   The third moral principle is that we should cause minimum harm. If we cannot help others, at least we should aim not to

hurt them. And while causing minimum harm, we should have compassion for all beings. We should treat them well.

(4)     The fourth principle is that we should seek the well-being of the whole. Any thing which contributes to the well-being of the whole is good, while anything which detracts from it is bad. We should treat it well.

Taken together, the import of these principles can be summed up in the idea of Reverence for the Being of beings, or simply the Reverence for Being.

Stated baldly in this way, these principles raise many questions. The first and second principles that nature has value in itself and all life is sacred imply that all life forms should have opportunities to realize their potential and attain their own good. They are all valuable parts of an interrelated whole – precious threads in nature's web.

If we accept that all life forms are intrinsically valuable, how do we discriminate between different life forms when there is a clash of interests? Do simple organisms like ticks have the same right to flourish as elephants? An obvious criterion might be the degree of consciousness or sentience (the ability to feel pleasure or pain), so that we might discriminate in favour of the elephant before the tick if one of them has to be sacrificed. But then we might say that although it may have less consciousness, the life of an oak is more important than the life of a mouse because it supports more life-forms. In the latter case, the life of an essential organism in an ecosystem is considered more important than an individual life. The consciousness of an organism is of considerable importance, but also is its place and function in the web of nature.

I can imagine certain circumstances where utilitarian and aesthetic considerations are more important than the right to life. I am prepared to dig out 'weeds' in my garden to make room for vegetables and flowers. Growing vegetables organically can be defended on utilitarian grounds as a means to life. But what about flowers? Since they are merely decorative, it would seem that killing them can only be defended on aesthetic grounds. Use value is not the sole criterion in this case – beauty is uppermost. In a dwelling, it is good not only to have objects which are useful and beautiful but also those that are beautiful but useless. These might include pieces of wood or stone collected from the seashore

79

or flowers from the garden. Indeed, the disinterested love of beauty is one of our finest sentiments and as a form of harmony is closely linked with virtue and truth. There is a fundamental connection between the beautiful, the good and the true.

In place of the principle of biocentric equality – which asserts that all life forms have an equal right to live and flourish – I propose the wider principle of ecocentric impartiality. This asserts that when there is a clash over the claims to life of different organisms, the ones most likely to enhance the well-being of the whole should generally be paramount. The well-being of the whole would mean the vitality of the ecosphere which is fostered by diversity, complexity, richness and stability. Cutting a few common cultivated flowers for the house on these grounds would be acceptable, but not the wanton killing of a rare wild orchid.

A concern for the well-being of the whole on the principle of ecocentric impartiality implies that we should give precedence to rare species before the common, the less resilient to the prolific, the endangered before the overpopulated, those essential for the health of the ecosystem rather than its parasites. At the same time, individual organisms should never be sacrificed for the good of the whole, unless that good is seriously threatened. Moreover, since nature is evolving towards greater diversity and consciousness, the well-being of the whole can only be achieved through the individuality and interdependence of its parts.

The kind of impartiality I am advocating is not based on cold analysis and disinterested calculation. It attempts to go beyond the narrow interest of humans for themselves, beyond the view of nature and all its creatures as means to our ends. It respects all beings as intrinsically valuable and celebrates the fundamental goodness of creation. Above all, it has an open heart and a great compassion which ultimately expresses itself in an all-embracing love for the universe as a whole.

But is such impartiality 'against nature'? In the evolutionary drive for the survival of our species, it might be considered 'natural' to give precedence to our own species. Certainly those who believe there is such a thing as the 'selfish gene' would think so. Yet in the struggle for survival in evolution, it is the most co-operative species which survive. For humans to survive now, they need to co-operate, not only with each other but with other species and the biosphere. The well-being of the earth, and therefore their own well-being, depend on it. As fellow voyagers in evolution, we should help each other. This does not mean changing the nature of predators and prey – even if that were possible – or expecting the lion to lie down with the lamb. But as countless examples show, ever since animals began to share the hearth with humans, friendship – one of the most 'natural' of feelings – has existed across the species. And not only is a man's best friend his dog; it is possible to establish deep and meaningful relationships with wild creatures, whether birds, badgers or bears.

Many people think only of themselves or their own, whether it be their egos, family, clan, nation, race or species. This is especially so in situations of scarcity. In a four-person life raft, where there are four humans and a large dog, most people would argue that the dog should be thrown overboard to prevent the life raft from sinking. But the person who loves the dog might have different ideas. Indeed, a yachtsman when his boat sank once got his dog and himself into a two-person dinghy and tied his cook to the side. When they were picked up the cook was dead and the two in the dinghy alive. Most people would argue that the cook should have taken precedence over the dog (children, women – and men, first). But on the principle of ecocentric impartiality, a dog has a claim to life and to realize its potential as much as a human. One should not necessarily be discriminated against on grounds of species any more than on those of sex or race.

This is not so outlandish as it might appear. A growing number of environmental philosophers and activists maintain that it should not be humans first but Earth First; indeed there is an environmental group of that name. Although I would not go so far myself, it has been argued that in certain circumstances it might be preferable to kill a man rather than a rattlesnake. It has even been asserted that the wanton killing of a flower is worse than killing a human in self-defence.

It is impossible to lay down a categorical imperative, a universal moral maxim to cover all cases and circumstances. However, if we are obliged to choose between saving one of two humans or a human or an animal in an extreme situation like the life raft, there are certain moral principles which should be taken into account. As we have seen, the first is that nature has intrinsic value and not simply as a means to our ends. Secondly, all life is sacred. Thirdly, we should cause minimum harm and have compassion for all beings. And finally, we should seek to contribute to the well-being of the whole.

In general, a dog has as much intrinsic worth as a life form as a human. But under the principle of ecocentric impartiality, if the dog in question is one of the last in the world, it might be considered more important to the well-being of the biosphere for it to survive than another member of an excessively numerous and destructive species. Having myself lived for seventeen years in a loving relationship with a dog, I can sympathize with the yachtsman who wanted to save his dog and can understand that a benevolent dog might be more worthy to live than a sadistic human killer. Yet as I write this my instinctive humanity – my species being – rebels in favour of my fellow human.

The dilemmas rise like gulls along a seashore: myself or others first? My dog or my enemy first? Humanity or earth first? Earth or cosmos first?

The principle of ecocentric impartiality asserts that all beings and things (individuals as well as groups) have inherent value, but it does not deny that there is a partial ordering of value. The more valuable something is in contributing to the well-being of the whole, the more worthy it is of being preserved. A definition of well-being in this context would take into account the ecological principles of diversity, complexity and stability. The greater variety in an ecosystem, the more overall harmony and vitality. The same is true for Gaia and the cosmos.

In normal circumstances, a human might be considered more valuable than a non-human, but if a group of animals or a species are threatened, then they might take precedence. Although in East Africa, humans are hungry for land, it is right to create nature reserves for threatened species like elephants or rhinoceros. While humans might like to drive a motorway through a rare and sensitive habitat in order to take a few minutes off a journey, the interests of the habitat and its creatures are more important. And the wilderness of Antarctica is better off – for our imagination and for the earth – without the presence of human beings.

The principle of ecocentric impartiality implies that the vital interests of organisms should on occasion trump human interests of a non-vital kind. It might well be right to sacrifice our local interests as humans to the larger interests of animals, plants and ecosystems. We might forgo our pleasure in climbing a mountain or visiting a wilderness area in order to let nature have a free hand to thrive and flourish in its own way.

In general, I would say that while all beings have intrinsic worth, their degree of consciousness and their ability to contribute to the well-being of the whole are relevant considerations. Except in special circumstances, a human would take precedence over a non-human since the former has a greater degree of consciousness and more opportunities to contribute to the well-being of the whole. In the final analysis, we must all make our own decisions in a concerned and sympathetic way according to the particular circumstances by following the voice of our intuition.

The third principle of liberation ecology that we should cause minimum harm and have compassion for beings also has its difficulties. All beings tremble before danger, all fear death. When they consider this, compassionate people do not kill or cause to kill. Yet given the inescapable web of relationships within nature, the endless net of cause and effect, it is impossible to avoid causing some harm. In order to live, we inevitably harm others, even unto death. If we do not kill animals to eat, we kill carrots and cabbages. But we can try and not kill or be the cause of killing. It is a question of degree. If we cannot avoid causing some harm to other life and the environment in order to live, at least we can try and cause minimum harm.

This might mean not breaking off an icicle hanging from a rock, not tearing a branch off a tree, not walking on snowdrops in the wood, not hitting grass with a stick. It might mean releasing a rabbit from a gintrap, a bird from a cage, a moth from a house into the night air. It might mean not killing off so-called 'pests' in the garden and sharing some of your produce with slugs, rabbits, squirrels, mice and wire worms. We should not begrudge their share of the bountifulness of nature. What right do we have to all the grain in the world? Would not the earth be the poorer by the disappearance of a single weed?

Living inevitably involves killing and we have to kill in order to live, but wanton killing or killing for sport is indefensible. Being aware of the consequences of our actions helps to prevent harm, but the most important of all is to have harmless intentions. No person deliberately wills harm, and cruelty is usually a result of ignorance, a damaged mind or a wounded heart.

It is, of course, difficult to draw the exact boundaries of justifiable killing in order to prolong human life. Since all life is sacred, we have no right to reduce the richness, complexity and diversity of life except to satisfy our vital needs. But what are vital

83

needs? What is vital to one, might be superfluous to another. Most people who are carnivores would say that taking the life of animals is justified to satisfy their 'vital' needs. Vegetarians, on the other hand, would argue – and I do so as one myself – that these needs are not vital, that is to say, essential for the continuance of their life. Indeed, since to produce meat protein requires seven times more land than to produce the equivalent value in vegetable protein, it will soon become vital for humans to eat less meat if they want to survive and allow other life forms to flourish.

The question of vital needs is a question of degree. I have no wish to lay down a moral law, only to offer certain guidelines. It is for each of us to define our own in order to live well in the light of the general principles of the sacredness of all life and the desirability of causing minimum harm. Even when we take life, eating a carrot in a salad or killing a lion which is about to eat us, we should honour the life of the plant or animal which is being sacrificed in order for us to live. And 'sacrifice' is an appropriate word, with its root coming from the Latin *sacrificium*, 'to make holy'.

If we believe in causing minimum harm, should we prevent others from causing harm? Some have made a distinction between self-regarding and other-regarding actions and have argued that people should be prevented from harming others. To harm others is a serious infringement of their freedom and autonomy. While it is still a harm to restrict the freedom of someone in order to prevent him or her from harming another, it is the lesser of two evils. Whatever the situation, minimum restraint should be used.

In the case of self-regarding actions, I would argue that people should to a large extent be allowed to harm themselves if they so wish. If people want to commit suicide or undergo euthanasia as a form of voluntary death, they should be allowed to do so if the decision is a conscious, uncoerced one. If people want to go to the dogs or fly with eagles, they should be allowed to do so, although those around should always be ready to lend a helping hand. If people want to experiment with drugs to expand their consciousness, they should be allowed to do so as long as they know the risks they are taking.

The last proviso is crucial. The risks should be clear. If there is only one bridge across a raging torrent, and the bridge is rickety, people should not be prevented by the police from using it but warned by a sign that the bridge is dangerous and they cross it at their own risk. If people want to smoke marijuana, they should be provided with the known information of the possible hazards and benefits at the point of purchase.

In reality, since people are sets of relationships as well as unique individuals, it is difficult to maintain a rigid distinction between self- and other-regarding actions. In the net of cause and effect all actions inevitably affect each other. You might say that people should be free not to wear a crash helmet on a motorbike – and I would – but if there is an accident and the rider is brain-damaged, the injured person would draw heavily on the resources of the rest of society. Yet in other cases the financial burden of providing collective health care might be less than the harm of curtailing personal freedom and increasing the power of the state.

But this whole discussion is riddled with the utilitarian calculus of profit and loss, advantage and disadvantage. If people did act benevolently and aimed to cause minimum harm there would be little need for such calculations. As a general rule – and, as such, a rule to be broken according to the light of particular circum-stances – I would say that people should be given as much autonomy and responsibility as possible, and only be restrained with the minimum of force if they are clearly hurting others.

The Jains, famous for wearing masks and sweeping the paths before them to avoid killing insects, take the principle of no harm (*ahimsa*) to the extreme. They extend the Buddhist compassion for all beings to things. They will not become farmers for when ploughing the soil they might injure plants and animals and the soil itself. They will not practise certain violent crafts, for the metal on the blacksmith's anvil and the wood under the carpenter's saw may experience excruciating pain.

I would not follow them into such extremes, but I believe that they are right to feel compassion for all things and beings. Animals and plants have a will to live and are capable of thriving or languishing. Plants appear to be sensitive to light and touch, and animals being so close to us clearly experience pain and pleasure. But even rocks as vibrating quanta of energy may have a degree of sensitivity.

In my view the principle of Reverence for Being is the most important overriding moral principle. It has two distinct merits. Firstly, it seeks to cause minimum harm, trying to find ways of minimizing suffering rather than of maximizing pleasure.

Secondly, it seeks to allow individual organisms, communities, and nature as a whole to realize their evolutionary potential.

The principle of Reverence for Being is not a law, but a general principle which is nothing more than a signpost pointing in the right direction. It may be likened to the craftsman's rule of thumb, not a rigid measurement but a rough guide. Whatever the case, it should always be applied in the light of the particular circumstances. There may be circumstances in which individual lives may have to be sacrificed for the well-being of the whole, as in the case of rhododendron ponticum invading oak-woods or of smallpox virus causing an epidemic. The well-being of the whole might also be compromised for the sake of individual lives, such as making room for fragile and endangered species in over-crowded ecosystems. The particular circumstances are paramount and ultimately every case should be a rule unto itself. The well-being of the whole can only be achieved with the well-being of the individuals who make it up.

In order to liberate Gaia and ourselves, liberation ecology therefore suggests that we use our imagination to go out of ourselves in order to become concerned observers of our needs and the needs of others. It recommends the use of intuition to appreciate the inherent value and equality of all beings. It calls for the sensibility to have compassion for all beings. Above all, it urges an open heart and a visionary mind so that we can all honour the creation, celebrate life and feel Reverence for Being.

# 8

# Liberation Ecology

*Horses live on dry land, eat grass and drink water. When pleased, they rub their necks together. When angry, they turn round and kick up their heels at each other. Thus far only do their natural dispositions carry them. But bridled and bitted, with a plate of metal on their foreheads, they learn to cast vicious looks, to turn the head to bite, to resist, to get the bit out of the mouth or the bridle into it. And thus their natures become depraved.*

Chuang Tzu

Liberation ecology is a system of ethics for the new millennium. Based on compassion for all beings and Reverence for Being, it combines ancient wisdom with modern insights. It is holistic, deep, social, libertarian and transpersonal.

Liberation ecology is holistic because it recognizes the interwoven and interrelated nature of the world. It does not place humans at the centre of the universe or consider them the measure of all things, but accepts that they are one species among other species, one strand amongst myriads of other strands in nature's bespangled web.

It is holistic in seeing the whole as greater than the sum of its parts, both in society and nature. The fulfilment of a part can only take place within the larger whole and the larger whole does not exist without the organic unity of its parts. It regards all parts from the point of view of the whole and recognizes the unity in the diversity of the world.

A mountain is high because of its individual particles of matter;

a river is large because of its individual drops of water. Complex wholes cannot therefore be explained by analysing the simple properties of their constituent parts. Individual organisms are not just separate entities but sets of relationships, threads in a web of relations. Individual organisms come and go while the whole remains; fish and seaweed are born and die, but the sea continues to flow around the planet.

There is, however, a danger in taking too holistic an approach for it can lead to the wanton sacrifice of individuals for the alleged well-being of the whole. In ecological terms, oceans, lakes, mountains, forests and wetlands are more important – of greater value – than individual animals. In nature's web, soil bacteria and plankton are more essential to life on earth than humans. But this does not mean that the interests of a forest or a wetland should always come before those of humans, only in most cases.

Extreme holism can also be authoritarian. Expressed in social terms, it often takes the form of rulers calling on citizens to sacrifice themselves for the 'good of the whole', whether it be in wage restraint or in waging war. It can flare up as a kind of herd instinct, a form of group identification which manifests itself in tribalism, racism, patriotism and nationalism. Rulers often claim special insight into the 'general good' and oblige rebellious and recalcitrant citizens to realize their 'higher selves' by identifying with the state, so that they are in Jean Jacques Rousseau's sinister phrase 'forced to be free'.

Those who put the earth first in all circumstances and are prepared to sacrifice humans for its alleged good are in danger of becoming a new breed of eco-tyrants. This anti-human stance has led some to argue that the degree of misanthropy in the modern environmental movement is a measure of its purity. From this perspective, humans are seen as little more than harmful parasites crawling on the skin of Gaia.

What is needed, and what liberation ecology proposes, is a holistic approach which is concerned with the well-being of the whole but which does not wantonly sacrifice individuals. We are undoubtedly part of the whole, in metaphysical, moral and social terms, but we are also unique individuals. If nature's web has an intrinsic value, then so do the threads which go to make it up. To tear part of the web, to wipe out a species or individuals of a threatened species, weakens the whole. Neither the whole nor the parts, neither the web nor the threads, are of paramount importance; they are equally valuable and mutually beneficial. It follows that we should recognize the claims of the whole as well as those of the individual parts and try to avoid sacrificing one for the other.

Liberation ecology is deep because it goes to the roots of our ecological and social crisis, asks profound questions and affirms fundamental principles. It is not concerned with the latest storm over a particular issue or event, but dives to deeper and calmer waters. It flows with the underlying currents of nature and settles in the primordial way of the cosmos.

The majority of those who express concern about the environment are not deep green but shallow green. Their measure is man: the value of anything is its usefulness to humanity. They value nature not as an end-in-itself but as a means to an end. They do not want to upset existing property relations, but seek limited access to the countryside as an enjoyable feature of life. They see nature as a colourful backdrop to the spectacle of society. They like the idea of having wild places and wildlife, but get closest to them on the television. Such shallow environmentalists want to clear up the planet in order to make it a better place for themselves.

As conservationists, they want to conserve nature for the well-being of humans. They appreciate that nature provides free goods and services for their life-support systems. They are keen to use resources efficiently; they create conservation areas and talk of 'sustainable development' and the needs of future generations. Some go further and call for preservation, wanting to maintain things as they are, drawing up preservation orders to preserve certain landscapes, species and natural systems (whether moorland, whales or Antarctica). Their defence of nature is largely based on its value as a resource for human science, as a pool of genetic diversity, and as a place of recreation, of aesthetic pleasure and of spiritual inspiration.

Translated into action, this shallow green approach usually means campaigning to preserve certain landscapes now considered beautiful. This not only overlooks the fact that taste changes, but also denies the potential for the dynamic evolution of habitats and ecosystems. Where I live in North Wales is a case in point. In the eighteenth century, its rugged and mountainous landscape was considered as 'rude' and 'horrid', but since the Romantics it has become sublime and inspiring. It is now a national park and its stewards wish to preserve it in aspic largely as it is, an accident of uncontrolled farming practices which have left it for the most part a green desert with woodland covering an area of only two and a half per cent of the total.

Much of the work that is done by conservationists is good. They enjoy the moods of nature and wish to protect what remains of its green and brown presence. They recognize the therapeutic value to be gained from contact with wild places, animals and birds. They appreciate a fine view when they see one and would like to keep the woods healthy and the ponds clean. Nevertheless, shallow environmentalism still reflects an instrumental and calculating rationality. It is mainly concerned with short-term fixes of conservation, preservation and pollution control. It lays the blame for the ecological crisis not on the human conquest of nature but on inappropriate technology, overpopulation, or excessive industrial growth.

The greatest limitation of shallow environmentalism is that it remains rigidly anthropocentric – man-centred. It sees nature as a park, a passive habitat of potentially useful objects for humans, a collection of resources for them to exploit, and as a theatre for their activities. Above all, it extends the domination in existing society to nature, placing humans and natural objects in the same master–slave relationship. It comes as no surprise that the root of the verb 'to conserve' is the Latin *cum* 'with' and *servus* 'a slave.'

Liberation ecology on the other hand adopts a deeper, greener and more radical approach. It is not just concerned with cleaning up the planet to make it a better place for humans, but seeks to develop a new understanding and relationship with nature, a new awareness and sensibility. It maintains that nature is not just a backdrop to our social spectacle, a collection of resources or a place for recreation. It is freedom; it is wildness; it is the primordial. It is not something alien, the Other, what is outside ourselves, for we are an integral part of nature. We experience nature, and nature experiences us. Nature drives our desires. It comes through in our dreams. It is the life force itself. It is absurd to imagine a wilderness faraway from ourselves. The sea is in our blood, the moor is in our belly, the stars in our brain. The primeval vitality of nature is deep within us.

Despite the constant efforts of humans, nature can only be tamed temporarily. It cannot be held down. It pushes its way up like grass between the pavements when human feet stop walking on the cracks. Its wild animals, whether foxes or mice, flourish in the nooks and crannies of towns. Its insects, whether mites or cockroaches, thrive in our presence despite our insecticides. Nature takes over in any derelict land, and if the land is left to itself it would eventually return to primeval forest.

Liberation ecology is social because it traces the causes of the present ecological and social crisis not only to a mechanical and authoritarian world-view but also to hierarchy and domination within society. Modern technology, industrial growth and over-population all play their part, but it is our exploitative and conquering relationships with each other and with nature which are mainly to blame. The domination of nature mirrors the domination of humans by humans: woman's domination of man in matriarchal society, man's domination of woman in patriarchal society, and the domination of men and women by each other in an unequal and unjust society.

Domination and hierarchy are not permanent features of our condition, but a particular historical and social development in the course of our evolution. Certainly, there is a potential in all of us for domination and aggression, as there is for equality and non-violence, but it is our social and cultural circumstances which encourage the one at the expense of the other. The will to dominate is not innate in human beings, but something learned and acquired.

It was hitherto considered necessary, by socialists and liberals alike, to dominate and conquer nature in order to transcend scarcity and create a just society. But such thinking is not only outdated but a positive fetter on developing a more enlightened and ecological society. Abundance is not a precondition of an ecological society nor is it essential in order to overcome the urge to dominate nature. Hunter-gatherers who survived in a world of comparative scarcity had no wish to dominate nature and lived harmoniously within its web. Whatever the level of material wealth, we need not be victims of nature nor conquerors of nature, but can become fellow companions in the odyssey of evolution.

What is needed is to re-interpret the world and to change society. Liberation ecology is therefore radical, going to the root of things, and calls for deep social change. Only by changing our relationships with each other to create a more just and equal society can we expect a new relationship with nature based on equality and justice to develop. There is no reason why this should not be possible. Although we are products of our society, history and environment, we are nevertheless free to shape consciously and purposefully our lives. We can gather up our past and launch ourselves into the future. By our present actions and thoughts and feelings, we shape our own destinies.

Liberation ecology is transpersonal. It begins with the individual, but does not end there. It sees the individual at the centre and circumference of the universe. It takes seriously the Sanskrit phrase *Tat twam asi* ('That art thou'), and recognizes that beings and things are interconnected and interdependent. Those who see all creatures in themselves and themselves in all creatures know no fear and grief. All is One, and One is All. Being aware of this, there is no need to feel abandoned, alien or afraid in the universe. The universe is our home and we are secure in it. It supports us and cares for us.

Because we have imagination and intuition, it is possible to identify with other aspects of nature, to think like a glacier or feel like a tree. It is possible to have trans-species experience and an empathetic understanding of other creatures. You do not have to be a shaman shape-changer to crawl with a snake, to soar with an eagle, or to dive with a dolphin.

True realization is only possible with the identification of the individual self with the larger Self of the universe. If it stops with the personal ego, it can degenerate into self-aggrandizement, self-assertion and self-interest. But by expanding the sense of self until it embraces the whole, by becoming the self-in-the-Self, both the individual and the universe can unfurl their potential and realize themselves. True realization is transpersonal by going beyond possessive attachment to family, clan, tribe, race or species, to identify not only with all beings but with the Being of beings. Charity might begin at home – people find it easier to help what is close to them rather than what is faraway – but it should not end there. True realization develops in an ever widening circle from the earth to embrace the entire creation. It passes from the social, the natural, to the cosmic. It realizes that no one is saved until we are all saved.

All beings have a right to continued existence. It is human arrogance to discriminate in favour of their own species, a kind of speciesism which is comparable to sexism or racism. True benevolence is not just for one's own. It is not anthropocentric but ecocentric, not humanist but trans-speciesist. It is love for all creation, not just for a particular manifestation.

At the same time, it is not the kind of benevolence or altruism which constantly meddles in the affairs of others. It helps by not interfering, by letting things be. The best way to help others is to attain self-harmony for oneself. The best way to help the world is to let it return to its own spontaneous order. By ordering one's own dwelling, the Earth Household finds again its own natural equilibrium and harmony.

Finally, liberation ecology is libertarian in seeking to free humanity, society and nature from their present burdens. It takes up the great aspirations of the French Revolution for liberty, equality and fraternity, and believes that you cannot have one without the other. It plants a liberty tree in the concrete of tyranny, a flower of love in the garden of cruelty. It refuses to treat nature as a slave, to subdue, control and exploit it, but seeks to liberate it from human domination. It aims to overcome humanity's sense of separation from nature and to reconcile the two in creative fellowship. We are the voice of nature's self-expression.

By freeing nature, we free ourselves, and by freeing ourselves, we free nature. Together we can unfold and realize our evolutionary potential. Finding our rightful place within nature as shepherds of being rather than lords of creation, we can free ourselves from our self-imposed manacles. We can become free to reach our full stature.

Liberation ecology thus offers a life-based, holistic ethics. It is not anthropocentric – man-centred – but ecocentric, taking into account the well-being of the biosphere as well as of humans. It does not wantonly sacrifice individuals for the well-being of the whole, but sees their good as inextricably entwined with the good of others. It has respect for the lives of particular beings – for deer, frogs, periwinkles, ash – but also for larger wholes of which they form a part – boglands, woods, meadows, lakes and mountains. It not only has compassion for individual beings, but celebrates the Being of all beings. It honours the goshawk and the sparrow, the shrimp and the whale, the buttercup and the orchid, the ocean deep and the mountain high, the land and the sea, the sun and the moon, the earth and the cosmos. It stands at the centre and the circumference, in the heart of the atom as well as in the main stream of the Milky Way.

Being holistic, deep, social and libertarian, liberation ecology calls for a new awareness and a new relationship with nature. In the past, humans have interfered deeply and with disastrous results. Humans did not appear on earth until very late in its evolution. It is possibly 15 thousand million years since the Big Bang which created the known universe, yet recognizable humans did not emerge until 3.5 million years ago in East Africa. Since then they have fanned out and colonized the world. Their remarkable lack of biological specialization has enabled them to flourish in virtually every type of habitat, from mountain to desert, the Arctic Circle to the Equator.

Early humans had little impact on natural ecosystems. The discovery of fire was the first great technological breakthrough, enabling them to cook food and destroy vegetation on a large scale. About the same time, the making of tools and weapons made them more powerful as predators. But while humans remained hunter-gatherers, their impact was comparatively slight. It was the invention of agriculture some 18,000 years ago in Asia and the Middle East and the domestication of animals which began to transform the landscape. Virtually every animal in our fields and plant in our gardens are a result of selective breeding and artificial selection. We are now trying to change through genetic engineering the course of human biological evolution.

The ecological impact of humans has inexorably grown with their numbers. Humans reached their first billion by 1830 but the agricultural and industrial revolutions which gradually spread throughout the world enabled the population to grow in leaps and bounds with devastating effects on the environment. Corn and iron may have 'civilized' humanity but they ruined nature. The twentieth century saw a phenomenal increase: 2000 million by 1930; 3000 million by 1960; 4000 million by 1976; 5000 million by 1986. Our forever proliferating numbers (an insane multiplication of human proliferoles) should reach 10,000 million early in the twenty-first century.

The effect of the human species on the earth is now vast and incalculable and set to continue. We have irrevocably used up much of its non-renewable resources. There has been widespread destruction of natural ecosystems. With the greenhouse effect of massive industrial pollution, the sea level continues to rise and the polar caps to melt. Humans have not only transformed the landscape but have begun to alter the weather. Every minute the trees of the rain-forests – the lungs of the earth – crash down. The resulting burdens on Gaia are enormous. She is just coping with the maintenance of the gases in the atmosphere, the key to life on earth; her seas are absorbing what they can; her land is suffering most and large swathes are turning into green and brown deserts.

The history of humanity has to a large extent been a history of their attempt to subdue, control and improve nature. Virtually all political movements have sought to bring about economic abundance through the conquest of nature – a vision shared by Adam Smith, Karl Marx, Peter Kropotkin, Adolf Hitler, Maynard Keynes and Mao Tse-Tung. The result of this headlong exploitation is that there is nowhere in the world which has not felt the impact of humanity, from the deepest ocean to the highest mountain, from DDT in polar bears, radioactive fall out in upland pastures, mercury in tuna, to PCBs in barnacles. The impact has been so great that it makes sense to talk of the 'end of nature' as a pristine world without the fingerprints of humans.

Apart from a few isolated voices, only in the late twentieth century did a widespread movement develop which sought to check economic growth, curb the use of what was left of renewable resources, and reverse the destruction of wildlife habitats. Only now as the new millennium dawns is there a growing song, rising from deep within, calling for clean land, rivers, seas and air and urging a more sustainable way of life in harmony with nature.

Is it too late? It might be. It might not be. It depends on us, on whether we wish to export our consumerist and materialist way of life until it chokes the very arteries of the earth, or whether we decide to rediscover the uncarved block and develop a quiet and simple life. There is no going back, any more than we can put our foot in the same river twice. We can only move forward, but we can also take up the best practices of the past and where appropriate make them our own.

The most important and urgent task is to develop a new relationship with nature, or rather reinvent the archaic one we have lost. We do not stand apart as subject and object: humans are as natural as wolves, oaks and rocks. Nature is the air we breathe, the land we tread, the body we move. But as a species with tremendous power through our science and technology, we have a responsibility to use the power well, a responsibility for ourselves and the rest of nature that is our only dwelling.

This can start with a new relationship with the land. Aldo

Leopoldo after the Second World War famously called for a 'land ethic' which would change the role of *homo sapiens* from conqueror of the land to plain member and citizen of its community. Since we are the most powerful species, we need to develop a new ethic in our dealings with nature, an ethic which treats it with love and respect and recognizes the right to life of animals and plants, soils and waters, whatever their use to us. The land is one organism; everything is interwoven and interdependent in nature's web. Harmony with the land, Leopoldo said, is like harmony with a friend; you cannot cherish his right hand and chop off his left. As a rule of thumb, he suggested that any decision about the land is 'right when it tends to preserve the integrity, stability and beauty of the biotic community. It is wrong when it tends otherwise.'

There is much to recommend in this land ethic but the criteria are not self-evident. Beauty is notoriously in the eye of the beholder: a stag is beautiful for most people, but not necessarily a frog. While stability is an important ecological principle, it does not alone allow room for dynamic evolution. To focus narrowly on the 'biotic community' also neglects the wider elements which support it.

The greatest shortcoming of Leopoldo's land ethic is that it overlooks the biotic rights of individuals. On the principle of the sacredness of life there should be compassion for all individual beings. The loss of individual lives in the economy of nature is inevitable if nature is to prosper as the whole. The culling of individual wolves might be acceptable if it helps preserve the community. But what if this principle of sacrificing individuals for the good of the whole is applied to the human community? It has not been without its advocates.

We cannot leave it to the so-called wildlife expert to decide alone what is the healthy functioning of an ecosystem any more than we can leave the medical expert to decide about the health of our bodies or the politician to decide on how to run the body politic. Any decision has to be a democratic one which takes into consideration the interests of all the parties concerned, whether humans, animals, insects, plants, water, soil, air, germs or even microbes. The well-being of individual members as well as the well-being of the whole community have to be taken into account.

Apparent 'non-resources' and those members of the biotic community whose disappearance would not greatly affect its healthy functioning should be allowed their place in the spontaneous order of nature. Even an organism like smallpox, which now only exists in a laboratory, should not necessarily be eradicated. Although its natural habitat is in the human body which its threatens, smallpox has intrinsic value as a life form and may well in the future be shown to have an important function in human ecology. Only if it is out of control, like malaria, should it be contained. There is a place for germs in the body, weeds in the garden, and wolves in the forest, as long as they do not affect adversely the healthy functioning of the whole. A healthy community can support parasites and population fluctuations. Indeed, disease is part of the total harmony. Just as a healthy human organism can rely on its own resistance to infection, so a healthy ecosystem can resist potentially harmful intrusions. Indeed, the health of an organism might be measured by the degree of parasites it can support and tolerate.

I suggest that any decision about land is right when it tends to foster the natural course of evolution towards greater diversity, harmony and vitality of the whole community with the minimum harm to individual members. It is wrong when it tends otherwise. And the general principle should be seen as a rule of thumb and on occasion the interests of individual members might trump those of the community if it is no great burden.

Land reform should be an integral part of a new land ethic. Rather than being controlled by larger and larger corporations of agribusiness which destroy the land and the communities it supports it should be redistributed to those who wish to reinhabit the countryside and nurture, restore and care for it. With land reform must go a new awareness that no one can strictly speaking own the land any more than the air, water or the sea. It is part of our common treasury, a treasury which we share with other creatures. Large swathes of land should be made into wilderness areas with very restricted human access while wildlife should be allowed to repopulate the fringes of farming areas. Hardwood forests should be extended, providing rich habitats and a source of renewable energy. In this way, humans and wildlife can be members of the same eco-communities.

It is absurd for someone to say, 'Get off my land!' Whatever the laws of the state might say, the land is morally a free gift from nature to all of us, humans and non-humans alike. Mixing one's labour with nature creates wealth and one is entitled to the fruits

97

of labour but it does not make nature an object to possess for exclusive use.

If we are responsible for portions of the land, if we are involved in ploughing and sowing and reaping, it is only for a time. Our dwelling on the earth is temporary. We come and go, while the land and all that it sustains continues. Those who occupy the land should be considered as tenants or stewards, not owners or managers. Good farmers enhance the land under their care during their lifetime, or at least allow nature to take its course. Their pride is not in increased productivity but in the improved quality of the land they pass on for future generations to enjoy. That is called sustainability.

The land belongs to nature and we belong to nature. The land is ours in so far as we are all part of nature. We come out of the soil and we return to the soil. It sustains life and absorbs death. It is the skin of Gaia and we have put it under stress. We can either deepen the wounds or apply balm to heal them.

While much has been written about the land ethic, little has been said about a sea ethic. Yet the sea covers about 70 per cent of the surface of the planet. Not only did life evolve in the sea a thousand million years before on land, but its depths, long considered relatively lifeless, are now known to contain more diverse life forms than a tropical rain-forest. New species are constantly being discovered, some unimaginable, like giant worms and crabs which live in the nutrient rich and warm waters near volcano vents at the bottom of the ocean.

The sea is the last great wilderness on earth. We have transformed the land, but despite the waste and chemicals we pump into it, the sea is still wild and free. We have tamed the land, but the sea remains untamable. We know more about the surface of the moon than the floor of the ocean. The sea escapes us, it defies definition, it cannot be imagined. The sea is called cruel because it is greater than us. For many it is the ultimate Other, and yet life emerged in the sea and it flows in our veins – our blood is the same chemical mix as the sea. It also contains highly evolved mammals – whales and dolphins – who in many ways are much wiser than we are with their co-operative and playful ways. I often wonder whether they are meditating in the deep, trying to hold the world together. The more we kill them, it seems, the more the world falls apart.

The sea not only provides the rain which makes life exist on earth but plays a key role, especially with its algae and plankton, in maintaining the equilibrium of the gases in the biosphere. Yet we fish it dry and use it as a dump and a drain for our foul effluent and noxious waste. Because of the noise of our boats, there is nowhere under the water which escapes the sound of our rapacious activity. The sea can absorb much, but it is already under threat along its shores. A sea ethic recognizes that the health of the sea is essential to the health of the land and that both land and sea are two aspects of the living organism of Gaia.

Liberation ecology does not stop with the land and the sea, but urges a Gaia ethic which celebrates the vitality of the earth as a whole. It still does not rest there and passes from a geocentric to a cosmic vision. Gaia is only part of the wider organism of the universe, with all its planets, stars, black holes, anti-matter and other wondrous mysteries of outer space.

To what degree should we interfere with the natural processes in the land and the sea? Should we try and manage Gaia and direct the future evolution of the cosmos? Many Victorians, triumphant in their apparent conquest of nature, believed that progress depended not on imitating but on combating the cosmic process. T. H. Huxley, known as Darwin's 'bulldog' for his spirited defence of his theory of evolution, proposed in 1893 'to pit the microcosm against the macrocosm and to set man to subdue nature to his higher moral ends'. His grandson, the biologist Julian Huxley, still saw a unique role of humanity to 'inject his ethics into the heart of evolution'. Indeed, he believed that 'man' is not only the sole agent for further evolutionary 'progress' on this planet but should become the 'business manager for the cosmic process of evolution'.

The prospect is alarming, especially given the past record of human interference in nature. Those who stand in this tradition are the modern scientists who are involved in genetic engineering, creating new hybrids of plants and animals, changing the structure of DNA, cloning sheep (humans next?), encouraging new diseases by their lack of care like BSE and possibly AIDS. They are the ones who split the atom, create the hydrogen bomb and nuclear energy without thinking of the long-term results. Those engaged in potentially the most destructive aspects of science and technology deny any responsibility for their findings. They hide behind slogans such as the 'disinterested pursuit of knowledge' and 'knowledge for knowledge's sake' without ever questioning what is real knowledge, let alone wisdom. Continuing in the rapacious tradition of Francis Bacon, who urged scientists to place nature 'on the rack' and 'force her to reveal her secrets', they break down matter, experiment with diseases, and cross natural boundaries, completely impervious to the eventual consequences of their research. They tear the veil off nature, and penetrate rudely her most intimate places.

It was Bacon, the great apologist of the sixteenth-century Scientific Revolution, who said that 'knowledge is power'. Many modern scientists have not forgotten his advice and use their knowledge chiefly to increase their power over nature. Unlike the true alchemists of old, they have not learned the responsibility which should accompany the pursuit of knowledge; they have inordinate power over nature, but little power over themselves. They do not know how to discriminate and when to stop. They abdicate all moral direction to the politicians and industrialists who finance their work – the least qualified to become business managers of the 'cosmic process of evolution'. By interfering deeply in nature, such scientists have gone far in subduing it to their own ends, but they have conspicuously failed to develop a sound evolutionary ethic.

This need not be so. Socrates believed that knowledge is virtue. Our present knowledge of nature could be transformed into the kind of wisdom which would encourage us to live harmoniously and co-operatively with the rest of the creation and to work out the boundaries which we should not cross. Above all, it would lead us to celebrate and nurture all life forms on the planet and not only ourselves.

Since virtually the whole world has suffered the destructive impact of humans, you might conclude that it is time not merely for preservation or even conservation, but for stern man-age-ment. But since men have been mainly responsible for the ecological crisis, it is unlikely that they will undertake the task with the necessary skill and sensitivity. Given their past record, they are not in a very good position to 'improve' let alone 'direct' evolution.

Are there any circumstances where we should interfere with nature, rather than just let it be? In the past, the only hand which we have offered nature is one of destruction. So-called *homo sapiens* has distinguished itself by multiplying its numbers, subduing nature, and ousting other species. If we cannot extend a hand of friendship, then I say: 'hands off!' Let nature follow its own beneficent course, without us interfering deeply in its evolution. We can trust that the creation is good. Left to itself, nature will find its own creative and life-affirming course. Nature flourishes best when least interfered with. This deep-seated trust in the wisdom and goodness of nature is the fundamental intuition of this book.

In general, it is best to withdraw as much as possible from areas relatively untouched in order to let them return to their primordial state. Where the damage is great, a degree of judicious and restrained damage limitation work might be necessary to re-establish the natural integrity and harmony. We can reverse the process of destruction of species and ecosystems and co-operate with nature in encouraging richness, diversity, complexity and stability. We can undertake a modicum of sensitive restoration work by clearing up the mess we have made, and by giving nature a helping hand to regenerate itself. In the long run, the best way to help nature is to live lightly on the earth, minimize our waste, control our numbers and refuse to meddle with natural evolution.

Despite the ambitions of scientists, there are no convincing grounds for 'managing' the future of the world. By what special right does humanity have to be the helmsman of evolution, the captain of nature? They cannot look after themselves, let alone the rest of nature. To attempt to 'humanize' nature and to open up new evolutionary pathways would seem to be courting disaster. Humans should never interfere deeply with natural processes or attempt to direct the course of evolution (whether it be splitting the atom, cloning sheep, or changing genes).

Stewardship rather than the management of the evolutionary process is a better role for humans. Stewardship implies care and concern. The country would benefit if farmers saw themselves as stewards rather than owners, holding the land in trust on behalf of the rest of humanity and for future generations. But stewards still represent particular interests, whether in the workplace or on earth. They care for something primarily for their own benefit. Stewardship also implies that we have a responsibility for something weaker than ourselves.

Then what about becoming partners with nature? Better a partner than a thrusting steward or an arrogant manager, for partnership implies co-operation and fellowship. But it also suggests that we are somehow separate: partnership bridges a gap. We are not separated from nature as subject and object, as 'I' and 'it'; to believe so is the ultimate alienation. Nature cares for us as much as we care for nature; we experience nature and nature experiences us. The mountain stream and the wild wood are within our breasts.

We have no God-given right to manage or even care for nature. We have had enough of Managers, Helmsmen, Stewards and Partners. Let us become Lovers of Being, celebrating the life force, dancing on the beaches and uplands and under the sheltering sky. Let us become fellow voyagers with other life forms in the great odyssey of evolution, not trying to steer the boat, but going with the currents, confident that they will take us to a safe shore. Let us ride the wind, exhilarated, joyful and free.

We can care for each other, help each other on our way, but we are all voyaging through something far greater than ourselves, something ultimately beyond our comprehension, something which can be deeply sensed but not fully understood. It is something beyond words, beyond concepts, beyond images: the primordial, the absolute, the Tao. Let it be!

We can develop a new relationship with the rest of nature, being close to the land and sea, recognizing our kinship with other beings, and having Reverence for Being. We can restore the original sense of the seamless unity of nature. Communing with nature in this way is making direct contact with reality so that the subject and object, the observer and observed, the human and the natural, are no longer experienced as separate but as one.

To be at one with nature is not a static identification but a process of creative self-realization. In this relationship, there is no longer any controller or controlled, ruler or ruled. To be at one with nature is to be open and receptive rather than assertive and domineering. It involves contemplation rather than imposing a grid. It means becoming like water which goes through rock, seeps into places that humans reject, and always finds its own level.

Ultimately, when humans begin to live in harmony with nature again, as they did thousands of years ago, they will no longer have to consider what is right or wrong, what are the good or the bad results of their actions. They will no longer deliberate over different courses of behaviour. They will act spontaneously in a way which enhances life and seeks no injury. The wise will be spontaneously good without any judgement or preference, without any utilitarian calculations of profit and loss, without any analysis of intentions and consequences. They will be creative and spontaneous. They will not force nature but let it organize and regulate itself. They will flow like water and be the stream of the universe.

# 9

# Of Dolphins, Pigs and Oaks

*In the south west of Ireland lives a dolphin which the locals call Fungi. He stays around the entrance to the harbour of Dingle opposite a small beach. They say that ten years ago his mate died and was washed up on the beach and since then he has never left the spot. Sometimes when schools of dolphins pass by he goes and joins them for a few days out in the bay but he always returns. Thousands of people each summer come from all over the world to swim with him. They say he has therapeutic powers. He is always friendly to humans, the dolphin of Dingle.*

Humans like to think they are unique on this planet. Certainly they have many unique characteristics. They are so unspecialized that they can live virtually anywhere on earth. They are so dexterous that their thumb and index finger can form a circle. They are so affectionate that they can make love at any time. As tool-making creatures, they can fly to the moon and dive to the floor of the deepest oceans.

At some stage in our development, natural evolution gave way to cultural evolution – the second nature of consciousness evolved from the first nature of biological life. Our bodies may not have changed since the Stone Age, but our knowledge has multiplied. Accumulated knowledge was passed down orally until the invention of writing some six thousand years ago when the process of cultural evolution accelerated. In the electronic age, communication is even faster.

But does this make us a unique species amongst other species on the planet? In the East, the widespread acceptance of the doctrine of reincarnation, in which individuals can move up and down the scale of being from one species to another, has meant that humans are not seen as uniquely separate from the rest of the creation. The self or soul of a person can take the form of many different kinds of bodies.

Western philosophers and theologians on the other hand have long argued that there is an unbridgeable gap between humans and other animals. In the creation myth of Genesis, God is said to have first created 'man' in his own image, next the different species and then given him dominion over them all: 'Be fruitful, and multiply, and replenish the earth, and subdue it: and have dominion over the fish of the sea, and the fowl of the air, and over every living thing that moveth on the earth' (1:28).

In the mainstream Judaeo-Christian tradition, humans are considered unique because, unlike other animals, they have souls and by extension they can do what they want with animals. The Christian Fathers were crystal-clear about this position. St Augustine argued that Jesus himself shows that 'to refrain from the killing of animals and the destroying of plants is the height of superstition, for judging that there are no common rights between us and beasts and trees, he sent the devils into a herd of swine and a curse withered the tree on which he found no fruit'. Surely the swine had not sinned, nor the tree. Again, St Aquinas summed up the traditional teaching of the Roman Catholic Church by maintaining a rigid distinction between humanity and the rest of nature and by arguing that 'plants, which have merely life, are all alike for animals, and all animals are for man'. Even St Francis, who treated the birds as his brothers and sisters and who has recently been made the patron saint of ecology, ate dead flesh.

The second traditional grounds for human uniqueness is that humans alone are said to have a moral sense. It is this moral sense which makes them feel guilty when they do wrong, which inspires them to heroic acts of self-sacrifice, and which makes them capable of perceiving the good. Animals do not have such a refined moral sense and clearly have no sense of sin; they enjoy themselves too much.

If it is not the soul or a moral sense, then it is reason which is said to make humans unique. Aristotle defined man as a rational animal; he accepted that animals might feel desire but argued that they did not possess the power of deliberate choice. The French philosopher René Descartes, the father of modern philosophy, maintained that only man could reason. Indeed, it is his reasoning ability that makes him able to prove his own existence: *cogito, ergo sum* (I think therefore I am). Descartes not only made a rigid distinction between mind and body but also between humans and animals. In his view, animals are merely unconscious automata – machines – incapable of experiencing pleasure or pain. They never develop to a point where any sign of thought can be detected in them.

The fourth great distinction between humans and animals is said to be language. Animals are dumb, humans talk. Indeed, Wittgenstein went so far as to suggest that the limits of our world are the limits of our language and that without language we cannot think. Even if we are part of nature, it has been further argued, there is a degree of separation from nature because of the imaginary sphere in human consciousness – the realm of the image, sign, signifier, symbol and metaphor.

These philosophical and theological attempts to drive a wedge between humans and animals on the basis of a soul, moral sense, reason or language cannot be maintained. They have been undermined by evolutionary theory and ethology as well as by a more holistic philosophy. On the one hand, humans have been dethroned from being lords of creation, and on the other, animals have been shown to be more than the dumb mechanical brutes that their exploiters would like to think them to be.

Darwin and other evolutionists have shown that the species are not fixed, travelling on a single track, but fan out from a common ancestry. Humans share the same roots as the higher primates. This so-called 'ape theory' does not reduce humans to gorillas, as Darwin's contemporaries feared, but shows that they do share the same remote forebears.

At the same time, ethology, the study of animal behaviour in their natural environment, has shown many examples of animals which reveal qualities long considered to be peculiarly human. Much animal behaviour is instinctive or can be explained by reflexes and conditioning. But there is increasing evidence to suggest that some animals are conscious beings, with a clear sense of self and a subtle understanding of their relationships with others. They show the ability to calculate risks and to learn from experience and from each other. Some primates, especially chimpanzees, are even capable of deception, and of seeing events from another's point of view.

I have been to the Serengeti and other wilderness areas in East Africa many times, and my own observations confirm that lionesses co-operate and show foresight in organizing a hunt, stampeding their prey towards members of their pride hiding in the grass. Elephants also live in tightly-knit groups, and if they separate to search for food when they reunite they go through a complex greeting ceremony. When giving birth, an elephant is usually helped by one or two 'midwives', often elder sisters. Elephants seem to show grief at the death of one of their family group: they try to get it back on its feet and when they realize it is dead they are reluctant to leave the corpse. They also rearrange the bones of their ancestors, paying particular attention to the tusks.

Having observed at home my old Welsh sheep dog whimper whilst asleep by the fire, I cannot help thinking he is dreaming of the chase. And when he is awake and responds to my moods, I cannot see him as Descartes' automaton, incapable of feeling, devoid of consciousness. Watching his fellows respond to the calls and whistles of a shepherd gathering sheep on a mountain-side, it is difficult to deny that they are alert, intelligent and imaginative.

Whales and dolphins perhaps have the greatest claim to animal intelligence. They live in tight-knit groups and look after each other. Whales have been sighted helping injured companions to the surface to breathe, suggesting that they have caring and highly developed relationships. Humpback whales in the northern oceans often hunt together, and off the coast of Alaska trap shoals of herring in a cylinder of bubbles which they produce by forcing air through their blowholes. Whales are thought to be sensitive to the earth's magnetic field: formations such as underwater cliffs and mountains cause slight variations in the contours of the field and whales may memorize these and navigate by them.

Whales and dolphins can communicate with each other over vast distances and seem to have a highly developed language. Orcas, known as killer whales but in fact the largest of the dolphin family, live in a community made up of different pods or groups which contain as many as 50 individuals. Their cohesion is connected to a common 'language' of calls and sounds, with each pod having its own dialect. Whales and dolphins not only communicate with each other by sound, but also navigate with it, measuring the interval between a click and its echo as it bounces of some distant object. The endangered 100-foot long blue whale, the largest creature to live on this planet, makes the loudest noise which lasts up to 30 seconds and carries over vast distances. The humpback whale also produces songs which are harmonious to the human ear. From low-frequency whistles to high-frequency clicks, the varied language of dolphins appears capable of expressing a great range of ideas and emotions. Crossing the Atlantic in a small yacht, I spent many hours in my bunk listening to the calls of dolphins to each other as they swam and played alongside the hull.

I cannot believe that dolphins and whales do not have consciousness, experience emotions, and have a language. With their brains much larger than ours in ratio to our bodies, they may well be wiser than we are. I often wonder whether the whales are trying to hold the world together as they meditate in the deep.

It is now clear that many primates also share characteristics which were long considered to be uniquely human. Chimpanzees fashion tools, using blades of grass to catch termites or stones to crack nuts. They recognize who is a member of their family and can use mirrors, thereby demonstrating a sense of self-awareness. As the famous case of the chimpanzee Washoe has shown, they can be taught sign language, and crucially can make new combinations of learned signs to express their thoughts and feelings. Washoe even taught it to a young companion. Chimpanzees observed in the wild know how to deceive others and shows signs of guilt after stealing from their clan members; they have a moral sense.

Although much animal behaviour is determined by inherited genes, some is learned from parents as well as by experience and observation. Even cultural evolution would seem to operate amongst higher primates: Japanese macaque monkeys on the Pacific island of Koshima have been seen passing down their acquired knowledge, showing their offspring how to wash the sand off sweet potatoes and grains of rice in a pool after one of their troop began to do it.

From my own experience and observations, I cannot but conclude that humans are not fundamentally different from animals, whether on the basis of a soul, moral sense, reason or language. There is a difference only in degree and not in kind. There are therefore no grounds for humans to consider themselves to be a unique species on earth or lords of the creation. We are members of the same community with other animals and we share many of the same characteristics. Animals, especially the primates, have consciousness, sentience, a sense of self and a moral sense. They experience pleasure or pain and are capable of happiness or suffering. They have particular natures which can be thwarted or realized.

Many humans consider animals as means to their own ends. They impose their own values on the animal community in the natural world. Living in an hierarchical society, they see hierarchy everywhere in nature. In the Middle Ages the Greek idea of a ladder of existence was transformed into the notion of a Great Chain of Being which stretched from angels, humans, animals to plants. Unequal subjects of a monarchy rather than equal citizens of a republic, the English talk about the 'animal kingdom', with the lion – the 'king of the beasts' – at the top and the 'lowly' worm at the bottom.

Many see the natural world as a mirror of their own political organization. Bernard de Mandeville in his notorious *The Fable of the Bees, or Private Vices and Public Benefits* (1714), not only read into bee behaviour the worst aspects of human conduct but then proceeded to argue that human society thrives like a hive of bees on a system of mutual exploitation and greed. Other animals are given human characteristics. Amongst the egalitarian rooks, those who squawk and squabble, there is said to be a parliament. Since ancient times, the fox has been cunning, the goat lustful, and the ant provident.

Different species in the Chain of Being were classified into friends and foes – as they still are in modern gardening books – according to their usefulness to ourselves. Amongst the friends are pets and domestic animals, amongst the foes are vermin, pests, and wild animals. To abuse humans we call them animals: a coward is a chicken; a policeman is a pig; the mob are swine; a difficult woman is a bitch, shrew, vixen or cow. The 'savage' aspect of our nature is described as 'the beast within'. These categories eloquently show what many people think about the long-suffering creatures which they exploit, coerce and eat on this planet. If animals could talk our language, I wonder what they would have to say about us.

The members of these categories are not universal: while people in the West perfume and cuddle dogs and have them on their laps and in their beds, in Africa and Asia, especially amongst Muslims, dogs are considered filthy scavengers. In Thailand, Western tourists try and save the puppies of dogs near the beaches from cobras although the locals are going to eat them anyway. The attitude to animals of the same species is often contradictory, depending on their closeness to humans. The hunter who revels in chasing the fox to death, can sleep by the fire with his hounds who are trained against their nature to kill their wild cousins. A farmer might keep his working dogs filthy, cold and half-starved in an outhouse, while his wife pampers an untrainable dog in the warmth of the fireside.

Although domestic animals in the past were looked after since they were so valuable, and even lived in the same house as their owners, the general response to wild creatures was to reach for a gun. In Europe, wolves and bears early on were virtually wiped out. When Europeans started to colonize the world, whenever they encountered a new wild creature, they either captured or shot it. In the nineteenth-century frenzy to collect and classify animals and birds, the public and private museums became stuffed with them: the taxidermist never had it so good.

It was common, and still is in some parts of the world, to treat people 'like animals'. Slaves were considered little different from domesticated 'beasts'. After their gruelling voyage across the sea from Africa to the New World, they were sold in the market-place like cattle, prospecting buyers intimately inspecting their bodies. The value of women was measured by the largeness of their breasts and that of the men by the quality of their teeth and the strength of their muscles. The women were bought to breed, the men to labour. And as with domesticated animals, if they got enough to eat, it was only to get the most out of them.

Until recently, the well-being of animals had few supporters in the West. The growing concern about the welfare of animals has been one of the great moral revolutions of the twentieth century, along with the increased awareness of the fragility of the planet. A new wave of green Christians have reinterpreted the God-given 'dominion' over all the creatures not in terms of control but of stewardship. The special position of humanity in nature, they argue, gives them the responsibility to look after the rest of the creation and not to conquer and exploit it. They point to Noah's covenant with God to care for every living creature 'for perpetual generations'.

The most common defence of animal liberation, however, has been on the basis of rights. Ever since Locke first defended the natural rights of humans to life, liberty and property, there has been a gradual extension of the notion of rights. The US Declaration of Rights reinterpreted them as the rights to life, liberty and the pursuit of happiness, while the French Revolution recast the principles in terms of liberty, fraternity and equality. Yet they continued to limit the ownership of rights to rational beings – which turned out to be people like themselves, white, property-owning males. It was only due to the struggles in the last two centuries that human rights have been extended to the poor, women and non-whites. Although they have become enshrined in the UN Declaration of Human Rights they are far from being universally respected.

In recent years, there has been a growing call to include animals in the moral community and to extend the notion of rights from humans to animals. Not to include non-whites was a form of racism, not to include women was a form of sexism, and not to include animals is to lay oneself open to a charge of speciesism. For centuries, the criterion amongst philosophers for moral consideration was rationality or speech. Since animals are not rational, it was argued, they cannot be said to have rights. Ironically, it was the utilitarian philosopher Jeremy Bentham who first challenged the criterion at the beginning of the 19th century. 'The question is not', he insisted, 'Can they *reason* or can they *talk*? but, Can they *suffer*?' Basing his case on the twin pillars of utility, that is, contributing to the greatest happiness of the greatest number, and of equality, in which each is to count for one, he looked forward to a time when 'the rest of the animal creation may acquire those rights which never could have been withholden from them but by the hand of tyranny'.

It is, of course, not always easy to define the boundary between sentience and non-sentience. One philosopher drew the line near a mollusc – somewhere between a shrimp and an oyster. Anyone who has seen shrimps trying to jump out of boiling water or any oyster squirm when squirted with lemon juice cannot deny their sentience. Octopuses are molluscs, and yet in tests they have shown considerable problem-solving intelligence, a powerful memory, and even feelings (they change colour according to

111

their response to a situation). In all this, they resemble the primates, which, of course, include ourselves.

But as a rough and ready benchmark, I believe that sentience, the ability to feel pleasure and pain, should be the criterion for moral consideration before rationality. If we accept by analogy to ourselves that other humans can experience pain and pleasure, then I can see no grounds for denying the experience in other animals which are so close to us. Animals are subjects of life as much as humans and have similar opportunities for satisfaction. As such they have intrinsic worth and a claim to life and liberty and respectful treatment. In some ways, it might be said that animals are closer to the divine than humans: they are complete in themselves and know no sin.

But does this mean all animals should get equal treatment? Although one should only count for one, and no one for more or less than one, the principle of equality does not necessarily mean equal *treatment*, but equal *consideration*. Although the needs and interests of all beings should be considered equally, some needs or interests are greater than or different from others. The needs of beavers, for instance, are different from those of ants. Animals, like humans, contribute to the general well-being and take from the common stock in different ways. Your needs can take precedence over mine while my needs can weigh more than those of a pig. It is up to all of us, both individually and collectively, to define the boundaries of these needs and where they clash to give equal consideration to the needs of all those involved. You might say that animals cannot voice their needs, but neither can babies and some disabled humans. That does not mean that we do not give them equal consideration.

What if my needs clash with those of a pig? Am I justified in killing and eating a pig in order to live? Are my vital needs greater than those of a pig? It depends on the situation. If there were no other means of sustenance, I might kill a pig. If a wild boar was about to kill me, I might kill it in self-defence. But as long as I can live from plants, I would not now kill a pig, even if I like the smell of bacon. And even if you do eat pig, there are no grounds for denying its rights to liberty and to the satisfaction of its natural instincts whilst it is alive. No argument can be made for a sow to be chained to the floor and its body held in an iron cage.

I prefer pigs alive rather than dead, in a wood rather than on a plate. They are by all accounts highly intelligent animals and if allowed will naturally live a complex social and family life. It is fortunate for them that Muslims find them unclean but unfortunate that most of the rest of the world find them so edible.

I should add that I once killed a pig in France which some friends had bought to celebrate my twenty-first birthday. Its name was Napoleon and it had a growth on its back leg. It is easier to call a male pig 'it' than 'he' as it distances me from the experience. Four of us tied him down on a wooden table – I held a rear trotter – while a friend tried to kill him by inserting a long knife between his ribs. Only after several bloody thrusts did he reach the heart. The pig in the meantime struggled with all his might, kicking ferociously with his legs and nearly breaking his bonds. He screamed and screamed and screamed as blood poured out of his mouth. I can still hear his screams reverberating in my head. It was roasted whole that evening and tasted good, but since we also ate some snails which had not been properly starved, I was sick for days afterwards. It served me right; I was no doubt paying my karmic debt. It was a critical experience in my life which eventually led me to become a vegetarian.

The advantage of appealing to animal rights to improve the welfare of animals is that it is a language that everyone in the West understands. The trouble with the language of rights is that it is based on a notion of possessive individualism. It assumes that certain individuals or groups 'possess' certain rights which they assert against others. Those who draw up lists of 'rights' often get tied in knots, as some rights clash with others. Most would agree that humans have a 'natural' right to life and liberty, but a right to private property is far more controversial. Many communities do not have a sense of mine or thine, so a right to private property can hardly be called 'natural'. At the same time, in certain circumstances, property is clearly theft, when for instance a few take from the many and then claim that they alone have a right to enjoy the usurped wealth. A starving man might think that the right to life overrides the right to property, and that he is morally justified in stealing bread, but the owner of the bakery might feel he is justified in reaching for his gun to defend his rights.

Again, rights are not always helpful when it comes to a clash between the good of an individual and the well-being of the whole. Is the vitality of a larger whole like an ecosystem more important than an individual member of its community? Does the right to life of an oak-tree, for instance, carry more weight than

113

the right to life of a mouse which lives in its trunk, even though one is an animal and the other a plant? I would argue that since the oak-tree is an important part of an ecosystem which supports a great diversity of life over hundreds of years, its life should generally come before that of a short-lived mouse. On the other hand, if the mouse were a rare variety and in danger of extinction, then perhaps its interests on the grounds of biodiversity, essential to the health of the ecosphere, should come before the oak-tree.

There are also circumstances where the vital needs of woods and ecosystems – as we perceive them since they cannot directly voice their needs themselves – should count for more than the non-vital need of humans. Knocking a few minutes off a car journey by building a motorway through an ancient woodland is a non-vital need. Creating jobs by extending a runway which will only increase the greenhouse effect cannot justify the loss of a unique green belt of fields and trees. Apart from the psychic value of woodlands, they play a key role as the lungs of the earth, helping to maintain the balance of gases in the atmosphere. From the point of view of the well-being of the whole, of the health of Gaia, individual trees and woods should not always be sacrificed for runways and motorways. Whereas the former heal, the latter pollute the planet.

In reality, rights are often little more than particular claims made by certain groups in pursuit of their interests. Although an appeal to natural rights has moral force, especially in Western culture, they are usually framed in legalistic terms and require the coercive force of the state to enforce them. When asserted, a power struggle inevitably ensues, whether it be the rights of man opposed to the divine right of kings, the rights of slaves opposed to the rights of masters, the rights of women as opposed to the rights of men, and now the rights of animals opposed to the rights of humans.

In the final analysis, I would argue that the grounds for moral consideration should be not so much whether a being reasons, talks, or even feels, but whether it *lives*. The 'life force' which pervades the universe is intrinsically valuable. This criterion would include not only all animals, birds and insects, but also plants, and living ecosystems like lakes and woods. If this were the case, entities like woods, lakes, plains, rivers and seas would have moral standing. Their vital needs and interests would be considered as well as our own.

114

A good case against cruelty to animals and for their humane and fair treatment can be made on the grounds that animals as conscious and sentient beings have rights to life and liberty as much as humans, but in my view the best grounds for their welfare is the principle of *minimum harm*. Liberation ecology seeks to achieve precisely this. Inspired by compassion for all beings, animated by Reverence for Being, it aims to cause no injury. Rather than trying to find ways of maximizing happiness, it wishes to minimize suffering. It avoids meddling in nature, and lets evolution take its own course. It celebrates the intrinsic worth of dolphins, pigs and oaks and allows all beings to live and flourish in their own way.

# 10

# The Family of Life

*Animals and birds wish as much as we do to preserve their lives, and do not have to borrow from man's wisdom to do so. Buck and doe mate together, mother and child keep close together; they shun the plains and choose inaccessible places; they avoid cold and seek out warmth; they live in herds and travel in formations with the young ones on the inside and the fully grown on the outside; they lead each other to water and call to each other when they find food. In the most ancient times men and animals lived together and walked side by side. In the time of the Five Emperors and the Three Kings, the animals were frightened away and scattered for the first time. In our own degenerate times, they crouch in hiding and flee to their lairs to avoid harm.*

Lieh Tzu

We have lost our original kinship with animals and use them as we will for our own narrow ends. At least hunter-gatherers had little impact on the environment, and the few animals they killed lived a free life in the wild until the moment of their death. Modern agriculture, on the other hand, is concerned with the maximum conquest and exploitation of nature in the drive for increased production and profits. Whereas traditional farmers had a personal and direct relationship with the land and their animals, in the age of agribusiness in the West that bond has been broken. Animals are now just items on a balance sheet, machines for manufacturing profit by the deft manipulation of the market and the system of grants and subsidies.

116

The 'successful' farmer sits behind a computer screen in an office, talking to his men in their air-conditioned tractors by portable phone. It is not bird song or the wind in the hedgerows which fill their ears, but the latest electronic music. Most modern farmers have lost interest in ploughing and sowing, except as a computer game. Soon the work will be done by robots in tractors directed by satellites. Farmers drive to work from their village along the causeway of tarmac with little thought of the sea of green on either side which they have turned into a desert.

At the beginning of the nineteenth century, the labours of one farmer fed four people; now a farmer in Europe feeds 42 people and in Britain more than 80 people. After the Second World War, 1.2 million lived and worked on the land in Britain; now the number is down to only 100,000. British farmers control 80 per cent of the land, and yet contribute only 1.4 per cent of GDP.

The growth of productivity is impressive, but it has been at a huge loss to rural communities, to wildlife, to the welfare of animals, and to the fertility of the soil. The close-knit communities have been broken up, with villages becoming dormitory towns in which young people can no longer afford the dwellings which their ancestors occupied for centuries.

The vast majority of farmers in Europe are not interested in being stewards of the soil or in sustainability. They do not see their land as a temporary gift of nature which they must pass on enhanced by their labour to future generations. Encouraged by successive governments, they have continually tried to increase production and mechanize their methods. Heavily subsidized, they have poured artificial fertilizers into the soil and sprayed their crops with pesticides and herbicides, thereby polluting the water system and the air. The old patchwork pattern of small fields and hedgerows and copses of Britain was to a large extent transformed in the twentieth century into barren ranches and prairies.

The water-meadows have been drained and grained, the uplands cleared and resown, the flower-rich meadows, full of grasses and sedges, reduced to one bright green rye grass or dusty wheat prairie maintained by artificial fertilizers and pesticides. The soil loss in East Anglia is a dozen tons per hectare per year; the greatest renewal capacity of soil is one ton per hectare per year. Those old farmers who once knew where their soil line had been now walk knee-deep in dust in the absence of soil.

Because the landed interest is so powerful, farmers are the last bastion of government support. The public through the government use of their taxes are not only paying farmers to prevent access to the countryside but are encouraging them to kill off the wildlife and pollute the land, the rivers and the air. It is not entirely the farmers' fault: successive governments have told them to expand, and given them grants and subsidies to do so. But the overall result has been devastating, both in terms of the untold suffering of animals and the irredeemable destruction of the land and habitats.

In the drive for higher yields, farmers have not only gone against the rhythms of nature, but have caused unnecessary pain to their animals. Some of the worse cases of cruelty have become highly publicized, such as the rearing of chickens in battery pens, the chaining of sows in iron cages, the raising of calves for veal in pens so they cannot move, the force-feeding of turkeys so that their excessive weight breaks their bones, and the transporting of live sheep for days from one end of Europe to the other. Even the migratory instincts of salmon are now being denied as they are overfed in 'farms'. Virtually the whole of the agricultural 'industry' is now a prison for animals, birds and fish, in which their rights to life and liberty are denied and the opportunities for leading a fulfilling existence ignored. Most farmers show little respect for life or compassion for their animals. Some are little better than torturers.

All these practices deny the natural instincts of animals and birds for movement, sociability and foraging. Many people have been rightfully horrified by the transportation and gassing of humans in the last world war, but we continue to do the same to animals who experience pain and pleasure, and are capable of happiness and suffering as much as ourselves. Animals have evolved similar bodies and not dissimilar minds. If we recognized animals as part of the same moral community and considered them worthy of moral consideration, we would no longer use phrases such as 'treating people like animals', since we would extend the similar treatment to animals as to humans.

If people wish to eat flesh, then it is preferable that the animals, birds and fish are allowed to fulfil their natures and have freedom of movement in a natural and appropriate environment. If they are going to eat salmon, it is better that it is wild than farmed. If they are going to eat chickens, they should at least be free range.

And if I am going to drink milk, then I should share it with other young animals and not push them out of the way.

If we were to farm organically, recycling energy in terms of manure, compost and green manure crops; if we were to farm ecologically, encouraging the diversity, complexity, richness and stability of the land in our trust; if we were to farm humanely, treating animals like friends and allowing them to follow their natural instincts, we would create a far more vital, joyful and fruitful land. If we were to reform land ownership, allowing more concerned people to become stewards of the land, we would create a much better society, in a more flourishing countryside.

The inevitable conclusion of a deep concern for animal welfare is to adopt a more vegetarian diet. The moral argument against meat eating is profoundly persuasive. The raising of animals for slaughter has become one of the principal causes of unnecessary suffering inflicted by humans on animals. It also has had a devastating effect on the environment at large.

Apart from the moral case, there are good health and ecological grounds for being vegetarian. Meat and fish are clearly not essential ingredients to good health. A third of Indians thrive, when they have enough, on a meat-free diet. Like many post-war children, I was brought up to believe that I needed a piece of meat every day to grow strong and healthy. If I continued I may well have ended up with heart disease. The amount of animal protein recommended by the British government after the Second World War was enough to kill sedentary people.

The strange belief that eating certain animals and different parts of animals makes humans strong continues throughout the world. The alleged food value of different animals is intricately bound up with culture. Babies in Europe are given brains to make them brainy, red meat to develop strong muscles. In China and Korea, the demand for rhinoceros horn as an aphrodisiac is leading to their extinction in East Africa. When I was in Cameroon, an acquaintance proudly announced that he was giving his baby the ground arm bones of a gorilla from the rain forest to make him strong, along with powdered baby milk imported from Paris. He had been given the arms by his former colonel in the army, who liked to eat gorilla and pythons for breakfast. The eating of monkeys is a widespread practice in Africa and Asia.

It is now acknowledged by modern nutritionists that we do not need to eat meat to be healthy and strong. Indeed the opposite might well be true: too much meat is not good for you. It is now widely known that vegetarians tend to live longer and get less cancers, especially of the colon, than meat-eaters. They eat less fat and more fibre, and tend to have a healthier lifestyle.

When I became a vegetarian in my late twenties, giving up my slab of meat and two soggy vegetables, I felt a surge of energy and still feel full of energy twenty years later.

Only now are consumers awakening to the dangers of modern farming methods to their health. The animals and birds are pumped full of hormones and antibiotics to put on weight fast, the land is covered in chemicals to increase yields, and both hormones and chemicals get into the food chain. The unnatural conditions of battery hens encourage salmonella in eggs, while the rough and tumble culture of slaughter houses, with carcasses covered in faeces, foster bacteria which kill when eaten.

To make matters worse, scientists are constantly breaking natural boundaries, by trying to turn herbivores into carnivores by feeding them processed offal and by turning chickens into cannibals by feeding them feathers and faeces. The process of artificial selection, breeding, hybridization and cross fertilization has developed to such an extent that is now possible to clone sheep. We already have cloned politicians; no doubt humans will follow suit.

But there are limits to what nature can take. Just as breeding a female horse with a male donkey produces a sterile mule, so crossing natural boundaries leads to a dead end. Human arrogance, in trying to transform nature often leads to tragedy. And there is an uncanny tendency for nature to take its revenge, as the outbreak of BSE has shown. Humanity's hubris is followed by nature's nemesis.

The other great practical argument for vegetarianism is ecological. It takes seven times less land to produce a kilo of plant protein than it does meat protein. This means that the less people eat meat, the more land there is for other purposes. Cows (along with cars and chainsaws) are one of the greatest threats to the biosphere: forests – the lungs of the earth – are cut down to create pasture for them while the methane they produce upsets the delicate balance of gases in the atmosphere. The Amazonian rain-forest crashes down every day for more pasture. Where I live in Wales the countryside has been turned virtually into a green desert. With a human population of 2.5 million, there are 11 million sheep and 3 million cattle munching away and releasing methane into the atmosphere every day. Travelling from North to South Wales, it is possible to see no person working in the fields.

If people reduced their consumption of meat, thereby releasing much land from the burden of 'livestock', would the familiar fields be empty, would the landscape change? Some green deserts called pastures might be for a while, but nature would soon begin to create a new diversity. It is not long before the untidy scrub in a field set aside turns into a woodland, and throughout the process it supports a great diversity of plant, animal, bird and insect species. The land would be able to support a far greater variety of wildlife. The wolves and bears might return to some forests, and wild goats and deer roam the upland pastures, symbols of the wild and free.

Without the huge burden of sheep and cattle reared for meat, there would also be more room for the old copses, woodlands and forests to regenerate and expand, thereby providing local timber and an important renewable source of energy. The great oak forests could return. The oak, once symbol of Britain's intransigence, would become a symbol of a new relationship with the land for a mature oak forest has the richest ecosystem in our climes and supports the greatest diversity of life. Where the dust prairies now languish, where the sheep and cattle graze, let the oaks and wildlife return!

For all these reasons – Reverence for Being, a good diet, and a healthy ecology – it makes sense to eat less meat and fish and more plant protein. But I do not advocate a vegetarian diet as an absolute moral imperative. It is a question of degree: in general, a vegetarian diet is better than eating meat, while a vegan diet is best of all since it causes minimum harm and suffering. It is for people to make their own choices, and to travel at their own pace. Indeed, it is difficult on ecological grounds to universalize the call for a vegetarian diet. To ask the Inuit and the Maasai to stop eating fish and drinking blood would be to ask them to stop being Inuit and Maasai.

Like all moral guidelines, the moral principles of Reverence for Being and minimum harm should be adapted to particular circumstances. I can imagine circumstances in Africa, for instance, in which to refuse a piece of meat would be a great discourtesy, especially if an animal had been killed in my honour.

**121**

If people live by the sea, then it seems reasonable for them to live off the sea, especially if there is little alternative food supply.

If eating meat is generally avoidable, what about using animals for experiments? Is vivisection unacceptable in an enlightened society? Scientists in the West ever since the Scientific Revolution in the sixteenth and seventeenth centuries have had few scruples about cutting up and experimenting on animals, allegedly for human benefit. Standing in the mainstream Christian tradition which asserted that animals are created by God entirely for human use, they had no compunction about using them in this way.

Great strides were being made at the time in the understanding of the structure of the body. The Flemish anatomist Andreas Vesalius was the first to argue that the physical correlative of the personality is the brain and not the heart. Vesalius conducted public dissections of live animals for his students, so that they could concentrate on the cries of the animals as he cut out different organs. He particularly recommended cutting up a pregnant sow: 'For a dog, after being bound for some time, no matter what you do to it, finally neither barks nor howls so you are sometimes unable to observe the loss or weakening of the voice.'

Anatomy became a great public spectacle, and lecture theatres were transformed into places of fashionable resort. In seventeenth-century Leiden, members of polite society paid to see bodies being cut up accompanied by music before they went off to dine and feast. In the process, the body became 'invented' as an object of study in its own right and as a metaphor for being human. Anatomy thus broke the medieval link between the microcosm and the macrocosm and encouraged the bifurcation of thinking between mind and body which has plagued the Western mind ever since. Until recently, children at school had their feelings hardened and learned that to dissect is not to murder when a frog came under their scalpel.

Dissections on live animals without anaesthetics are not now undertaken in lecture theatres, but behind the scenes countless animals undergo a slow death in laboratories in the name of objective science or the 'disinterested pursuit of knowledge'. The scientists refuse to be held individually responsible for the experiments they undertake, saying that they are merely in the employ of politicians and businessmen who must take the final decision on the application of their findings.

Vivisection – the act of making experiments on live animals – has never been so widespread or organized on such a massive scale. In laboratories throughout the world, animals are subjected to agonizing stimuli. Dogs are obliged to smoke tobacco and get cancer. Rabbits test shampoo in their eyes. Chimpanzees, the closest primates to humans, are kept in small cages, infected with AIDS and then injected with all manner of chemicals in search of a cure. Mice have human ears grafted on their backs. British scientists have cloned sheep in order to breed organs which will not be rejected by the human body. Japanese scientists have reproduced a cow without the use of a bull. Are humans next? When will it stop?

Genetic engineering has been one of the main growth areas in human and animal biology in recent years. It has been defended on the grounds that it creates more 'productive' animals and might eradicate certain inherited human diseases. There are genes, we are told, for selfishness, genes for violence, genes for criminality, genes for homosexuality. The corollary is that they could be bred out or those with them would not be allowed to breed. The whole programme evokes the eugenic campaign of the Nazis to create the 'master race'.

The trouble with genetics – and molecular biology – is that it tries to isolate one element responsible for particular types of behaviour, namely the inherited gene. In doing so, it focuses narrowly on a part of the whole and misses the complexity of the system. It is the very opposite of the holistic approach to the human body which sees the mind as an open system interacting with its own history and environment. The geneticists are offering a new vision of original sin located in the body. Not surprisingly, the salvation on offer is not a spiritual transformation or a social revolution but the use of drugs, whether it be drugs to dampen down violence, criminality or sexuality. By the year 2020, the World Health Organization forecasts that if we continue our present way of life, depression will be the cause of the majority of illnesses. And the proposed answer? Not what is really needed – a fundamental change in consciousness and society so that people can lead more meaningful and purposeful lives – but accelerated research in genetic engineering and the increased manufacture of mood-changing drugs.

What about hunting and fishing? I have not hunted animals but I have fished, and fishing is a form of hunting. Having spent many hours sea-fishing as a boy, I can understand the thrill of the chase and capture, the excitement of the sudden tug on the line after a long period of expectancy and repose. Fishing took my brother and me far out in our little open boat in the bay off Bognor Regis on the south coast of England, teaching us the ways of the weather and the sea and the nature of the creatures of the deep. At the time, I did not fully grasp the suffering I was causing, as I threaded lug worms on to hooks attached to a trot line which was then weighted down for hours on the floor of the seabed. Flat fish would swallow the hooks; to get them out would involve ripping the barbed metal out of their stomachs. Following my grandfather's advice, I would try and kill them swiftly by smashing their heads with an iron rollock, or by cutting their backbones with a knife. I thought I was being humane by killing them rather than letting them flap for hours, gasping in the sun, in the bottom of the boat.

I appreciate the arguments that hunter-gatherers had the least impact on the environment, while settled agriculturalists transformed the landscape by clearing the land and growing crops. As the ancient cave paintings and the beliefs of modern indigenous hunters show, the hunter traditionally honoured the spirit of his prey and only took what he needed. He enacted rituals to ensure the fecundity of nature and the continuation of the species. In the process of hunting, with light weapons and with the real possibility of becoming hunted himself, he was close to the earth and a keen observer of his environment. There was an ancient tradition in West Africa, now virtually disappeared, that you only took two harvests of honey from the bees of the forest; to raid three hives would be greedy and would bring bad luck.

Some of the great naturalists and lovers of nature started out as hunters. It was the look in the dying eye of a mighty stag which the American naturalist John Muir had killed which led him to question hunting for pleasure. Many factors have now made hunting unacceptable. Firstly the balance of power has changed totally in favour of the hunter. Take the example of whales. For the men of the Azores to go after whales in light boats, there was still a possibility that the whales could escape and the men could lose their lives. But now with huge harpoons which explode inside their bodies, the whales have no chance. Secondly, the scale of slaughter has multiplied to such an extent, with vast factory ships plying the seas, that the whales have been hunted to virtual extinction. Even though protected, the blue whale faces extinction because of the difficulty of finding a mate over vast distances.

I can still accept the arguments for hunting for the pot, especially amongst peoples whose traditional way of life depends on it. You cannot tell the San in the Kalahari Desert not to hunt without changing their whole way of life. In East Africa, the only way to encourage local people to respect the wildlife in the parks and reserves is to allow them to take a few of the numerous species for their families. While their own children go hungry, you cannot expect them to look on calmly at the white hunters who take no risk with their high-velocity rifles and four-wheel-drive vehicles to get a trophy for their suburban drawing rooms.

I also accept the need to cull animals (although not human beings) in certain circumstances. We have intervened so deeply with the natural rhythms of nature that in some places a degree of intervention is necessary in an attempt to restore the natural equilibrium and diversity. Elephants strip the bark of trees to eat. When there is enough land for them to move around freely the trees naturally recover. But since the elephants are now often restricted in small 'game parks' there comes a time when their numbers have to be controlled if they are not to destroy their own habitat and themselves at the same time.

Hunting for the pot is one thing, but hunting for sport is another. It seems a strange distortion of the personality to find pleasure in inflicting suffering on others. Oscar Wilde was right in describing fox hunters as 'the unspeakable in full pursuit of the uneatable', and it is a sign of our animal-friendly times that the phrase has become a cliché. The defenders of blood sports are also right in saying that they just want to continue an ancient rural tradition – a tradition steeped in the mire of blood, in the torture and cruelty to animals, both wild and tame, and in spreading terror throughout the countryside. He who for the sake of happiness hurts other creatures who also want happiness is unlikely to find happiness himself.

I have experienced the ire of hunters first hand. One day when I was working with some friends in the walled garden of our community in Buckinghamshire, when babies and toddlers were playing on blankets in the sun, hunting dogs suddenly appeared. They were baying and barking in full pursuit of a fox, terrifying the children, chasing cats onto roofs, and utterly destroying the quiet balance of the afternoon. Then careering down the long drive to our country house were the fox hunters on their horses, dressed in traditional red jackets. I went out to meet them with other members of the community, our garden tools absentmind-edly still in our hands. I told the front runners as they pulled up their horses that the estate was under new ownership and they no longer had the right to ride across it for the hunt.

They were furious, the colour of their cheeks matching the bright red of their uniforms.

'We've been coming through here for centuries. You don't understand country matters', said one of them, rearing up on his horse and spinning him round.

'Because something has been done for a long time' I replied calmly, 'it doesn't mean it's right. They burnt witches in the country for centuries...'

'We're doing everyone a favour!', he countered.

'Not here and not to the fox either!'

The horses were milling round, their blood up, wanting to gallop together. I did not blame the horses; it is the nature of horses to want to gallop together as a herd. I looked round and saw some of my fellow communards had half raised their forks and spades and rakes. It was a little like the Diggers facing Cromwell's cavalry on St George's Hill; they believed that the land was a common treasury, and had dug up the common land and sowed carrots, parsnips and cabbages.

We stood our ground and the cavalry was forced to retreat. The Master of the Hounds, almost apoplectic by now, was the last to leave. He gave me a 'V' sign, swore and shouted: 'We'll get you! You'll see!'

'You'll be hearing from us', I replied.

So much for our friendly new neighbours. I imagined them sending round their men during the night to cut our tyres, break our windows and destroy our carefully tended gardens. We wrote to the hunt saying that we had turned our land into a wildlife sanctuary. In the event, their men did not come round and the hunt did not cross our land again. Toddlers can now play safely in the walled garden, the cat can sleep curled up in the sun, and the fox can slink by in the shady woods.

Animals cannot shout at us:

'We want our rights to life and liberty! We demand equal consideration of our interests and respectful treatment! We

126

claim our birthright to realize our potential, to follow our particular natures! We assert our equal right to be free!'

So we express these aspirations on their behalf to persons who understand our language, who have asserted their rights against the privileged and powerful, and who would also like to be treated equally and fairly.

But while the language of rights is a useful slogan in the struggle to create a fairer world for animals, what is really urgent is liberation. Hence the need for liberation ecology. Animal liberation does not require a new bill of rights to be enforced by some political authority but a moral revolution which throws off the chains, opens the cages, takes down the fences, so that animals can move and breathe freely again and follow their natures. It requires a thoroughgoing transformation of our unjust and unequal relationships with each other, with animals and with the rest of nature. It means an end to hierarchy and domination, coercive power and imposed authority. It asserts that all beings have intrinsic value, are worthy of our respect, and are ends-in-themselves. It encourages a new relationship across the species which is based not on conquest but mutual aid, not on domination but fellowship, not on cruelty but love. It replaces the 'family of man' with the family of life.

# 11

# Giving Birth to a Dancing Star

*One day the emperor offered to resign the empire to a smallholder who was reputed to be wise.*

*He responded thus: 'I am a cell in the organism of the universe. In winter I wear warm clothes. In summer I wear cool clothes. In spring I plough and sow, toiling with my body. In autumn I gather in the harvest, and devote myself to rest and enjoyment. I eat when I am hungry, I go to sleep when I am tired. Contented with my life, I pass through life with a light heart. Why then should I trouble myself with the empire? Ah, my friend, you do not know me!'*

Chuang Tzu

Without authority, the centre will not hold and anarchy will be let loose upon the world. Such is the view of authoritarians, people who are as keen to obey orders from their superiors as they are to issue them to their so-called inferiors. Having been brought up in an hierarchical society with an authoritarian culture and trained to do what they are told, most feel at a loss when they have to decide for themselves. They are no longer able to act and think on their own, to take control and responsibility for their own lives. They feel the need for some authority to order them, whether it be God, king, president, general, leader, or guru. They insist that there has to be some ultimate authority at the end of the table, on the judge's bench, on the throne, or in the heavens; if not, all will fall apart.

Society no more needs political authority in the form of a state to hold it together than nature needs an interfering God to make the flowers grow. The alternative to political authority is anarchy, but not anarchy in the sense of chaos, but as natural and spontaneous order. The Greek root of the word *anarchos* means the condition of being 'without a leader', which is usually translated as 'without a ruler'. Leaders, rulers, and authoritarian types will naturally argue that without their rule, there would be chaos, but in reality their rule is the principal cause and not the remedy for social conflict. Far from leading to confusion or anarchy, a society without political authority in the form of the state would lead to the most desirable form of ordered and creative existence. Indeed, anarchy is order as much as nature is anarchy.

Authority can take a political form as the state as well as an economic form as capital: both are in the saddle in existing society and hold us on a tight rein. The principle of authority is more fundamental and exists prior to both. But do we really need authority? Do we really need people who assert the power or claim the right to enforce obedience, to control, command, judge or prohibit the actions of others? I would argue that most authority is not only evil, but an unnecessary one. We do not need people *in authority*, in positions of power, to issue commands and establish laws. We do not need *authorities*, whether an external government or police force, which claim the right and power to control our actions. We are all capable of governing ourselves, of judging our own moral constraints, and of running our own lives.

There are of course many different senses of authority. A *person of authority* is a person who has power over the opinions of others or has the ability to influence their conduct. There is little wrong with the authority of the wise if you voluntarily make their wisdom your own. Elders can offer useful guidance to young people because of their experience and knowledge of life. But there is nothing worse than aged ignorance cutting the wings of youth. Old fools who think they are wise are fools indeed; they have never known the path of wisdom as the spoon never knows the taste of honey.

Again, we have all at different times in our lives learned from teachers or gurus, but there is a grave danger if we become dependent on a charismatic guru for all our beliefs and actions. A guru can be a great inspiration and model of right conduct, but to

129

remain slavishly dependent on one is to check one's own moral and spiritual growth. Buddha specifically said that we should work out our own salvation with diligence. Any guru or teacher should be a stepping-stone across the river of knowledge; a ladder which we throw away in our ascent to a better understanding of the world.

A person can also be *an authority* in the sense of having special knowledge in a particular field, such as quantum or car mechanics. While such people may be consulted, their knowledge does not confer on them the right to command or control others. Because you may be an authority in a particular area, it does not mean that I should obey you. Scientists may have authority in their area of research, but given their past record they are the least qualified to command others. Whatever Plato might think, philosophers too do not make good kings. There are a few good philosophers but there is no such thing as a good king.

To bow to the authority of others because of their alleged superior knowledge is to undermine one's own independent judgement and self-confidence. By relying on experts, we cease to rely on ourselves and become open to manipulation. We want to be told the 'truth' and give up trying to work it out for ourselves. Whatever our knowledge, we are all capable of managing ourselves and deciding on those issues which most affect our lives. You do not have to be an expert to know that government is not good for you.

Inevitably some people have greater ability and understanding to carry out a particular task. Clearly a cobbler knows more than I do about mending shoes, and a surgeon more about a heart operation, but whether I want my shoes repaired or my chest opened should be my decision, not theirs. Experts should always be accountable to those for whom they claim special expertise and their advice accepted only on the basis of voluntary consent. The rule of the person in the white coat is no better than the rule of the person with a gold chain or chain mail. If we are to accept temporarily the authority of competence, it should always be based on accountability and consent.

The case is the same with leaders. Guides serve a useful purpose when hiking in unknown territory, but travellers should decide for themselves in which direction they want to go. Pilots with local knowledge can lead foreign sailors into a strange haven, but the sailors have made the decision to make the voyage there in the first place. True guides and pilots know their limits; their task is to help others, not to travel for them. On the other hand, leaders who demand unquestioning obedience usually lead people into the wilderness where they soon become lost without the compass of their own will and judgement. A leader with charisma is perhaps the most dangerous of all for he or she can bind followers to them so tightly that they become voluntary slaves, abandoning all personal autonomy and conviction.

It is common for politicians to talk about the ship of state and of the need for a strong hand on the helm. It is also widely accepted that a captain has supreme authority and ultimate responsibility on a ship. But it need not always be the case. Traditionally on Scottish trawlers, the crew would elect their skipper. A skipper on a dhow in the Indian Ocean has the support of his crew only because they have come to trust his wisdom through long experience. As a yachtsman, I know that it is quite possible to share decisions, although in an emergency it might be best to follow the advice of the most skilled and experienced. Even then, they should make suggestions, not issue orders.

Customs officers always assume that on a yacht there is only one skipper and he is male despite the increasing number of women going to sea. After anchoring with my brother and some friends in a yacht off Alderney in the Channel Islands, the customs officer came on board and asked 'Who is the skipper?' We replied: 'We all are!' But he still insisted on taking one person's name: the bureaucracy of the state could not cope with true democracy at sea any more than it could on land.

No one deserves unquestioning obedience, whether it is a captain, general, teacher or parent. If someone makes a right decision it is right; if they make a wrong decision, it is wrong, whatever the cap on their head. The less people in authority govern, the more people do for themselves. The more people rely on themselves and shape their own lives, the less need there is for government and leaders. Participatory and direct democracy is best whatever the situation. If people are directly involved in the decision-making, they know what is going on and can then act out the collective decisions with conviction and clarity.

In a free society, political authority would be decentralized and eventually dissolved as the state would be replaced by a federation of local, district and regional assemblies. A local assembly might still be able to 'authorize' a delegate to express its view in a regional or national assembly. But this kind of delegated authority is only acceptable if those authorized are always accountable and dismissible and cannot issue commands or directives of a legal kind. Such delegated authority is non-coercive, non-compulsory, and is exercised collectively to a particular end. Ultimately, in a free society, both political and economic authority would be dissolved and the only acceptable authority would be the 'authority' of nature – the force of things, the way of the universe, the Tao.

Good leaders dare to lead from behind, not making their presence felt, but the best leaders do not lead at all. They enable people to lead themselves. If they are allowed to manage their own affairs in their own way, when the people complete a task, they say: 'We did it'. In this way, they develop confidence in themselves and pride in their work. Charismatic individuals may be yeast in the social dough, catalysts in the crucible of life, but they should not direct or command. The wise are aware of the dangers of wielding power, like well-trained masters of martial arts. They have the power but do not use it. They reject authority if it is offered, refusing to command or order others.

If coercive authority is always wrong, what about power? Those in authority, those who govern, have the power to control, command, judge, and enforce obedience. Authority is a manifestation of power, although they are different. In its broadest sense, power is the ability to do something, to achieve intended effects.

Unlike authority, power can have its positive aspects. A powerful creature is like a tiger who burns bright in the forest of the night. A powerful idea carries its own weight and will have its time, like the idea that anarchy is order. A powerful person is a strong person, like a man who delivers sacks of grain. A powerful mathematician can make impressive calculations. Power as vigour and energy, power as mental and physical strength are fine; indeed, they are worth cultivating.

But what about *those in power*? They are not so attractive, for they assert the right to command and control and issue orders. What about *the powers that be*? As the government or administration, they are even less appealing. A *power in the state* is a person to be feared and obeyed. Power in these senses is to have control or dominion over others. It is not pleasant to be under the sway of such a powerful individual.

132

Power is always negative when it is used in a coercive way to control or command others. It is not good to be in someone else's power, whether the Devil, a charismatic leader, a guru, a dictator, or a government. To misuse one's power is to have mastery over others. The God of the Old Testament allegedly gave humanity dominion over all the creatures and look how they have misused it.

Because in existing society *the powers that be* have accrued power to themselves and have dominion over others, most people experience a sense of powerlessness. They are unable to realize their projects, satisfy their desires or achieve their ends. Among such people are the poor, the dispossessed, ethnic minorities and the majority of women. Their call for 'empowerment' is therefore a positive thing if it increases their ability to control their own lives and realize their ends.

It becomes negative, if the powerless try to exert power over others once they have acquired power. A powerful female prime minister is no better than a male prime minister; indeed, in some ways she is worse for having experienced a lack of power and seeing the state of her sisters, she should know better. Revolutionaries who seize the power of the state and then wield it against their enemies, as did the Bolsheviks in the Soviet Union and the Maoists in China, inevitably end up becoming tyrants themselves. Lenin might have talked about smashing the power of the state, but he only strengthened and centralized it when he came to power on the back of the revolutionaries. Revolutionary power by its very nature is counter-revolutionary and the worst power of all comes out the barrel of a gun.

With power should go responsibility: the more power one has, the more responsible one should become. Francis Bacon, the apologist of the Scientific Revolution, said that knowledge is power. He was thinking of the knowledge of nature which would give humans more control over nature. But, while the scientists have achieved enormous power over nature, they have not developed power over themselves. Like Faust and Frankenstein, they do not know when to stop. And unlike the Taoist or the Zen monk, they do not know how to use their physical and spiritual power well.

Is the will to power a universal drive in humans? Living in troubled times, when all scramble over each other for a pot of gold or a seat on the throne, it is understandable that many should think so. But there are many traditional societies from the African rain-forests to the islands in the Pacific in which people do not have such a drive. Indeed, they feel embarrassed if someone breaks social etiquette by putting himself or herself forward and becoming bossy.

In existing Western society there is undoubtedly a widespread will to power – power over each other, power over other species, and power over nature itself. It has led to disaster for all concerned – those exerting power and those on the receiving end. Brought up in an hierarchical and authoritarian society with an unequal distribution of power, many individuals compulsively seek coercive power relationships, wanting to dominate or be dominated. Often the roles are reversed. The authoritarian politician likes to be spanked by a prostitute. The crushed worker crushes his wife and children. The helpless old man kicks his dog. The frustrated boy slashes a tree with a knife. The child told off will take off the wings of a butterfly. Victims too become executioners: some so-called 'freedom fighters' become the worst tyrants when they seize power only for themselves.

Power over individuals is often diffuse and concealed. You may be coerced in many different ways: by physical power, when exerted by a bully, police officer or soldier; by economic power, through a system of rewards and sanctions, by an employer's wages or a government's taxes; and by political power, through propaganda in schools, the media, churches, parties and government.

The will to power amongst aggressive and competitive individuals has meant that in existing society power is concentrated in the hands of a few. The state claims a monopoly of physical power within its boundaries and the government uses the police force and army to ensure that it remains in its hands. The demand to decentralize and dissolve political power as far as possible comes from an awareness of the corrupting nature of power. Power corrupts and absolute power corrupts absolutely; it is true, however much a cliché. The greater the degree of power, the easier it is for those in power to abuse it, and the more difficult it is for those without power to do anything about it.

There will always be a degree of power in the form of external influence on individuals – the influence of reason, of persuasion, of example, of public opinion, of natural forces. But a free and enlightened society would try to decentralize political and economic power as much as possible. In a transitional stage, it would seek to disempower those who control and command others, and empower the existing powerless. Hence the call for 'Power to the People', 'Black Power', 'Gay Power', or 'Girl Power' – all groups who historically have been without power. In the long run, however, in a truly democratic society political power would be dissolved along with government as people gained more control over their own lives. Economic power would at the same time lose its coercive force as they began to share the good things of the earth. All would then be able to develop their own physical and mental powers, and have more opportunity to fulfil their aims, without seeking power over each other.

Many kinds of power are positive. Power over oneself is fine in the sense of self-determination and self-discipline. Power to overcome our fear of death and to end our craving for pleasure leads to self-harmony and tranquillity. Power to develop our talents is to turn ourselves into a work of art. Power as energy and vigour, as physical and mental strength is great, if it is used in a creative and life-enhancing way. We all need the power to realize our intended ends. But power becomes destructive as soon as it seeks to control or command others.

Living in an uncertain world and having been pushed around by 'the powers that be', some people become 'control freaks'. They want total control over their lives and those of others. But to want to control everything is to close oneself off from some of the most creative impulses in life: from the playful, the unexpected, the spontaneous, the absurd, the chaotic. It is to have everything four-square and safe and predictable. It is to banish change and growth. It is to turn life into a pension plan rather than a happening, to keep to a rigid timetable rather than to dive into a continuous flow of tumbling energy. The unexpected enables us to cleanse the doors of perception.

Despite the pleas of the power-hungry and the power-intoxicated, it is possible to have human relationships based on love and trust, not on power and suspicion. It is feasible to create a society without rulers and ruled, masters and servants, leaders and followers, kings and cannon-fodder, sadists and masochists. It is possible to become free and equal partners in a non-hierarchical world without domination. It might be difficult to realize, but the ultimate goal of the complete absence of coercive authority or power would herald a new era of freedom, creativity, joy and fulfilment.

135

Freedom is not just a 'negative' condition of being left alone, or the 'positive' state of recognizing necessity. It is the unfurling and realization of potentiality. If we are free, we are free from constraint and free to realize our potential. Since we are part of nature, the self-expression and consciousness of nature, we cannot be free if the rest of the planet remains enslaved by us and unable to realize its full evolutionary potential. It follows that we should allow nature to take its course with as little human interference and control as possible.

The wild is the free. The wild exists not only in the world around us but also deep within us. It is not just the pristine state of nature but the spontaneous and creative impulse at the heart of civilization. It reveals itself in the unconscious and dreams, in the imagination and intuition, in the dance and the carnival. As Nietzsche observed, one must have chaos within to give birth to a dancing star. The wild gives rise to creativity. It is also the source of the wonder felt in the face of the mystery of the universe and of the sense of the sacredness of all things.

In order to live well on earth, it is not enough simply to reject coercive power relationships amongst humans. It involves abandoning dominion over other species, 'dominion over the fish of the sea, and over the fowl of the air, and over every living thing that moveth upon the earth'. It means leaving the old path of multiplying our numbers and subduing the earth. We have no God-given right to become the lords of creation, whatever the Old Testament might say.

At the same time, we must also give up the Western fantasy of having complete power over nature through our scientific knowledge. In order to pass from economic scarcity to relative abundance, it is not necessary to rape and pillage nature. Real progress, progress towards creating a harmonious, fulfilling life, does not depend on the conquest of nature but on a creative fellowship. We do not have to fight the so-called hostile forces of nature or struggle against its alleged disharmonies.

Earlier peoples were awe-struck in the face of nature. They recognized its great power and celebrated it in their rituals and ceremonies. They sensed a joy deeply fused in nature, a joy too deep for tears. They had an overwhelming sense of the wonder of the life force. They orientated their monuments and cities towards the stars so that they became a mirror of the heavens. They knew that pride comes before a fall and that if they vied with the gods disaster would follow. We can learn from earlier peoples before nature has her revenge on us.

If we are to live well, we should recognize our limitations, use our power responsibly, and respect the greater power of nature. There is no need to fear nature; there is nothing in the infinite spaces to fill us with dread. We should simply understand its ways and go with its deep and underlying flow. All will be well if humankind follows the earth, for earth follows heaven, heaven follows the Tao and the Tao follows what is natural.

# 12

# The Beast, the Octopus and the Sword

*The more laws and restrictions there are,*
*The poorer people become.*
*The sharper men's weapons,*
*The more trouble in the land.*
*The more ingenious and clever men are,*
*The more strange things happen.*
*The more rules and regulations,*
*The more thieves and robbers.*

Lao Tzu

The present crisis is a social problem as well as a question of consciousness. It is important to interpret the world afresh, but it is equally important to change how we live. If we are to survive the present crisis and to live well in the coming millennium, we must develop a new philosophy of nature and create new relationships between ourselves and the rest of nature. If we are to unfurl and realize our potential, we must create a new society for a new humanity. We must dwell lightly and lovingly on the earth and be in tune with the harmony of the universe. We must end the antagonism between different groups of humans and humanity and the rest of nature. We must enable the individual self to become part of its larger social and ecological self, and find its rightful place in the universe as the self-in-the-Self.

There is no need to hold up our arms in despair for the roots of the present crisis are in our history, society and culture. It is not just the result of unchecked technology, industrial growth and overpopulation, although they have all played their part. It is mainly due to the emergence of hierarchy and domination and the institution of private property. Both led to the establishment of a centralized state which protected the unequal distribution of power and wealth in the hands of a few. They also led to the blight of government affecting every aspect of our lives.

It often seems that the state has always been with us but in fact it is a comparatively recent phenomenon. As a coercive legal order claiming a monopoly of force within a certain territory, it first clearly emerged some six thousand years ago with the establishment of civilizations and empires in the tropics, especially along great rivers – the Yangtze in China, the Indus in India, the Euphrates in Mesopotamia and the Nile in Egypt. Like all civilizations, they rose and fell; the early civilizations in the Middle East, for instance, were followed by the Greek and Roman empires.

Ever since humans emerged in East Africa and spread out throughout the world, they have lived in stateless communities. They fall roughly into three groups: leaderless societies, in which there is scarcely any political specialization; chiefdoms, in which the hereditary prestige of the chief is largely based on his ability to bring security; and big-man systems, in which the charismatic big man collects dues and distributes gifts for the rest of society.

While many of these societies are characterized by sexism and ageism and have strong moral and religious taboos and strict social controls, they all show that humans are not naturally grasping and egoistic but capable of co-operation and mutual aid. They further demonstrate that a society without the state is not a Utopian dream but a central part of human history and experience. If authority exists, it is delegated and rarely imposed, and there is little concentration of force in the hands of a few.

Although early civilizations rose and fell over thousands of years, most of the world's population continued to live in clans and tribes, organizing themselves without governments and laws, political administration, courts, or police to maintain order and cohesion. They managed their affairs through well-established traditions, conventions, customs and voluntary agreements. Having evolved as social beings, with an instinctive sympathy for their fellows, humans co-operated with each other peacefully until unequal property relations and coercive government began to distort their affections. Such societies formed by a loose coalition of groups have continued into the modern era, from the vast coalitions of the Santals in East India or the Tiv in West Africa, to more marginal groups like the Kabal of the Atlas

139

Mountains, the Inuit of the Arctic circle, the San of the Kalahari desert and the pygmies of the central African rain-forest. When Rudyard Kipling boasted that the British Empire brought 'the rule of law to the lesser breeds', he overlooked the fact that they had for thousands of years managed very well on their own.

The origins of the state lie in the emergence of domination and hierarchy in society and on the foundation of private property. The domination of nature by humans mirrored the domination of humans by humans: woman's domination of man in matriarchal society, man's domination of woman in patriarchal society. The powerful and cunning in such hierarchical societies established a state in order to defend their interests against the many. The institution of private property only aggravated matters. The real downfall of humanity was when a few put up fences around the common land and said 'this is mine' and managed to persuade or coerce the many to respect them. The barbed wire of the colonizers also disregarded the ancient and harmonious relation-ship of indigenous peoples with the land, whether they were the aborigines in Australia or the native Americans of the New World. If they had only been able to pull out the stakes, and convince others that the land is a common treasury what great calamities might have been avoided!

Once private property was established, it became the principal aim of the state to protect it. The rich and powerful called on the support of warriors and priests to enforce and sanctify their rule. Decrees were made to protect their property and power. The embryonic state emerged as an apparatus claiming supreme authority within a given area. Ever since, people have had to live under the twin burden of capital and the state.

While the Roman empire was undoubtedly a state, with order emanating from Rome, the Greek city states before it and the medieval European city republics after it, were not. In Europe the modern state barely dates from the sixteenth century, when the centralized administration claimed ultimate authority and took over the powers of the self-governing cities and their federations. It was primarily the work of an alliance of the aristocracy, lawyers, priests and merchants who formed the elite of society and saw it in their interest to concentrate most of the functions of society into the hands of a few. In Italy it followed the reunification of the city states and in France the emergence of a unitary monarch from the struggle between the barons. Louis

XIV summed up the desired result when he declared: '*L'état, c'est moi*' ('I am the state'). The centralized state which emerged not only crushed local initiative and autonomy but developed new coercive relationships between members of society who had hitherto co-operated voluntarily and lived together peacefully.

While some like to conflate the two, the state is not the same as society. Unlike the state, society, the sum of voluntary associations, is always a blessing. 'Society' derives from the Latin word *socius* for companion; it is a relationship between companions, a household within the Earth Household. Society is produced by our collective needs, purposes and aspirations and promotes our happiness by combining our affections. It flourishes best when least interfered with. It is always changing and evolving. It creates its own spontaneous order. Like water, the more you try to block its flow, the more it will build up pressure to overcome the dam in order to find its own course. Without the state, society will find its own level and follow its own beneficial direction.

Human beings are social beings and sets of relations. Society sustains us and enables us to realize ourselves as individuals, to become aware of 'I' and 'you'. There is no conflict between society and individuality. Throughout known history and throughout the world, humans have lived in groups and formed families and clans. Society brings out the best in us. It thrives by mutual aid and voluntary co-operation. Society needs the laws of government as little as fish need nets; they both serve to catch the unwary.

We cannot reach our full stature outside society. Even if we decide to live alone in the forests, we have been born and raised in a family and society and take that experience with us. Even the so-called 'wild' children reared outside human society have grown up with the society of other animals.

States and governments have many features in common. Government inevitably restrains, punishes and coerces. It is not only an evil but an unnecessary evil. The best government is one which least governs, but the best condition is no government at all. The state, based on authority, power and domination, also casts a dead hand on the spontaneity and life of society. It is a heavy burden, a dead weight imposed on suffering humanity by a few in the pursuit of their own interests. It checks the flow of society and denies its individual members their instinctive solidarity, initiative, autonomy and independence.

Although the terms are often used interchangeably, the state is not the same as government. Governments come and go, while the state remains with its apparatus of army, police force, judiciary, executive, financial institutions and civil service. A government is the body within a state which claims legitimate authority. It make laws and directs the state apparatus. It is a tradition within liberal democracies that the legislature – government – which makes laws is separate from the judiciary which interprets them and the executive which applies them, but all three are organs of the state. Governments usually follow certain known procedures for obtaining and using power, based either on custom or a constitution. During the campaign before an election, the government of the day is dissolved but the state remains firmly in place.

The state may be defined as a coercive legal organization which claims supreme authority within a given territory. It asserts the sole legitimate right to command its subjects and to be obeyed. Ultimately, it relies on a monopoly of physical force – the sword – to enforce its rule.

There is a wide chasm between the intended end and actual effect of the state. Its apologists claim that the state brings order to the chaos of society, but in reality it is not the remedy but the principal cause of social conflict. It claims to protect its subjects and their property against the invasion of a few, but in fact it chiefly protects the interests of the few who control its apparatus against the many. Far from preventing inequalities and injustices, it only preserves and perpetuates them. Once established, it checks the dynamic spontaneity, initiative and creativity of society. Its tendency is to prolong abuse rather than to end it. It looks back to precedence rather than forward to improvement.

The state asserts the legitimate right to make, interpret and enforce laws within its boundaries. Its coercive nature is clear in its panoply of army, police, prisons and schools. If you don't pay its taxes, you are imprisoned. If you refuse to allow your children to undergo its compulsory scheme of schooling, they are taken away. If you don't go to war at its bidding, you are imprisoned or shot. Indeed, the coercive nature of the state is most transparent when it goes to war. Its politicians, army and police then come to the fore and reveal the iron fist behind the glove of legitimacy. War is thus the health of the state in that war reveals its true nature and its primary end.

Thomas Hobbes gave the classic apology for the state which he called the Leviathan in the seventeenth century. Living in a period of great social unrest and with the imminent threat of civil war and foreign invasion, he pictured human beings as naturally power-seeking, aggressive egoists and the 'state of nature' as a war of all against all in which life was solitary, poor, nasty, brutish and short. Every individual was prey to the violent invasion of his life and property by his fellows. To avoid the resulting chaos and conflict, Hobbes argued that rational beings should come together and form a covenant to transfer their natural right to all things to a person or body who had sovereign power to make laws and to enforce them. The coercive nature of the proposed state was made clear when he insisted that the sword is essential to oblige subjects to obey the laws: 'Covenants, without the Sword, are but Words.'

The title page of Hobbes' *Leviathan* shows a crowned sovereign whose body is made up of a multitude of individuals. The sovereign wields a sword in one hand and a mace in the other, symbols of power, and is flanked by a castle and a church, symbols of political and ecclesiastical authority. By calling his absolute state Leviathan, the fabled sea monster in the Bible, he wished to conjure up a huge and powerful beast. And that of course is what the modern state has become, whether in socialist or liberal countries.

John Locke, writing a generation after Hobbes, when the upheavals of the English Revolution had passed, gave a much more benign picture of the alleged 'state of nature' without government and the state. People are naturally in 'a state of perfect freedom to order their actions, and dispose of their possessions and person, as they see fit, within the bounds of the law of nature'. Although a state of liberty, it is not a state of licence. People have sufficient reason, Locke argued, to follow the law of nature which teaches them that all beings are naturally free, equal and independent and no one ought to harm another in his life, health, liberty and possessions. In the state of nature, people live according to reason without a common superior on earth, able to resolve disputes amongst themselves.

This is a highly desirable kind of life, the very opposite of our grasping, irrational, violent modern states. But Locke went off course when he argued that there are certain inconveniences in this state of nature, especially when individuals try to punish the transgressions of others. He therefore urged that people should consent to set up a limited government with known and settled laws in order to protect their natural rights to life, liberty and property. They could then enjoy them in peace and security.

Of course Hobbes' and Locke's accounts are clearly hypothetical and not historical accounts of the foundation of the state. Nevertheless, they bring out well the nature and purpose of the state and try to base political obligation to the state on the principle of voluntary consent. But there is a fundamental flaw in their accounts. If people were sufficiently rational to make contracts in the state of nature and could be trusted to keep them, then there is no need to set up a state in the first place. Since most people who have lived in stateless societies, and even in modern states, generally keep their word and can be trusted, there is no need for the sword to enforce contracts. If individuals fail to keep their word, they very soon find few people to enter into any agreements with them.

The modern state is an octopus as well as a Leviathan. Its tentacles penetrate the most intimate relationships of everyday life. It is there from the foetus to the coffin: our births and deaths are registered, and in between we are taxed, ordered and surveyed. If we fail to accept the laws of the state, we are punished, fined and imprisoned. If we wish to marry, it is easy and cheap; if we want to divorce, it is expensive and protracted. If our children are born out of wedlock, they are 'illegitimate', as if the state is the sole source of legitimacy in life.

The tentacles of the state not only grasp the bodies of its subjects but reach into their minds. State jugglers dupe and manipulate them to such an extent that they begin to believe that they cannot live outside its confines. By mystifying its naked power with ritual and ceremony, by appealing to patriotism and citizenship, and by trying to become a centre of sympathy, the state wins over the allegiance of its subjects. In a subtle process of reification, a spook in the mind begins to appear as solid as an immovable rock. The state ends up in the saddle, keeping a tight rein on its subjects, making sure by whip and by spurs that it cannot be thrown off. Brought up to do what they are told, trained to obey orders, its subjects finally become voluntary slaves, cannon fodder at war, and docile hands during peace.

The apologists of the state claim that the state expresses the 'general will' of the people and the 'spirit' of the nation. Statists, whether communist or fascist, have further argued that the people can only realize their 'higher selves' within the confines of the state. If they mistakenly oppose its laws or decrees, then it is quite legitimate for the agents of the state to puncture their illusions, to mend their ways, to make them obedient subjects once again. Modern states have developed their propaganda to such a fine art that they even try to define reality. They not only change historical records but restrict the use of permissible language so that people can think only in a particular way. Even the titles of the servants of the state are invidious euphemisms for their true role: the minister of the 'environment' promotes motorways; the minister of 'defence' wages wars abroad; and the 'home' secretary keeps people in prison.

The state is not just a collection of bureaucratic and coercive institutions but has become a state of mind, a means of ordering reality. In liberal democracies its naked power has been curtailed to a degree, but it has become more subtle and intrusive so that it is difficult to define the exact boundary between society and the state. It mixes political with social institutions, punishment and welfare, usurpation and distribution. Its subjects find it difficult to imagine that its main institutions and provisions – the army, police, courts, prisons, civil service, education, health care, and welfare – could operate outside its tight control. But by taking over most of the services of society, the state undermines self-reliance and fosters a sense of powerlessness. It further celebrates at the public expense no end of anniversaries and rituals in order to give it a spurious legitimacy, to create an appearance of tradition and stability, and to evoke majesty and awe. The result is that the state has become so much a part of everyday living that it now seems essential to the social fabric. It has almost become a way of being.

The struggles of the workers and reformers have increased the representation of the people in government and state and have ensured that it provides a degree of welfare in the form of education, health and pensions. But even today, after centuries of struggle to widen the scope of civil rights, about two-thirds of laws in Western states are to protect private property. While some gains have been made, the state has systematically undermined local initiative, self-help, self-management and mutual aid. The neighbourhood can provide better help for the young, elderly, sick, or disabled than faceless bureaucrats at the centre. Local people know their needs and how to satisfy them.

The alternative to state welfare is not privatization of services or the free market but the community providing its own care at the local level. This is best achieved through a voluntary redistribution of wealth.

The real nature of the modern state is most clear in Africa. Villages live peacefully in co-operative harmony, farming their land, educating their children, celebrating the fecundity of the earth and the mystery of the universe until the representatives of the state arrive to cause trouble. They are the taxman, who takes off a percentage of their crop; the soldier, who acts like a bully and takes what he wants; the policeman, who tries to impose an alien law; the teacher, who insists on schooling the young in useless information and citizenship. In most cases the most the villagers ever see of the politicians, to whom they are meant to be indebted and grateful for bringing the civilizing force of the state, is a cloud of dust behind newly imported limousines. Almost without exception, the nation state in Africa has been a disaster, cutting through natural and ethnic boundaries, stealing from its people, stoking ethnic wars, creating false and artificial desires. Like an elephant, its destroys most things in its path and leaves a pile of steaming dung in its wake; and unlike an elephant, its dung does not lead to new growth.

The first step towards liberation from the state mentality is to realize that it is a cancer on society, a dead weight of institutions, a spook in the mind, an unnecessary evil. The defenders of the state claim that the alternative to the state is anarchy. It is, but not in their interpretation of anarchy as chaos. It has been in the interests of leaders and rulers to argue that without their leadership and rule, society would become chaotic, confused and uncertain. Those opposed to 'archy' or imposed rule argue on the other hand that anarchy is the most desirable form of human society where people can flourish in self-managed and mutually agreed order. Rather than being the remedy for disorder, rulers and their states have for most of human history been one of the principal causes of social conflict. People flourish best when least interfered with. When left alone, they live simple and harmonious lives.

The second step towards liberation is for people to create new relationships with each other within, alongside and outside the confines of the state. To contract out of the state, we can revive convivial forms of social organization which are always there like

**146**

seeds beneath the snow. By acting differently, by creating alternative institutions and relationships within the organic community, we render the rule of the state obsolete. By thinking and acting for ourselves, we render its interference unacceptable. By making voluntary agreements based on trust, we make its legal order intrusive. By reinvigorating ancient traditions of mutual aid and co-operation, visible in countless voluntary organizations, clubs and societies, we make its welfare provisions inadequate. Above all, by leading peaceful, creative and co-operative lives, we show the state up for what it is, an unnecessary evil, a disease of the body politic, a hang-over from a barbarous age. In the new era of the coming millennium, the state and its government will become superfluous as people begin to govern themselves and manage their own lives in their own way.

I am not calling for a return to a mythical golden age of perfect equality and freedom, nor to a so-called primitive society with few wants and few opportunities for satisfaction. I propose the taking up of the best of the libertarian, voluntary and co-operative traditions of the past and a move towards creating a society without government and the state which enables individuals to unfurl and realize their full potential. Leaving behind the taboos, superstitions and big men of traditional society, it would create a new era of self-conscious freedom.

Such a free and enlightened society would develop a form of communal individuality which would combine the maximum degree of solidarity compatible with the greatest degree of individuality. It would seek not only to overcome the antagonism between humans but between humanity and the rest of nature. In its full growth, such a society would reflect the ecological principles of unity in diversity and harmony through complexity. It would express the spontaneous and natural order which is at the heart of the universe.

Since freedom is the father and not the son of order, without the artificial restrictions of government and the state, without the coercion of imposed authority, a harmony of interests amongst humans would emerge. It is not necessary to rely on the hidden hand of God to co-ordinate different human interests. The natural instincts of sympathy and co-operation are enough, instincts which have been revealed throughout history when not repressed or distorted by hierarchy, domination and scarcity.

To bring about this desirable state of affairs, I am not

recommending the violent overthrow of the state or government. Violence only breeds violence, and he who lives by the sword dies by the sword. The way forward is to develop a new consciousness which rejects hierarchy and domination and seeks to form relationships based on trust and co-operation. It is to forge voluntary institutions and associations based on affinity and sympathy. It is to create a new society within the shell of the old so that when the state eventually cracks and falls apart under the pressure of creativity, new life will emerge, stretch its wings and joyously ride the wind!

# 13

# Wading Through the Sea

*When the eccentric old man met the brilliant young pupil, he asked him what he had learned.*

*'I've been taught about the laws and regulations which rulers make and which no one would dare ignore or disobey.'*

*'That is a false teaching indeed', replied the old man. 'To attempt to govern mankind thus is as impossible as to try to wade through the sea, to hew a passage through a river, or make a mosquito fly away with a mountain!'*

Chuang Tzu

Clearly not all governments and states are as bad as each other. A representative government within a republic is preferable to monarchy, aristocracy or despotism. An elected president is better than a king. I would rather live under a liberal government which respects the basic rights to life and liberty than under a despotic one that does not. It is better that soldiers are ordered to prevent the lynching of innocents than to shoot strikers and dissidents.

But the type of centralized state and representative government which has become established in Europe and which has been exported throughout the Western world is not the last word in democracy. There have been greater democracies before, and there is no reason why there should not be better forms in the future. Society constantly changes, new needs and challenges emerge, and our social arrangements need to adapt to express our evolving aspirations. A timid reverence for the past, a paranoid clinging to hoary traditions, should not prevent an imaginative and life-affirming change for the future. In their time, the revolutionaries who founded the American Constitution and who drew up the French Declaration of Rights certainly saw the advantage of new beginnings. But many of their beliefs are still entrenched and it is time to think again about new social arrangements for a new era. We need to move away from representative forms of government, in which a few govern the many usually in their own interest, to a more direct and participatory democracy.

There have been many inspiring examples in the past. The case of ancient Greece, at the dawn of Western civilization, stands out and has never been equalled. In the fifth century BC, up to 6000 citizens met in regular assemblies on a hill outside Athens to decide on the affairs of the day. The administrators of the Council of Five Hundred were not elected but chosen by lot (sortition). The system not only prevented the creation of a permanent bureaucracy but encouraged active and responsible citizenship. The fact that citizenship was extended only to free men and not to women or slaves, shows the limitations of the Greek polis but it does not undermine the intrinsic value of the form of direct democracy.

Other examples come to mind. Traditional Icelandic democracy was direct and convivial. The medieval free communes were self-governing and efficient. The lively seventeenth-century town meetings in New England, in which all the townsfolk participated, remain as an inspiring example of direct democracy at work. The independent Swiss cantons also show how well a decentralized society can work.

In times of civil war and revolution, popular movements have emerged which created a form of participatory democracy in which men and women were directly involved in governing themselves. These include the Levellers, Diggers and Ranters in the English Civil War in the seventeenth century and the *sans culottes* and the Parisian sections during the French Revolution at the end of the eighteenth century. The Paris Commune in 1871 and the Russian Revolution in 1917, particularly in the Ukraine, saw a conscious attempt of the people to govern themselves without representatives. The greatest social experiment so far was undoubtedly during the Spanish Civil War when large swathes of the republic, especially in Catalunya, were organized without a centralized government by the people managing their own affairs.

Yet the main trend in the West has been to establish centralized states and representative governments. The philosopher John Locke in many ways justified the birth of the modern liberal state in the 'bloodless revolution' of 1689 in Britain. His doctrine of natural rights to life, liberty and property and his model of government with known laws to protect and enforce them inspired the great American and French Revolutions in the eighteenth century. But the rights were still limited to property-owning white men, thereby excluding women, black slaves, or the poor. It was only during the nineteenth century that a growing number of thinkers, workers and peasants began to realize that the representative parliamentary system was flawed; indeed, that in many ways government is tyranny, property is theft, and anarchy is order. Even Marx and Lenin came to dream about the withering away of the state, although their followers have only increased and centralized its authority whenever they have been in power.

Britain has been called the mother of democracies and the parliamentary system set up in the late seventeenth century remains largely intact 300 years later. The franchise has been recently broadened to include the propertyless and women and the House of Commons has more power, but the unelected House of Lords and the monarchy still hold sway and interfere with the democratic process. The presence of lords and bishops in the upper house reflect the power of the church and aristocracy in the modern British state. The hereditary principle, based on blood rather than merit, is alive and well. The state apparatus is still controlled by the same elite – the Establishment – with graduates from Oxford and Cambridge forming the majority in the higher echelons of the army, judiciary, civil service, financial institutions, parliament and church. By retaining the right to inheritance, the state has ensured that society continues to be grossly unequal and unjust. Wealth and power continue to cascade down from generation to generation within the same families.

There are fundamental flaws in this representative system of democracy based on majority rule which has been exported throughout the world. Strictly speaking no one can be represented by another. If people allow themselves to be represented, they abrogate their right to independent judgement and autonomy. A parliamentary representative is expected to represent tens of thousands of people. Such representatives usually end up not expressing the will of their constituency, or their own conscience, but the line of their political party. In the meantime, the people are forgotten until they are briefly wooed again in an election with false promises and wild claims. They then sign away dutifully their freedom for another few years by putting a cross on a piece of paper. Once in power again, the so-called representative government invariably fails to promote the national interest or the general good, but furthers the interests of those with power, privilege and wealth. In Britain and the USA, there is as much choice between the political parties as there is between detergents in a supermarket. All are concerned with whitewash and are wedded to the centralized state, mixed economy, industrial growth and the status quo. The fundamental choice of whether we want a representative system or not is not on offer.

Majority rule and representation are the two pillars of the liberal theory of the state. During elections people are asked to vote for different representatives, and then those representatives vote in Parliament on specific issues. If decisions are based on majority vote, then the waverers end up with the greatest influence as they hold the balance of power. If the majority imposes its views, we then have the tyranny of the majority, especially if the majority expects the minority to carry out its commands. The great irony of modern representative government based on majority rule is that the government is invariably elected by a minority of the people (about a third in Britain) and as such ends up as a tyranny of the minority over the majority. In some cases, the real majority is formed by those who abstain, who are never represented. Yet the majority has no more right to dictate to the minority, even a minority of one, than the minority has to dictate to the majority.

Universal suffrage was once a great rallying cry for the dispossessed, but now that it has been achieved in the West, people are beginning to realize that they are still disenfranchised in the most fundamental ways. By giving up in a general election their right to manage their own affairs, they give up their liberty to decide on the most important issues of their life. At the same time, they remain disempowered both socially and economically. The net result is that whoever talks of political power under representative government means domination and hierarchy. Despite its claim to protect liberty, government always ends up restricting freedom. And whichever way you vote, the government always gets in; if it did not, voting would be made illegal. As a result, voters have become so alienated that some states are now making voting mandatory.

The liberal theory of the state is based on the notion of a contract between the government and the people. Unfortunately it is a myth. Even for the American Constitution, the people did not make a social contract to set up a government. The will of the 'founding fathers' is moreover imposed on subsequent generations, for each generation is not asked whether they accept their proposals or not. The practice of voting or paying taxes cannot be taken as an expression of tacit consent. The state ensures that there is no alternative: those who do not vote are denied any real public voice and those who refuse to pay their taxes are put in jail.

Whether it be with a government or between individuals, legally binding contracts (with the sword of the state always hanging overhead) are not the best way to manage and regulate our affairs. The only people to benefit from contracts are lawyers who draw them up and defend them. To base our relationships on contract implies a lack of responsibility and trust, but the fundamental flaw with all contracts is that they fix relationships at the moment the contract is made. A contract is made in particular circumstances with limited information by individuals who are at a certain stage of development; it does not, as a result, allow room for change, for new circumstances, for new knowledge, for personal growth. On the contrary, it ensures that past folly governs future wisdom. The same is true of a promise. It is made in certain circumstances with certain information, but if either change, then it might be reasonable to break the promise in the interests of truth and justice.

This is especially so with the marriage contract. There is strong pressure on women to marry to avoid the stigma of being categorized a spinster or mistress and on parents to avoid the stigma of 'illegitimacy' for their children. If people truly loved and respected each other, there would be no need for a marriage contract, for even if they fell out they would not fight over children or common possessions. If they did have problems over access to children, they might wish to have an adjudicator or seek advice from experienced negotiators but they would not rely as at present on an isolated and anonymous judge deciding the terms of their divorce in an obscure office with the minimum of information. Individuals should only stay together as long as their relationship is fulfilling and meaningful, not because of the legal bonds of marriage. The very term 'wedlock', like padlock or gridlock, reflects the restrictive nature of the contract. The state has no place in the most intimate and loving of human relationships.

I am not opposed to voluntary agreements to regulate our affairs. If contracts are nothing more than declarations of intent, open to change in changing circumstances, then they are fine. But if they are binding in the conventional sense, legally enforceable and carrying coercive sanctions, then they are not. They encourage us to reach for our lawyers rather than to consult our consciences. If an action is right, it should be performed because it is right; if wrong, avoided. The moral obligation to do what we say should be enough; we do not need the additional obligation of a legal contract which may subvert our judgement and check moral and spiritual growth. In an enlightened society, it would be enough to manage our affairs with such voluntary agreements and declarations of intent.

The other justification for the state and representative government is that they rule through known procedures established by laws so that their citizens can enjoy peace and security. The legislature, judiciary, and executive of the state make, interpret and enforce its laws with the threat or use of physical force. The state therefore claims to be the supreme authority and asserts a monopoly of force within its boundaries.

Defenders of the state argue that its threat or use of physical force is necessary to override the coercion of individuals or groups of individuals. It is the duty of the state, they claim, to protect certain civil liberties and rights, such as the liberty of thought and expression, the right of public meeting and association, and the security of property and persons. Yet in reality the state not only fails to protect all these goods but they can be achieved more easily without the coercive force of the state.

However much it claims to protect civil liberties and rights, the state invariably overrides them in its own interest, whether by forcing its subjects to go to war or the poor to respect the property of the rich. Even the state with its powers reduced to a minimum – the 'night watchman state' advocated by libertarians – would be used by the rich and powerful to maintain their power, wealth and privileges.

The notion of a free state, which the Irish called their country after independence, is a contradiction in terms. No state is free. Instead of providing healthy stability, it hampers creative change; instead of imposing order, it encourages social conflict; instead of fostering enterprise, its undermines initiative; instead of providing genuine welfare, it brings about helpless dependence; instead of uniting people, it turns them into a lonely crowd; and instead of bringing about security, it only increases anxiety, despair and a sense of powerlessness.

What are the laws that governments make and the state interprets and enforces? Laws are rules made by rulers who govern by means of organized violence. Those who break the laws are punished, either by being fined, imprisoned, or in many states, executed. In theory, laws are impartial and universal, but ever since the emergence of the state they have been made in the interests of the rulers and the privileged. If some have been passed to protect civil rights, it is only reluctantly under the pressure and agitation of the people.

Where there is morality, there is no need for law. Indeed the call for law and order arises when the social morality in a community has already broken down. Traditionally, people have managed their own affairs through customs, without a codified set of laws. When hierarchy first began to emerge in society, rulers issued decrees which the priests sanctified and the warriors enforced. They were later codified into laws by the ruling elite along with those customs which served their interests. But the net result was that the more laws and regulations there were, the more thieves and robbers appeared in the land and the poorer the people became.

The only acceptable laws are the laws of nature, and they are only observed regularities, interpretations of the way nature works. All man-made laws are arbitrary and artificial. They restrict liberty by making people act or refrain from acting. They operate like high hedges which are intended to keep people on the straight and narrow road, and not wander off into the open plains or trackless woods. The greatest shortcoming of man-made law is that it tries to reduce the myriad of human actions to one common and uniform standard. As such it operates like Procrustes' bed, which either stretched or cut the limbs of those who lay in it in order to make them fit.

Rulers find their standards of right in themselves rather than in nature. They thus coerce people into obeying artificial laws of their own making. By asserting themselves, they accomplish only disaster. Yet if they let go, if they abdicated their rule, there is nothing that the people would not accomplish. Society knows best what is good for society, not government and rulers. Since it is not possible to coerce people into being good, better let them be good of their own accord.

In existing Western parliamentary democracies, laws fall roughly into three different categories: constitutional law which protects the administrative machine of the state and government; property law which protects the interests of property owners and thereby the unequal distribution of property and the unjust appropriation of the good things of the earth; and the protection of persons and civil rights. In most modern states, the latter make up about a third of laws; the great majority are to protect government and property. If the causes of crime in the unequal distribution of property and in the coercive force of government were eradicated, there would be little occasion for anti-social acts. If property were evenly distributed about two-thirds of crimes – the crimes against property – would disappear. If government were simplified and eventually dissolved, there would be no need for constitutional law. All that would remain would be crimes against persons. In a society based on mutual aid rather than individual assertion, on peaceful co-operation rather than on aggressive competition, there would be fewer aggravations to promote violence between individuals. Overall, a far greater harmony of interests would prevail in a society without law, government and unequal property.

The inevitable sanction of law is punishment – the deliberate infliction of suffering. But punishment, whether in the home, school or in prison, is not the way to improve human behaviour. There can be no moral justification for punishment, whether it be for retribution, deterrence or reform. Retribution, an eye for an eye, is the most ignorant form of instinctive cruelty. Better forgiveness than revenge; better turning the other cheek than demanding a pound of flesh. Punishment intended to deter others by making an example of lawbreakers only hardens their hearts and the hearts of others, and makes would-be criminals more vicious. As for reform, punishment can inflict fear but it can never create lasting improvement. Harming people simply makes them worse. The rod might provide a motive not to be caught but it does not inspire good actions. Coercion can never inspire and enlighten; it only spoils and alienates the mind. Even on a practical level, punishment is not effective for there is no simple correlation between crime and punishment; the severity of punishment simply does not lessen the amount of crime in society.

All punishment is a confession of ignorance on behalf of the punisher. Indeed it is worse than the original crime, because while the latter may be committed in a moment of passion or folly, the former is a cold and deliberate act of cruelty. Being cruel is never kind. Hurting someone when you have been hurt may make you feel temporarily better, but it does not break the cycle of violence. In the long run, you reap what you sow: the more you hurt others, the more you hurt yourself. Evil will return to the one that commits it, like dust thrown against the wind.

To lock someone up in prison is asking for trouble. Prisons are universities of crime. By locking people away from their friends and family and the rest of society, you make them all the more anti-social. By locking them up with other criminals, they just learn from each other how to become more proficient. By locking up their hearts, with harsh treatment and blows, they become hardened and revengeful. And by regulating every detail of their life in a totalitarian institution, they lose all responsibility and initiative. The more prisons are reformed, the more invidious they often become. Modern penitentiaries have total control and surveillance of their inmates, allowing them no private space or autonomy. No wonder when people come out of prison, they have lost their bearings, do not know what to do next, and all too easily fall back into their old ways.

Since people rarely wish ill unless badly treated, friendly persuasion in most cases would suffice to prevent anti-social behaviour. By encouraging people to think and act for themselves, it would be enough to demonstrate the benefits of working for the well-being of the whole. And if that failed, the few individuals who still persisted in harming others would be restrained with the minimum use of force as a last resort. Instead of being locked away in prisons to become hardened and embittered recluses, they would be looked after with care, understanding and kindness within the community, amongst their friends, family and associates. They would, as in most traditional societies without law and external government, be considered unfortunate rather than guilty. They would be reasoned with rather than admonished. Respecting their dignity, autonomy and individuality, they

157

would be helped to find a meaningful and purposeful role in life and to become full members of society.

If not by law and punishment, then how do you deal with cruel behaviour? By good example, by better motives, by education, by persuasion. There is, of course, a danger that persuasion could become as oppressive as punishment and even more insidious. It is the nature of totalitarian regimes to make their rebels 'confess to their crimes', to encourage 'self-criticism' and to 're-educate' them into becoming good and pliant citizens again. Such psychological manipulation and brainwashing can be more harmful than prison: while the latter chains the body, the former shackles the mind. The use of psychiatry to control dissidents is well established in totalitarian regimes. Even in liberal democracies, mainstream psychiatry sometimes tries to 'cure' the so-called 'mad' by denying the wisdom of their unreason, and by obliging them to adjust to the existing reality, however mad and sick it may be. It is perhaps no surprise that some mental hospitals resemble prisons which resemble barracks, factories and boarding schools. They are all in the business of disciplining and punishing and curing; they all try to create docile workers and malleable citizens.

Many reformers look to the influence of public opinion or the moral censure of neighbours to replace the force of law to discourage anti-social behaviour. The censure of neighbours can take many forms – ostracism, boycotting, sending people to Coventry (in Britain at least), open criticism, satire, invective. These sanctions, of course, can have a powerful effect. But there can be a tyranny of opinion as well as the oppression of law in making people conform. Propaganda can curb free enquiry and creative thought. Moral force might be preferable to physical force, but it can still have a degree of coercive power. This is especially true of certain religious sects which exercise godly watchfulness and collective vigilance to prevent any nonconformity or moral weakness. Political groups can also practise a kind of fraternal terror against those who might deviate from the party line. Some gurus and spiritual leaders can exert great powers of persuasion which lead people into timid obedience and subservient dependence.

A repressive morality can be as invasive as the state, preventing people from acting and thinking for themselves. This is the case in theological states where religion and government are closely intertwined. No one wants interfering busybodies legislating for all and telling them what to believe and to do. To be governed by a narrowly defined 'reason', 'truth' or 'love' can be a greater curb to creativity and independent thought than a state religion. Censorship prevents free enquiry and a lively and tested apprehension of the truth. Repressive morality should not (say I tendentiously) replace repressive laws. We do not want 'Thou shall not' written over our doors, or lists of rules distributed amongst the community telling us what we can or cannot do.

If the state fails to protect liberty and is unable to ensure security, can it offer anything to its hard-pressed subjects? Although the state is by its very nature oppressive, under the pressure of reformers and the working-class movement it has provided a degree of welfare. Not all state institutions are therefore equally bad: hospitals and schools are better than prisons and workhouses. But the benevolent face of the welfare state has created a surly and overblown bureaucracy which increasingly interferes with the lives of its subjects. From the cradle to the grave, we are registered, regulated, supervised, noted, surveyed, spied on, watched over, inspected, controlled, commanded, pursued, hassled, taxed, extorted, assessed, evaluated, means-tested, censored, stamped, priced, pensioned, authorized, recommended, admonished, reformed, mystified, pressurized, preached at and exhorted all in the name of our so-called welfare.

The welfare state undermines self-help and mutual aid and creates a sense of helpless dependence. Its experts allegedly know what is good for us and tell us how to think, live, move and act. They impose a bland and grey uniformity, and try to squeeze organic, evolving social forms into a straight-jacket of mechanical conformity. The welfare state claims to offer security, yet people grow more anxious and bewildered. Rather than looking to their friends and neighbours and community for assistance, the dispossessed and unfortunate must face heartless bureaucrats, meddling investigators, and smug taskmasters. No wonder that by the year 2020 the World Health Organization estimates that half the illnesses in the West will be caused by depression.

Welfare can be better supplied within the community by voluntary associations than by state agencies. Voluntary associations organized locally are better able to satisfy the needs of the people and can involve them more easily in their running. Medicine and education do not need state sponsorship any more than industry and agriculture. Schools and hospitals are much better when in the control of the communities which they are meant to serve and are adapted to local circumstances and needs.

Socialist states throughout the world have been unable to escape the contagion of all states. While redistributing wealth a little and providing a degree of welfare, they have spawned a vast and corrupt bureaucracy which stifles the life and initiative of the community and undermines the work of voluntary associations. They have created a new elite of bureaucrats who administer the public wealth in their own interest. They encourage dependency and conformity by rewarding those they favour, by withdrawing aid to those who question, and by silencing those who oppose. Totalitarian socialist states, as in the Communist bloc, further sought total control of mind, body and spirit. By oiling the cogs of the state machine with blood, they amply demonstrated the truth of the maxim that power corrupts and absolute power corrupts absolutely.

For all the rhetoric about the 'withering away of the state', whenever authoritarian Communists have seized power, they have only strengthened and centralized the state administration in the hands of a bureaucratic elite. All the major Communist revolutions in the twentieth century – in Russia, China, Vietnam and Cuba – demonstrated the danger of the 'dictatorship of the proletariat' becoming the dictatorship of the Communist Party, and in most cases the dictatorship of the party leader. Not content with ruling by the threat of naked force, Communist states denied all dissent and attempted to brainwash their citizens. They even attempted to redefine reality, by manipulating the processes of thought through the control of permissible language. The freedom of assembly, of travel, of thought and of speech were all seriously curtailed. The State is Ultimate Reality and the Party is Truth was their message. Those that disagreed were forced to be free from their illusions. If I were living under such a regime, I would not be able to publish this book and would no doubt end up in a state prison or psychiatric ward.

But what about the nation state which has triumphed throughout the world and is the aspiration of most subject and colonized peoples? In Europe, most nation states are the products of historical conquest and geographical distortion rather than the organic growth of natural and cultural boundaries. In Africa, nation states are even more artificial, having been created largely by colonial administrators who drew lines across a map, regardless of the geography, history and culture of the people living on the land. The resulting mess has led to countless wars.

A nation is different from a state; they are not synonymous. The nation exists outside and alongside the state and sometimes in spite of the state. It is a community of peoples sharing common ways of life, languages, traditions, customs and memories. Indigenous Americans before the arrival of Europeans lived in tribes and nations but they did not have states; they still live in nations on their reservations within the United States of America. Scotland and Wales are nations but they do not have their own states; they were forced by military conquest to sign Acts of Union with England to become part of a larger state called Great Britain under a monarch.

It is understandable that a colonized or subject people should aspire to become an independent nation. A nation can include many different peoples, although it usually shares a common tradition, language, living conditions, culture and customs. State jugglers have tried to make the state the main object of a people's loyalties and a nation's identity; they have tried to show that it expresses not only the will of the people but the spirit of the nation. The idea of the nation state plays on a herd instinct and can have a strong emotional pull. By doing so it sinks the life of the individual into an abstract being, a spook of the mind. But the state is not the prerequisite nor the guardian of a nation's identity. A nation can exist outside and alongside a state.

There is undoubtedly a deep-seated desire to be part of a larger whole, especially in our society where families are breaking up and individuals are becoming like nounless adjectives floating in the lonely crowd. Many have lost the feeling of belonging to an organic community. They have little sense of a shared destiny. They experience life together as if they were queuing at a bus stop: they might objectively be doing the same thing, but subjectively they are completely isolated, forming an arbitrary collection of solitudes. Standing in a queue is very different from going on strike or having a party. People now barricade themselves in their homes in a desperate attempt to create an oasis of security, beauty and warmth in a desert of hostility and fear. Public spaces are no longer convivial meeting places but danger zones to be avoided, especially at night.

Western society has become deeply fragmented, with class solidarity an experience of the past. As a result, groups of individuals are finding their identity by aligning themselves intransigently with a sports team, a race, a political party, a religious group or a nation. Nationalism, patriotism, racism, xenophobia, and hatred of the Other are on the march, tight-lipped and jack-booted. By making people first and foremost sons and daughters of the fatherland, patriotism makes them slaves of their governments. They then act like puppets in the hands of their lead-ers, hating foreigners within and without, acting against all reason and conscience. Patriotism, a belief that one's nation comes first, right or wrong, is a dangerous and destructive impulse and the major cause of war. It is, as Oscar Wilde observed, the last refuge of the scoundrel.

Countervailing the pull of the nation state are larger federations like the Commonwealth, the European Union or the United Nations. Their supporters believe that by establishing a world government with a military force, war between nation states will be kept in check. Much is praiseworthy in this inter-nationalism: by thinking in global terms, we overcome local prejudices and blind loyalties. Being cosmopolitan means taking the *cosmos* for your *polis*, becoming a citizen of the world. But world government or a European super state would have all the shortcomings of the nation state writ large, denying local autonomy and riding roughshod over regional differences. Large international political organizations just multiply the difficulties of national governments and have even less accountability and flexibility. In the end it is the most powerful nations which tend to dictate terms to the others.

It is abundantly clear that the nation state claims to suppress injustice and oppression, but it only aggravates them. It is meant to bring peace, but it encourages national rivalries and war. If it provides a degree of welfare, it creates dependence and crushes creativity and self-reliance. Its powers of maintaining control of the economy, organizing distribution, providing welfare, main-taining peace between rival interests, and providing defence can all be better performed by society at large. While society is always a blessing, government even in its best condition is an unnecessary evil. And while a limited state is better than a strong one, the best society has neither state nor government.

Without them, people would be able to live creatively and peacefully in their organic communities and nations. They could draw on ancient traditions of self-help and mutual aid and combine age-old patterns of co-operation with a modern sense of individuality. A free community is not new; it is the unfurling and realizing of something always present, always there, something buried in society like seeds beneath the snow. As the thaw begins, the seeds of creativity and conviviality will begin to grow and blossom once again. Freed from the strait-jacket of the state and government, the nation will be able to become a community of self-governing communities, a ring in the widening circle of humanity which goes beyond nation, race and species to embrace the whole world.

# 14

# After the Leviathan

*A small country has fewer people.*
*Though there are machines that can work ten to a*
*hundred times faster than man, they are not needed.*
*The people take death seriously and do not travel far.*
*Though they have boats and carriages, no one uses them.*
*Though they have armour and weapons, no one displays*
*them.*
*Men return to knotting rope in place of writing.*
*Their food is plain and good, their clothes fine but*
*simple, their homes secure;*
*They are happy in their ways.*
*Though they live within sight of their neighbours,*
*And crowing cocks and barking dogs are heard across*
*the way,*
*Yet they leave each other in peace while they grow old*
*and die.*

Lao Tzu

While politics is usually defined as the art of government, in its widest and original sense it is the common pursuit of the good life. The good life covers all areas of social interaction – production and consumption, work and play, ritual and celebration, the social and the spiritual. It enables people to realize their potential as individuals and social beings. A good society would go beyond conventional politics and create new structures so that people in their regions could attain their own good within the wider community of nature.

There is an alternative to the state, to the present forms of

164

representative government and parliamentary democracy, to the rule of law. We do not have to be ruled by the sword. A much more democratic way of organizing society is on the twin principles of decentralization and federation. Decision-making would be decentralized in the local communities who would federate for common interests and endeavours. Power would no longer spread from the centre out or from the top down, but remain at the bottom and on the periphery. Institutions for organizing social life would be non-hierarchical, life-affirming and creative. They would be rooted in the culture and ecology of the regions and based on direct and participatory democracy. Society would resemble a network rather than a pyramid, thereby reflecting the self-organization of nature itself. The welfare state would give way to the commonweal. Democracy would spread out from the household, the neighbourhood, the local community, the region to embrace the wide world.

The basic cell of society is the individual, but the molecule is the family. We are all born into a family and however individual we become, we remain a set of family relations. Family life provides a haven and encourages some of the greatest of human qualities – generosity, sympathy, love and disinterested care. Domestic affections foster the culture of the heart. The nuclear family, a recent develop-ment in human history, can be limiting and oppressive, but for children at least it is better than a single-parent family. All things being equal, two loving parents of the opposite sex who love each other are better for a child than one because he or she is exposed to a richer emotional experience. But better still is an extended family with many other relations of different ages and a wider community which offers sociability, sympathy, care and support.

A family need not be based on common blood ties. We are all members of a biological family but we can form voluntary families as well. Outside these we can become members of affinity groups, convivial and voluntary associations of free and equal individuals which meet for a common end. Any community is made up of different affinity groups and they would undoubtedly become more widespread in a free society. Love of family and locality would lose their exclusive nature. Charity might begin at home and neighbourliness might flourish best in the immediate community, but they should not stop there. We can go beyond the narrow ties of family, clan, tribe or race to consider the needs of all humanity. We can even see other species as members of the same family and the Earth Household (*oikos*) as our home.

In place of a central government and the state, a form of direct and participatory democracy would evolve in a free society. The fundamental forum for expressing needs and aspirations and for making decisions within the community would be the local assembly or commune. Each community would manage its own affairs through open assemblies for all those who wished to attend. Decisions as far as possible would be made through consensus. The local assemblies would send delegates to district assemblies who in turn would send delegates to the regional and national assemblies. Their role would be to co-ordinate production and distribution, resolve disputes, and organize defence and foreign affairs. The national assembly would have little to do except facilitate communications and deal with international relations. It would have no coercive power to force local assemblies to toe the line, but merely make considered recommendations. It would lose its coercive nature as a legal order and be nothing more than a co-ordinating body.

The nation would thus become a decentralized community of self-governing communities. At the same time a loose confederation of independent nations could provide a forum to solve disputes, co-ordinate common ventures, and encourage a sense of fellowship amongst the whole human species. Such a federation, however, would have no central political or military authority which enabled it to force member nations to follow the will of the majority or the most powerful. All federated nations could withdraw whenever they wished and only co-operate when it suited them.

Rather than making decisions on the basis of majority voting, people would try and work through consensus, which expresses all shades of opinion and leaves no group or individual out in the cold. If it is impossible to achieve consensus on some issues, then the view of the majority might be acted upon initially. If the outcome is still not satisfactory, then the majority should be ready to let the minority view prevail. Whatever the circumstances, neither the majority nor the minority should oblige someone to act against his or her conscience and judgement. It is quite possible for one person to be right and a thousand people wrong. Truth cannot be decided by casting up numbers: something either corresponds to reality or it does not. We know it through our intuition and experience; we feel it in our bones.

166

If these structural changes were to be successful, they would have to be accompanied by a change in political culture. Genuine democracy would need to transcend the old gladiatorial model of assemblies in which parties attack each other and combative personalities rise to prominence. The art of listening would be more important than the science of rhetoric, and there would be room for the expression of feeling and sensibility as well as for reason and argument.

It would not be a welfare state but a welfare society. Without the aggravation of the state, the primary cause of social conflict and war, the more co-operative and gentle tendencies of humans would come to the fore. People would also control their own resources rather than give them up to state administrators who then think they are doing them a favour by redistributing what is theirs in the first place. No longer would the state decide on what and how their enforced contributions are spent. Rather than having providers telling people what to do and think, the people themselves would decide on the degree and kind of care they wanted. Local initiatives would blossom again and a myriad of co-operatives, clubs, unions and friendly societies, funded and run by and for the members, would re-emerge to meet the needs of each community. Learning and health care and prevention centres would be voluntary and local.

Without political and legal coercion, a new way of living and being would arise in which individuals govern themselves and manage their own lives while contributing generously to the well-being of the whole. Without the artificial divisions of unequal property and accumulated capital, a social morality would emerge which would think in terms of the whole as well as the individual, which would satisfy real desires, and which would encourage respect for the freedom of others and honour their individuality. Without coercive relationships and a repressive morality, there would be enough solidarity, reason and good will amongst humans to live in comparative harmony with each other and the earth.

A free society is a tolerant, pluralist and open society. It would be wary of the tyranny of public opinion replacing the tyranny of government and the law. It would encourage people to question authority and think and act for themselves. It would allow complete freedom of thought, of expression and of living. People would be able to think, feel, imagine and act as they saw fit, as

167

long as they did not prevent others from doing the same. My neighbour would be free to censure me as much as he or she wished, but must remember that I am to act according to my own judgement. My neighbour can place a hand on my shoulder, but cannot tell me what to do. He or she may advise, but not dictate to me.

Tolerance and forbearance would replace the orders of the day. There would be no rigid censorship to fetter free enquiry and thought, or to prevent the flowering of reason, imagination and intuition. Many experiments in living would flourish. The only limit would be a recognition that the freedom of one is the condition of the freedom of all: no individuals would assert themselves by curtailing the freedom of others.

There would be the maximum amount of individuality compatible with solidarity. Individuality would flourish as never before and everyone would be able to realize their own particular potential; indeed the health of the society could be measured by the degree of eccentricity it tolerated. Just as unity in nature is achieved through diversity, so in a free society the greater the degree of variety, the more overall harmony there is. A diverse, complex community is a resilient community, capable of adapting to changing conditions.

In any society there are bound to be some disputes and conflicts. But there is no need to resort to lawyers and courts who quibble over the interpretation of words and trip over precedents. Rather than trying to reduce the myriad of actions to one common standard, each case is best considered in the light of its particular circumstances. There can be no better guideline than every case is a law unto itself. Instead of professional judges who look to their hoary texts rather than to their consciences, to what went before rather than to what confronts them, popular juries could arbitrate. Their aim, as with the advice of elders in many traditional societies, would not be to apportion guilt, to take revenge or to make an example, but to try and make amends between the disturbers of the peace and their victims and to re-establish social harmony.

In the long run, it should be enough to recommend a solution between grieved parties rather than imposing a judgement by the threat of force. If people return to the simple life and dwell in supportive communities which tolerate individuality, the only laws they need to follow are the laws of nature and the freely

168

agreed customs of society. As people become more awakened and enlightened, there will no doubt come a time when morality as a conscious, calculating activity will be forgotten. A good people would be good spontaneously, contributing to the well-being of the whole, living in harmony with each other and nature, without analysis or prompting. They would no longer say, 'I ought to do this' or, 'You should do that'; they would instinctively do the right thing and perform the appropriate action. 'Ought' would become 'is'.

Such a free society, based on decentralization and federation, would consist of a community of communities. A more organic and voluntary grouping of peoples would emerge, based on ecological, geographical, historical and cultural lines. The bioregion – a living area and ecological whole shaped by natural boundaries such as mountains, watersheds, rivers and sea – would replace the arbitrary lines of the bureaucrat's ruler drawn across a map. Rebuilding regional cultures would give depth and strength to world culture. Unlike the state, a region has no clear boundaries and can occupy natural and imaginary spaces, ecological and mythical realms. At the same time, a free society would see the community and region as a base but not the limit of life. Rejecting exclusive love of one's country and xenophobic nationalism, people would go beyond the old ties of class, tribe, race and nation to embrace the entire world.

Power would be decentralized and remain with the people in their communities. It would lose its coercive influence and be replaced by calm persuasion. At the centre and the periphery, people would be self-sufficient, self-reliant and free, able to act, think and stand up for themselves. No longer a pyramid, society would be more like a circle: the individual would be at the centre combining with others to form voluntary associations and free unions. The outer circles of society would not crush the inner ones but all would gain in strength from each other like the rings of a tree. Free of the strait-jacket of the state, society would appear like a web of self-governing communities. The web of society would mirror nature's web, in which individual strands are interwoven to sustain a dynamic and living whole.

But how would such a society defend itself from internal disruption or foreign aggression? Not by violence, for you cannot use destructive and violent means to achieve creative and peaceful ends. Fighting for peace is like trying to cut a passage through water: it cannot be done. To travel with a gun invites aggression. Aggression only leads to more aggression, until you end up in a spiral which eventually turns into an all-consuming tornado. A person of peace and good will, on the other hand, has his or her own protective aura. If you pose no threat to an aggressor, they often lose their aggression. There are many examples of calm and clear-headed individuals turning the situation around and not only disarming their would-be aggressors but actually helping them to change their ways.

But is pacifism possible in all situations? Most people if they had a gun in their hand might be prompted to shoot a person who was about to rape their daughter. It may be instinctive and understandable to want to protect your child, but is it right? How can you be sure that the rape will actually take place? Even if it did, would killing a person be justified? Even if the man killed your daughter, should you take a life for a life? If you failed, the aggressor might end up killing you and your daughter while only rape had been on his mind. In such circumstances, the best policy might be to try and dissuade the person from his intended action in a calm and friendly way, and, if that was not successful, to employ the minimum restraint to control him until he came to his senses.

In the absence of a professional police force, and with fewer causes of crime, a community is quite capable of maintaining security for its members. They have done so in the past and still do in many parts of the world, especially in Africa and Latin America, where the police and soldiers are by far the most disruptive elements in society. Wrongdoers would not be sent to prison or punished but rehabilitated within the community. Disputes would be solved by arbitration and popular juries among neighbours rather than by lawyers and law courts.

Clearly anti-social individuals, who try to restrict the freedom of others, would have to be dealt with. If persuasion and example failed they would have to be restrained as a temporary measure. But they would not be ostracized, put away, beaten or brainwashed but helped in a friendly and respectful way to see the harm of restricting the freedom of others and the benefit of using their own responsibly. The aim would be to restore the harmony of society, not attribute guilt or enact revenge.

What about defence on a larger scale? How could you prevent a free and sustainable society from being destroyed from without?

To deal with an external threat, it is better to have a people's voluntary militia than a professional and standing army. An armed militia – as in Switzerland – is far more democratic and flexible and only with difficulty can be used against the people themselves. But by forming militias you are still empowering some individuals who have a personal affinity for weaponry, fighting and the military life. By doing so, you are preserving and encouraging the most aggressive tendencies of society.

The best form of defence is non-violent direct action of the kind Gandhi developed in India which seeks to dissuade and win over the attackers rather than to kill or maim them. If a country were invaded, autonomous peace brigades who knew their region well could meet the invader and oppose them non-violently at first. If they still persisted then the whole country would come to a halt in organized civil disobedience.

In defence, it is better to roll up like a hedgehog rather than launch your quills at an enemy like a porcupine. A decentralized, self-governing society without a state would be prickly and uncomfortable. With no centralized apparatus to take over, it would be difficult for an invader to seize control. Without major military bases, there would be no targets for massive assaults. A people united in their desire for freedom and peace would be impossible to rule as rulers inevitably require the formal or tacit consent of the ruled.

Passive resistance is not the same as turning the other cheek, although those who do carry their own moral force and powers of persuasion. Active measures could be taken to make an invasion or occupation extremely difficult and costly. The people as a whole could be trained in civil disobedience, non co-operation, passive resistance and sabotage. A general strike has an uncanny habit of bringing a country to a halt.

An occupying force would soon find it impossible to govern a people who blocked all its moves. Even if the occupying force was ruthless enough to begin to kill individuals who refused to defend themselves by violent means, their moral force would soon oblige their executioners to cease. Rather than trying to kill the invaders, the invaded would appeal to their common humanity and win them over to a peaceful settlement.

There have been successful historical precedents for this kind of defence and strategy of change. Gandhi and his supporters ousted the British from India through a careful campaign of civil disobedience, non-co-operation and passive resistance. Many people in Scandinavia prevented the full consolidation of Nazi rule during the Second World War by refusing to collaborate. Widespread sabotage of the Polish economy in the months following the imposition of martial law in 1981, helped overthrow the regime. Many of the former Communist regimes collapsed in Eastern Europe by massive peaceful demonstrations. Power certainly comes out of the barrel of a gun, but there is also the power of truth and example. However much the oppressive forces throughout the world would like to silence free enquiry and dissent, in the end the pen is mightier than the sword and truth will triumph over error.

# 15

# The Common Treasury

*One day Diogenes was sitting quietly in the sun in front of the tub which was his home when a great crowd of people arrived. There were many finely dressed men surrounded by soldiers carrying swords and long spears. The most splendid of all was a young man with steely blue eyes and blond hair. He was Alexander the Great, fresh from his conquests in Asia Minor and North Africa. Diogenes looked up, unperturbed.*

*'Diogenes', Alexander began, his tall figure casting a dark shadow over him. 'I am the most powerful man on earth. I have it within my power to give you anything you desire. I have heard that you are a man of wisdom. What would you like?'*

*'There is only one thing that you can do for me, Alexander', Diogenes replied, slowly. 'And that is to get out of the way of the sun!'*

*Alexander, furious, withdrew with his noisy entourage, leaving Diogenes sitting quietly in the sun.*

The earth is the ultimate source of all value. It is the common treasury. It is bountiful and abundant and gives freely. The value of the earth is enhanced by those who mix their labour with nature. In the process, they create material wealth, whether in the form of wheat or cotton, iron or coal, beds or books.

In a simple economy, there is a direct relationship between producer and consumer: the farmer brings vegetables to the village market where the price will largely depend on supply and demand. When the vegetables are transported to the town by a middle man, he takes his share and the prices go up. Buying cheap and selling dear, he makes a profit and exploitation begins. If a man of wealth comes along and buys the land of the farmer and his or her neighbours and gets them to work for him, he becomes a landlord. They lose their independence, become wage slaves, and are at his beck and call. If the landlord receives more than he gives, he indirectly lives off their labour. Capitalism thus begins and injustice and inequality multiply. In the process, both producer and consumer invariably suffer as well as the original source of all wealth: the earth itself.

In our present society, the circulation of energy produced by work takes the form of money to facilitate the exchange. But the trouble with money is that it disguises the point of work, the process of the worker mixing his or her labour with nature. Money seems to have the magical quality of reproducing itself without effort for those who have it, while it disappears for those who have to borrow it in the form of interest. Yet ultimately any increase in wealth is always indirectly related to someone's labour in the world, whether near or far. The overall result of the system is that the rich live off the surplus labour of the poor who do not reap the full reward of their labour. This is called exploitation. The justification for the high return on the wealth of the rich is that they undertake a risk. But all the capitalists risk is their capital. The persons who really take a risk — a risk with their physical and mental health — are the workers who are compelled to work in order to live. One group gambles with pieces of paper, the other with their lives; one lives in luxury and ease, the other in penury and anxiety.

The problem with the present economic system is that in order to increase profits, it is wedded to growth which increasingly uses up the world's limited resources, and to exploitation, through which the rich live off the labour of the poor. Above all, it sees abundance as only possible through the conquest of nature. In the process, it creates oases of beauty and abundance in a desert of ugliness and scarcity. It forges ugly workplaces, ugly cities, ugly fields, and above all ugly relations between humans. They are relations which are not based on harmony and love but on competition, violence, arrogance and resentment. As the world's resources begin to dry up and the human population increases, these relations are likely to get even uglier.

We are told that we will be happy if we own things and if we consume things. We are therefore offered ever larger, shinier and more colourful apples. We can eat them all the year round. They are transported from the other side of the globe. They are coated in pesticides so that they come to us without blemish. The trouble is in this age of so-called consumer choice the variety of apples decreases and the taste becomes more bland. The resulting apple might be good for the eyes but not for the palate or stomach.

We have a different proposal: we can replant our own apple trees in the dying orchards. Bees can take the blossom and bugs the leaves. By eating enough but not too much, we can keep the doctor away. When we bite into an apple, we can say, let your flesh become mine, your fragrance my breath, and your seeds, my thankfulness. We can rejoice in the fecundity and bounty of nature in which one pip can create a thousand apples.

If we wish to create a freer and more sustainable society, we need to develop real economics. The root meaning of economics is the *nomos* (laws or principles) of the *oikos* (household); it is concerned with organizing life within the Earth Household. The two models on offer in the twentieth century were a form of state socialism, in which production, distribution and exchange are controlled by the state, and *laissez-faire*, in which the market decides all. Most countries in the West adopted a mixture of both, but after the failures of the state experiments, the market triumphed virtually throughout the world. International financial institutions now impose it on so-called developing countries (which are usually going backwards). Even communist China has created zones of rip-roaring capitalism with no limits on the exploitation of workers and no safeguards for the protection of the environment. Free trade, regardless of the unequal distribution of power and wealth, has become the order of the day.

The triumph of the market at the end of the second millennium has meant that both within nations and between nations, the rich have got richer and the poor poorer. The gap between the third richest industrialized nation and the rest of the world is not narrowing but growing. The same old story continues: the poor nations sell their primary products on the world market cheap and then buy back manufactured goods dear. In the meantime, the advanced industrialized countries are becoming more and more service economies, where people make their living from providing services rather than manufacturing goods. Yet the goods provided by the services still have to be made somewhere and by someone. Even an aromatherapist will

175

use oils which are made from plants grown by a farmer somewhere in the world.

Governments in the South complain of the unfair terms of trade and crippling debts owed to the North, yet virtually all of them want to follow in the footsteps of the North and develop a highly industrialized, highly materialistic, and highly consumerist economy. The tendency is encouraged by the great international economic institutions, such as the World Bank, the International Monetary Fund and the World Trade Organization. They impose Structural Adjustment Plans on Third World countries crippled by debt which eliminate subsidies for food and reduce public spending on education, health and other goods. They all recommend free market economies with no trade barriers, on the assumption that wealth in the hands of an elite will stimulate production and trickle down like honey to the poor.

In reality, wealth has an uncanny habit of sticking to the soft hands of the rich. The market alone cannot develop an economy, for it only responds to present information and does not visualize a future. It is simply not possible for the countries of the South to develop along the same lines as the North, as the wealth of the North is based on the impoverishment of the South and the present economic development in the world is reaching its biophysical limits. At present, the richest 20 per cent of the world's nations consume 80 per cent of the world's resources.

Increasingly, it is transnational companies and not national governments which set the agenda and direct the pace of economic change. Globalization has meant that some companies not only run the economies of smaller nations but even decide what governments hold power. They seek the free movement of capital, free trade, and the cheapest and most docile labour force. The alliance of transnationals and global consumers rides rough-shod over local interests. A classic example is fishing in which international fleets take no account of the local needs of coastal peoples or the ecology of the sea in their region. Megatechnologies have further facilitated and promoted the process of globalization. High-speed computer networks, satellite communications and more extensive transport systems have all helped huge transnational corporations to dominate the global economy.

The economic and technological effects of this world-wide revolution are creating the biggest social upheaval since the Industrial Revolution. It is breaking up communities, under-mining local democracy, and destroying biological and cultural diversity. More than any other recent development, globalization shows the close link between transnational capital, the state, modern technology and the growing social and ecological crisis throughout the world. The more efficient the corporations become in their organization, the more irrationally they behave in their treatment of people and the planet.

Those who are aware of the problems but who are still wedded to the idea of economic growth are calling for 'sustainable development', especially in the so-called 'developing world'. Yet it is simply not possible to sustain, let alone develop, the existing consumption of resources if we are to hand on a livable world to coming generations. There is a direct opposition between the need of a growing human population for more agricultural land, housing and purchasing power and the need to protect soils, forests, animals and the atmosphere.

In the short term, the best the industrialized nations of the North can do for the South is to develop fair trade, cancel outstanding debts, and to stop intergovernmental aid. Rather than reaching those who might benefit from it, such aid invariably ends up in the hands of an elite to enhance their own power and wealth. It undermines initiative and self-reliance ('they know better'); encourages profligacy ('they will always bail us out'); and creates stifling dependence ('we have to do it their way'). The more things go wrong in the economies of so-called 'developing nations', the more money their governments demand. But it only makes matters worse. You cannot sober someone up by offering them more champagne. The answer is not to give more aid to governments, but to encourage more local autonomy and self-reliance. Aid through voluntary agencies intended to help people to help themselves is acceptable as an emergency measure, but lasting solutions will only be made by people doing things in their own way in the context of their own society, culture and environment.

In the short term, it is better for industrialized nations to stabilize their economies, to redefine GNP (Gross National Product) in terms of the quality of life, and to offer a basic income to all. A new indicator of the health of the economy might be created – GNH – Gross National Happiness! It also makes sense to consider the environment as an asset, to cost environmental services, and to impose pollution taxes and depletion quotas (to reduce extraction rates of non-renewable resources). A broad new

177

spectrum of self-managed enterprises, from individual producers and small partnerships to large co-operatives could be encouraged, especially if they incorporated ecological values. But this is only tinkering with the system. The system itself is fundamentally flawed.

In the long term, what is needed is not more growth and consumption, but a fairer distribution of the resources of the world, the elimination of waste, and a voluntary check on population. The continued impoverishment of the so-called Third World is directly related to the economic growth of the rich world. Rather than the poor nations 'developing' in the same direction as the rich industrialized nations, the rich industrialized nations should 'de-develop', or rather go off in a different direction. Only in this way will the earth be able to provide enough for all humans to have their vital needs met.

What is needed is a new economics for the people and the planet, an economics which has an ethical and ecological dimension, which is concerned with the well-being of the whole and the future vitality of Gaia. We need an economics geared to the locality and the bioregion, which is controlled by those who are affected by it, and which enhances rather than destroys the natural world. Above all, we need an economics which operates *economically*, with thrift and without waste, and which stresses the *oikos* rather than the *nomos*, the Earth Household rather than the principles of Man-age-ment.

There are economic models other than the market or the state. One is based on barter. In the informal economy, which in some countries is greater than the formal one, much barter takes place in which one type of good or service is exchanged for another of roughly equivalent value. This is the kind of exchange which took place before the invention of the medium of money and still continues in many parts of the world. Until recently, Cuba and the Soviet Union bartered sugar for oil, thereby bypassing the international market and normal terms of trade. The LETS system is also a form of barter, in which individuals exchange their different skills in labour time through a local currency.

While in some ways an advance on the market, the problem with barter is that the value of a good or service is still based on supply and demand or the measuring of equivalent values. Better still is a moral economy based on the gift which does not analyse what is 'fair' or 'equitable'. In this type of economy, which still exists in some traditional societies and in some pockets in industrialized nations, individuals and communities give voluntarily according to their abilities to the common stock, and take from it according to their needs. The result is a form of *voluntary* communism. It does not necessarily mean equal work or equal shares for all, for people not only have different capacities but have different needs. If put into practice on a large scale, an equality of unequals would no doubt evolve, celebrating the rich diversity of human character, need and desire.

This gift relationship mirrors the 'natural law' of giving in the universe and the dynamic interchange of energy in Gaia. The flow of life is the harmonious interaction of all the forces and elements in nature. Giving and receiving are different aspects of this flow in the world which circulates its natural abundance. The cup of life floweth over. We are naturally affluent, because the energy of nature flows all around us, meeting all our vital needs. The word 'affluence' comes from the Latin word *affluere*, meaning 'to flow to'. But if we interfere with the flow, if we do not give freely, the circulation of energy in the world is blocked and scarcity will prevail.

To live is to give. The sun shines and expects nothing in return. The tree gives shade without thought. The rose fills the air with its scent spontaneously. The dog gives his love unconditionally.

The gifts of nature are free. The four elements – water, land, fire and air – are part of the common treasury. That is why no one should try and appropriate them for themselves and get others to pay for them. Whatever the laws of a particular country might be, if someone says 'Get off my land', they need to be informed that the land is common and belongs to no one. If someone says, 'This is my river', then they need to be reminded that the crystal rain falls from the heavens which knows no bounds. If someone says, 'This natural gas belongs to me', then they need to be told that the dragon of the earth breathes fire for all. If we are not careful we will soon be asked to pay for the air we breathe. The sun shines on us all equally, whatever artificial distinctions society might create, and in her bounty nature gives us all that we need.

Wealth in a particular country cannot be the exclusive right of a few. All wealth creation is a result of people mixing their labour with nature. It is the result of many hands, in town and country, field and workshop, over many years. The existing means of production and transport are a form of collective labour of countless human beings, whether it is the canals dug by our ancestors with spades, or the latest computer produced by young girls in a faraway country. The wealth of any nation is the result of the labour of past generations and should therefore be held in trust and nurtured for future generations.

Receiving is similar to giving, different aspects of the flow of energy in the universe. It seems the way of the universe, the way things are, that the more you give, the more you will receive. If you give joy to others, you will become joyful; if you love, you will be loved; if you affirm life, life will affirm you. On the other hand, the more you hoard, the less will be given unto you. If you give begrudgingly, then you will only be given with reluctance. But if the act of giving is uncalculating, disinterested and spontaneous, it will circulate round and round the neighbour-hood, society and the universe.

Everybody can give something – whether it be a sack of potatoes, a chair, a poem, a compliment or a silent wish. Some of the greatest gifts are not material at all, such as the gifts of concern, affection and appreciation. Indeed, the most precious gift of all – love – costs nothing and requires no effort. The greatest gift is giving of yourself. Giving money to children is no wealth compared to loving them and spending time with them. When you give some of your possessions to others, you give little; you truly give when you give part of yourself. Real poverty is fear of losing possessions when you have more than you need. Real riches is giving what you have.

It is sometimes as difficult to receive as it is to give. All my life I have tried to be independent, standing on my own feet and taking no assistance from others. I have not wanted to be beholden to another, or to feel gratitude for their help. If they offered to con-tribute more, I have insisted on equal shares. I have calculated my turn to buy a round, regardless of the ability of my drinking companions. But I now realize that although this yeoman spirit may be better than deliberately exploiting others, my desire to remain completely independent is in some ways mean-spirited and narrow-minded. One should give spontaneously and receive with good grace. To be too independent can be too proud and arrogant.

Although it is difficult not to feel thankful when someone helps you, gratitude is a misplaced feeling. Gratitude can become a chain on the giver and the receiver. If an action is right, it should be performed. If it is a result of spontaneous generosity, it enhances the giver and receiver. In a sense, the receiver should be thanked for providing the opportunity for the giver to help. In that way, one person does not feel inferior to the other. And the best way to repay a gift is to give a gift to someone else.

Charity for those less well-off than you can remind them of their failure to stand on their own feet, however temporary their difficulty might be. It is often inspired by pity and expects gratitude. Pity and gratitude are part of a master–slave relationship and not part of the gift relationship. At different stages in our life, we all need help in one form or another. There is charity in receiving as well as in giving. The truly generous person expects nothing in return, while the graceful recipient accepts with good cheer; both are joyful that they have an opportunity to share and to confirm their friendship.

A free and sustainable society would reflect the economy of nature which gives without thought of return. At the core of the new economics should be the notion of the gift. This is not only virtuous and ecological but also efficient. In studies of blood donorship, for instance, the voluntary system in Britain not only meets the needs of all, but is three times cheaper than the commercial system in the USA.

The gift relationship is not the same as charity, which evokes negative feelings of pity and shame, superiority and inferiority. Nor is it a form of aid which often undermines local initiative and self-reliance. It is a voluntary sharing of the good things of the earth, based on the voluntary principle 'from each according to their ability and to each according to their need'.

With the notion of the gift at the centre of social relations, the value of people would no longer be their price on the market-place but their generosity and neighbourliness. The value of goods would not be defined by supply and demand, but how useful, beautiful and ecologically sound they were. A person who was not working would not be considered a drag on the economy or a wasted resource but a human being with his or her own intrinsic dignity, needs and aspirations.

If people give voluntarily according to their ability to the common stock, without the medium of money, capital would lose its exploitative and oppressive dimension. All would be able to have their vital needs met and enjoy the good things of the earth. At present, there would be enough for all if it was fairly distributed: the scarcity which exists for two thirds of the world is largely the result of uneven and unjust distribution. If people consumed less and restricted their numbers, if the available wealth were more evenly distributed, there would be sufficient for all to live in stable and sustainable societies. No longer having to struggle to survive, people would begin to thrive. A great burden would then be lifted from the earth and all the creatures would sigh with relief.

The needs of a potter are different from that of a computer programmer, but all would be met. Indeed, with basic security guaranteed, and production geared to satisfy vital needs with the minimum of waste, there would be more leisure for people to develop different interests and skills. Everyone would have the opportunity if they so wished to be a gardener in the morning, an artist in the afternoon, and a writer in the evening, without becoming gardener, artist or writer. Individuals would not be defined by their work, but by their humanity.

The appropriate use of technology could lessen the drudgery of unpleasant labour for some, while others might welcome the opportunity to work with their hands and be involved in labour-intensive work. I for one would prefer to cultivate a small plot of land with rake and hoe rather than sit in an air-conditioned tractor on a deserted prairie.

By recognizing that people have different needs, a rich equality of unequals would emerge in society. It would be up to people in their regions to decide what needs they wanted to fulfil and whether they had the resources to do so. After the satisfaction of vital needs, there would even be room for some luxuries. But the greatest luxury would not be material rewards but a sense of leading a meaningful and fulfilling life in harmony with each other and with the earth.

The provision of welfare and other services would be based on the voluntary principle. Perhaps the most outstanding example in Britain is the Lifeboat Association, which draws on voluntary contributions and provides a free service to those in need. There are also many public services provided free according to people's needs, such as libraries, museums, schools, hospitals, roads, street lighting, parks and beaches. They are part of an ancient tradition, symbolized by the commons, of people enjoying free goods according to their needs. In general, people do not use more than their fair share, even in a society which has made selfishness a public virtue and tried to turn public goods into privately owned commodities.

In the eighteenth century, the radical economists celebrated *laissez-faire* as the best way of bringing about the general good, but in fact the free market only helped the wealthy, powerful, cunning and unscrupulous. In the nineteenth century, the dispossessed and poor opposed the prevailing ideology of competition and self-interest in favour of co-operation and mutual aid. Many trade unions and co-operative societies were set up outside the state in order to meet the social and economic needs of working and agricultural communities. Their names reflected their nature: Credit Union, Friendly Society, Sick Club, Co-operative Society. They were voluntary associations organized by those who chipped in the little they had in order to help each other. When I was involved in setting up a rural community in the late 1970s, it took the form of a Friendly and Mutual Society. Building societies are a remnant of this co-operative tradition, although most are now turning themselves into banks run in the interest of shareholders rather than members.

If people are allowed to take according to their needs, will they take more than their fair share? Until recently, the provision of water was a great example of a service made available according to need. Water is a free gift of nature and has long been enjoyed freely by all the community. When families collected free water from the village well or pump, they only took what they needed. Farmers along rivers who rely on irrigation let the water flow through their land to the outlying fields. Even in shanty towns, where water is scarce, people quietly queue up for their fair share according to the needs of each household.

Only recently has water, a free gift of nature, been turned into a commodity. Private companies in Britain now appropriate the water which falls from the heavens and runs into our rivers and lakes and claim it as their own. They then sell it to people who have no choice at an inflated price and the profit is distributed amongst their shareholders. The rain which falls on Cornwall, for instance, the rain which is the birthright of every free-born Cornishwoman and man, is now collected and controlled by a transnational corporation based in Atlanta in the United States. As the black clouds sweep in from the Atlantic Ocean, the drops of crystal rain have an invisible dollar sign stamped on them.

Water is a free gift of nature, it cannot be repeated enough. In general, people turn off the tap when they have taken what they need. Only a few selfish individuals continue to water their lawns during a water shortage. Despite the deadening hands of capital and the state, the public spirit, the sense of good neighbourliness, the love of community are not dead. What happens with water could also happen with other public services and goods: people taking according to need, mindful of the needs of their neighbours and the condition of the supply.

In a genuinely free and sustainable society, the narrow spirit of selfishness, in which everyone is out for number one, would give way to a feeling of solidarity and mutual aid amongst the members of the community. No one would be forced to work and yet everyone's vital needs would be met. Indeed, the health of a community might be measured by the number of idle people it could support. Reflecting the interwoven web of nature, society would embody the deeply ecological principle of all for one and one for all. The common treasury of the earth would be enjoyed by the commonweal of society.

# 16

# Dwelling Lightly on Earth

*One day a rich man visited an old woman who was living alone in a hut by a stream. She was reputed to be very wise. It was his birthday and the man asked her to write something down for the continued prosperity of his family. She asked him to come back the next day at dawn. When he knocked on her door again, she handed him a piece of paper which had six words written on it:*

*'Father dies, son dies, grandson dies.'*

*When he read it, the rich man was furious. 'What sort of joke is this?', he exclaimed. 'I'm a busy man and you're just wasting my time. They told me you were wise!'*

*'There's no joke intended', the old woman replied gently.*

*'If your son should die before you, this would upset you greatly. If your grandson should die before your son, both of you would be broken-hearted. If your family, generation after generation, passes away in the order I have named, it will follow the natural course of life. That is what I call real prosperity.'*

In a good society, people would dwell lightly on the earth and share the bounties of nature with each other and with other species. Although they could make complicated machines, they would not be needed. They would know how to fight, yet they would live in peace. While they knew their neighbours and could hear them sing, they would not disturb them. Their food would be plain but varied, their clothes fine but simple. Their dwellings would be beautiful and secure. They would live long and well.

A good society would be a free society in harmony with its members and with nature. It would not be reduced to grey conformity or clocklike regularity. It would allow a thousand flowers to blossom, recognizing that there is a unity in diversity and harmony in variety in society as well as in nature. It would be an open and pluralist society in which many different ways of living would flourish. A form of communal individuality would no doubt develop, combining the greatest degree of individuality compatible with the greatest degree of solidarity. The freedom of one would be the condition of the freedom of all. Indeed, the health of the society might be judged by the degree of eccentricity it could tolerate and the number of non-productive souls it could support. Such a society would provide rich soil for creativity and the development of the whole self. No longer harassed to survive, people would begin to thrive.

A good society would be a sustainable society. There is no necessary connection between economic growth and increased welfare. Indeed, after the satisfaction of vital needs, the opposite might well be the case: the more we consume, the less happy we become. Pain follows the endless pursuit of pleasure as night follows day.

A sustainable society would develop an economy which encouraged stability, diversity and vitality. To begin with it would be a steady economy but not a static one. It would not be enough merely to apply limits to the present kind of growth; we would need to develop a more ecological way of producing and consuming the good things of the earth. This means using less of the earth's non-renewable resources (oil, coal, minerals) and more of its renewable ones (fertile soil, clear water, forests). It means recycling as much as possible and causing the least pollution. It means using renewable energy, conserving energy and keeping energy resources available for future generations. In the long run, the economy might well reach a steady state, that is, with a comparatively steady population and stock of physical wealth maintained by a low level of energy, resources and production.

'Sustainable development' is a catchword associated with the Third World, usually implying that any development should try and enhance the natural resource base and be appropriate to the culture. In one sense, the notion is applicable to all societies, regardless of their degree of industrialization. But in the final analysis, 'sustainable development' is a contradiction in terms, like the notion of a 'free state'.

Given the rate of soil erosion, deforestation, and depletion of non-renewable resources, the present kind of 'development' simply cannot be sustained. We now need to make not so much a U-turn to a former condition of life, but to go off at a tangent towards a new way of living which combines the best of traditional practices with the insights of new technology, science and philosophy. Both ancient wisdom and modern ecology confirm that we live in a fragile, interconnected world and what is good for one is good for all.

For society to be genuinely sustainable, we must therefore reverse the present trend and seek to minimize the extraction of resources and the production and consumption of goods. We should aim to pass on the planet to future generations in a condition as good if not better than when we entered it. We should try and limit our burden on Gaia by checking our numbers and reducing our destructive industrial activities. And we should release more land to return to the wild so that Gaia can heal herself and maintain the right conditions for life in the biosphere for both humans and non-humans to flourish together.

Both modern physics and ecology offer lessons for a sustainable society. The first law of thermodynamics means that, strictly speaking, we do not produce or consume anything but just rearrange particles in the universe. The second law of thermodynamics implies that the rearrangement involves a continual reduction in potential for future use in the system as a whole. It follows that the world's resources and energy are limited and have to be used frugally and carefully if they are to last.

It is fundamental to ecology that all life is based on interdependent relationships. The relationships amongst members in an ecological community are non-linear, with no simple pattern of cause and effect, and involve multiple feedback loops which are cyclical. What is waste for one species is food for another, so that communities of organisms have evolved over billions of years continually recycling the same molecules of minerals, water and air. The lesson for humans is that sustainable patterns of production and consumption need to be cyclical, with the minimum of waste, rather than linear with great waste as at present.

Whereas ecosystems are largely closed in regard to the flow of matter, they are open with respect to the flow of energy. The sun is the chief source of energy for the earth. Transformed into chemical energy by the photosynthesis of plants, solar energy powers most ecological cycles. It comes in many forms, such as sunlight, wind, water and biomass. It is the only kind of energy that is renewable, cheap and relatively harmless.

If we carry on at our present rate, non-renewable energy sources could run out in half a century. There will soon come a time when it will cost as much energy to mine a ton of coal as can be produced by a ton of coal. Even uranium on which nuclear energy is based is a non-renewable resource. There is no certainty that a new form of clean energy will be discovered. Even if it were – as in the dream of nuclear fusion – it would no doubt only accelerate the exploitation of other resources. It therefore makes sense to develop soft paths of technology based on renewable resources of solar energy with a benign impact on the earth. And the most important energy resource is conservation.

There is no technological solution to the problem of growth. It is naive to believe that humans will always solve the problems which beset them and that some 'technological fix' will be discovered to deal with the looming ecological crisis. We can have little faith in technology to get us out of the mess which it has helped to create. No one thought 50 years ago that uranium could be a source of energy, but neither did they imagine its destructive and polluting power.

At the same time, we are not victims of a technological determinism in which new techniques dictate how we are to live. It is we who control the technology, not the other way round. Computers may be able to beat chess players, but only at one particular task for which they have been programmed. They do not have the chess player's strengths and weaknesses as a human being. They cannot make love or appreciate the rising sun or the smell of bread baking. The problems facing humanity at the beginning of the third millennium are not technical problems but economic, social, cultural and spiritual ones.

What is needed is not the abandonment of all technology, a return to the Stone Age, or a new King Ludd who smashes the machines threatening the old way of life. What is essential is the *appropriate* use of *soft* technology. The type and size of technology should be decided for the task involved and in the context in which it is used. For some societies, it might be more appropriate to continue to make bricks from mud, for others to fire them in a kiln. In certain circumstances, human power might be better than a tractor. Weaving your own wool might be more appropriate than building a textile factory. On the other hand, the intermediate technology of a pump might be better than a traditional bucket in a well. It depends on the needs and resources of a community and its type of economy.

Apart from being sustainable and genial, soft technologies by their very nature tend to be more democratic and flexible. Whereas hard technologies associated with coal, oil, gas and uranium are usually controlled by remote and unaccountable centralized bodies, soft technologies linked to solar and wind power are more convivial and participatory. A nuclear power station requires a centralized grid and high security and poses a major threat to life and the environment, while windmills can be put up or taken down on an open hill for local consumption. I would rather have wind generators or solar panels in my backyard, even if they did temporarily spoil the view, than a potential nuclear bomb.

Some modern technology by its very nature is destructive, such as nuclear weapons or cars. Even so-called green technology such as refuse incineration, sulphur extraction in coal power stations, and catalytic convertors on cars costs energy and creates new pollutants. Although it has a clean façade, the present manufacture of electronics involves many harmful chemical processes. But clearly not all technology is equally bad and some is more kindly than others. A lot depends on how it is made and used and what quantity and kind of energy it consumes. A sustainable society would create soft technologies which are humane, convivial and benign and which serve and foster ecologically-balanced communities.

The revolution in information technology, especially the high-speed computer networks and satellite communications, can be used for good or ill. It can be used to increase surveillance by the state of its citizens and enemies, but it also enables individuals and groups to communicate freely with each other across national boundaries. The Internet was developed by the US military, but the millions all over the world who now use it can exchange ideas and information without censorship or central control. It can enable businesses to find cheaper work forces to exploit more and more markets; it can also help to decentralize production and distribution. It will certainly prevent a return to the kind of xenophobic parochialism of pre-industrial communities in Europe. With the new information technology, one can live locally and communicate globally.

In a post-industrial, sustainable society, the type and level of technology would be decided by individuals and communities in their regions. Some might want labour-saving technology to have more time for other pursuits, others would find satisfaction in intensive labour such as traditional weaving and planting. Universal automation, if it were possible, is no solution to scarcity. It would, moreover, deny one of the principal sources of satisfaction which is to be found in meaningful and creative work.

In a free and sustainable society based on soft technology, how would the economy be organized? Since it would be a decentralized society consisting of a federation of communities, the decisions for the kind of production and distribution and the level of consumption needed would be taken by the local and regional assemblies. The national assembly would act merely as a co-ordinating body for the other federated assemblies without any coercive authority. Voluntary agreements would be made through free negotiation.

This already happens to a degree in the international economy, although it is geared to making a profit rather than providing a service. A good example is the way the highly complicated airline timetables which cross national boundaries and use common facilities are negotiated through voluntary agreement without a central authority. The railway system in the self-governing Swiss cantons is organized in a similar way. Recent advances in information technology make this type of freely negotiated agreements all the more feasible.

The decentralized economy would aim at self-reliance and self-management. Field, factory and workshops would come closer together. There would be smaller units of production and distribution geared to local needs and resources. Vast is sublime, like the sea or the sky, but small is also beautiful, like a water-wheel or hand pump. It is good to look up at the stars and planets. It is also good to know and work with your neighbours.

Self-reliance means that local materials and local labour are used as far as possible to meet local needs. The use of resources would take into account long-term sustainability. This would encourage local autonomy and independence. Free trade at present usually means the freedom of the rich nations to exploit the poor. To depend on importing and exporting is to put oneself in the power of others (Cuba's economy is largely dependent on the world market for sugar); it is to cater for artificial wants as opposed to needs (African governments export out-of-season delicacies to buy arms while their own populations do not have enough to eat); and it is to cause considerable waste (Channel Island tomatoes are exported, packed and then shipped back for consumption).

Self-reliance is not the same thing as self-sufficiency, that is, complete economic independence. Trade in a form would still exist, but not based on the market, and goods and services would flow between the regions. Clearly some regions might be better at growing certain crops or have access to more resources, but those with a surplus would give freely to those with a shortage.

Living and working locally does not mean that one would have to stay in one's region or spurn outsiders. While tourism at present is the world's largest industry and one of its main sources of waste, travel can be a means of fostering understanding and peace between peoples and a way of appreciating the cultural and geographical diversity of the planet. Without looking through the window, one may see the ways to heaven. One can know the whole world without leaving one's home. But this does not mean one should be chained there. Some people develop a strong sense of place, and wish to live in their neighbourhood for all their lives; others like a life of movement and new horizons. There should always be room for nomadic and sedentary peoples, for travellers and for settlers.

There is a long tradition of travel as a form of pilgrimage in which travellers find their selves and their place within the universe. Travellers can also draw out the hospitality and generosity of the people they encounter. They bring first-hand knowledge and experience from afar and can enlighten as well as entertain. Travellers and pilgrims can strengthen the web of society and our contact with nature by journeying along their colourful threads. They can keep the song lines alive.

If society became a federation of self-managing communities with a decentralized economy, a new relationship with the land and sea would develop. No longer the artificial and arbitrary borders of administrative or political convenience, the boundaries of life would grow more natural. Communities would begin to

**191**

appreciate the intimate ways of the places in which they lived, their own particular geology, ecology and history. Becoming familiar with the natural contours and rhythms of their bioregions, people would learn to live with them and not work against them. By knowing their limits and capabilities, they would be in a better position to satisfy their needs.

Living close to the land, the sea and the sky, people in their bioregions would reconnect with the primordial and the essential. Dwellers in the land, they would live in place. They would be in touch with the spirit of the earth, and be touched by it. They would rediscover their sacred places and times. Lying on the ground, climbing the hills or mountains, swimming in the rivers, lakes and sea, they would be able to feel more keenly and to think more deeply.

A new awareness would develop which recognizes that we are what we eat, how we live, and where we dwell. The fruits of nature and the good things of the earth would be for everyone to enjoy. Being self-reliant and dwelling lightly on the earth in this way would not necessarily mean a narrow life. There would be some choice in necessities and some degree of luxuries, and a surplus to support non-productive members of the community. There would be time for celebration and for occasional excess, as well as time for frugality and care.

The trend of moving from the country to the town since the Industrial Revolution would be reversed for those who wanted it. The town would come to the country, with more local workplaces and opportunities for sport and culture, while the country would come to the town, with more green areas and wildlife. There would be a general loosening of boundaries. Both would be enhanced. Following a major land reform, the country would be reinhabited by people who cared for the land and held it in trust for others and coming generations. The land is a common treasury, so it should be communally cared for. The bounty of nature is a free gift and all should enjoy its fruits. All would have equal access to the inspiration and healing power of nature, refreshing their spirits, exercising their bodies, and being reminded of the basis of all life. At the same time, areas of wilderness and of special ecological interest would be expanded so that other species could flourish with the minimum of interference from humanity.

We have tamed and devastated the land, so a sustainable

society would try and renew the fertility of the soil and encourage biodiversity. This is best achieved through organic farming, which seeks to maintain soil fertility indefinitely by using renewable resources. Where conventional farmers see 'weeds' and 'pests' as enemies to kill off with chemicals, organic farmers recognize them as part of nature's web, essential threads in the overall stability and balance of the living world. They have a sense of the extraordinary complexity of ecological relationships and know the key role played by soil bacteria. They seek to produce food with the minimum impact on the land by following the natural path of diversity, balance and permanence through crop rotation, under-sowing, and avoiding monoculture of animals or plants. They use manure and compost rather than chemicals; they allow earthworms to flourish rather than spray insects. They would rather lose a little of their crop to other species than lose the long-term fertility of the soil. They would place mulch on top rather than turn top soil under. They also practice 'permaculture', which tries to establish a permanent and resilient form of cultivation through the careful mixture and balance of plants and animals.

True farmers have a reverence for the life which gives life, and see themselves as one species amongst a community of species. They know that they do not own the land, but the land owns them. In short, they seek to preserve the integrity, stability and beauty of the little portion of the earth which temporarily comes under their care.

While the country would be regenerated in a free and sustainable society, the city would also be revitalized. A city is not a monolith but a community of communities. It can be organized as a federation of districts. With people controlling their own dwellings and running their own neighbourhoods, a new sense of solidarity, conviviality and creativity would emerge. The inner city would no longer be a desert for office workers and the homeless and impoverished. It could become again a place where civilization flourishes, not where people choke and spit. The city could live up to its original meaning, derived from the Latin word *civitas*, a forum for citizenship. Public spaces would be for the public, not for anti-social tyrants, places of beauty and care, not of squalor and neglect. Some areas within the city might be more densely lived in, and others more sparsely populated, but light and air and natural growth would enhance the man-made structures of concrete and glass. The city would become a work of art, a place of beauty and use, constructed from natural materials but expressing the best of human creativity.

A sustainable society would need to consider carefully its level of population. By working out a healthy and just balance between humans and other species in their regions, people would seek to meet their own vital needs while not neglecting those of others. They would seek to hand on to future generations a world enhanced and not impoverished by their activity in the biosphere. At present starvation in some parts of the world is undoubtedly caused by the uneven distribution of resources or inappropriate methods of production. But there is also great pressure on the earth because of the relentlessly growing human population. The human species has probably already displaced nearly half of the world's potential life. Their population pushes towards six thousand million, with about four thousand million more expected by the year 2030.

If life is to be sustainable for humans and other creatures on earth, our population will have to be adjusted – through voluntary means – to the available food supply and resources. The population growth of humans has to be stabilized or even reversed in order to maintain the life expectancy of those who are to be born and to secure the long-term sustainability of their environment. But it should not be through bribery or coercion. Any check to reproduction should be through voluntary self-restraint or contraception. Although early abortion might be justifiable in certain circumstances, killing life is never a way to celebrate life. Each region will have to work out its own appropriate balance between humans and other species and choose its own methods of restraint appropriate to its culture.

A sustainable society would be a frugal society to ensure that the vital needs of all are met and that no one goes hungry. But it is absurd to advocate frugality to those who are poor and destitute; it is the rich individuals and nations which need to be more frugal now. The rich need to live more simply in order that the poor can simply live. Being frugal is not a punishment but a pleasure. It means enjoying the good things of the earth without waste and pollution and with the careful use of resources. It takes the cliché 'waste not, want not' seriously. It means dwelling simply and lightly on the earth and leaving little in your tracks.

Being frugal is not a new puritanism. In a free and sustainable society, there might be less concentration of material possessions in the hands of the few, but there would be better food, healthier bodies, fulfilling work, cleaner air, fresher water, and a more supportive and convivial community in a safer society. The world as a whole would be a better place to dwell in.

Nor would it mean a restriction of freedom. The desires of a few for amassing wealth and power would be curbed, but the vast majority of people would experience an expansion of their freedom. In our interconnected world, excessive property is theft. If you possess more than you need to satisfy your vital needs (which include food, shelter and the means to lead a creative and meaningful life), then you take more than your fair share from the common stock. What you have and don't need is stolen from those who need it and don't have it. If the exclusive right to property were curtailed, the rights to life and liberty would be expanded. Excessive private wealth would be returned to the common treasury. The choice of consumer goods might not be so great for some, but people as a whole would have more opportunities to realize themselves. They would be free *from* anxiety and frustration and be free *to* develop their talents and unfurl their potential.

These desirable changes in patterns of ownership, production and consumption would not be imposed by the state, for a precondition of a free and sustainable society would be the dissolution of political power and centralized control. They would be collectively agreed and voluntarily adopted through the federated assemblies.

It is clear that if all humans are to have their vital needs met without the destruction of the earth, then we must consume less as a species and adopt a more simple way of life in harmony with nature. But what are vital needs? They are basic needs such as food, drink, clothing and shelter which are necessary for survival. But if people are not just to survive but to thrive vital needs also include non-material goods such as fulfilling work, loving relationships and a meaningful life. Artificial wants on the other hand are not essential for a good life, but the result of our false desires.

In our present society our desires have been directed towards gaining material wealth, power and status; they have become artificial wants and are often experienced as needs. In a free and sustainable society, our desires would be expressed and find

195

satisfaction in more creative and life-affirming ways. Since means are ends-in-the-making, the way we live our lives here and now will determine the kind of society which will emerge in the future. One cannot live an exploitative life in order to bring about a just society. If one wants to create a sustainable society, then one cannot continue to consume vast amounts of the world's resources and energy.

In order to live well on the earth, one needs to live more simply. But living a simple life satisfying vital needs does not mean living in poverty; on the contrary, a simple life is most likely to bring about a rich social, aesthetic and spiritual life. It is a condition of beauty and joy. Nor does simplicity necessarily mean austerity; once the vital needs of all are met then there may well be room for occasional excess in times of celebration. It is for each individual and community to decide the rhythm of their production and consumption. True affluence is not the circulation of money, but the flow of creative energy. The art of making money would thus be replaced by the art of living and loving.

Already many people are realizing the value of a way of life which might be materially poor by today's standards but which is socially and spiritually rich. A whole swathe of society has adopted a form of voluntary poverty not simply because they cannot get a job in the system but because they do not want one. They prefer to work in the informal economy and to share their limited resources. They have tried to reclaim the commons and get access to the country. They have dropped out of the modern culture of consumerism and tuned in to the voice of the earth. Some are part of the so-called underclass, often without permanent homes and with few possessions, but they do not feel poor. They are not victims but rainbow warriors. They are the modern equivalent of the medieval wandering monks and nuns.

At the same time, there are many with lucrative jobs who have chosen to earn less in order to live more. They have eschewed promotion and tried to cut down their hours, so that they can spend more time developing their talents and skills outside paid employment. They have put the quality of their lives before the accumulation of possessions. They do not want to burn out at 30, and then dull their minds and bodies with drink and drugs. The process is sometimes called 'downgrading' but it is really jumping off the treadmill into a more creative way of life.

What else can one do in the present economy while working

towards a more free and sustainable society? There are many alternative economic experiments, from producer and retail co-operatives, non-profit-making organizations providing services, to local currency initiatives in which individuals trade their skills. But far the most influential development in recent times has been the attempt to green capitalism and to develop a form of green consumerism.

Consumer power has proved a great marketing ploy. Its advocates argue that markets operate like representative democracy, so that you can vote with your money with the goods you buy just as you choose what party you want to represent you with a cross on a piece of paper. The more you consume, the argument goes, the more influence you have: democracy is finally reduced to the credit card. And in the growing fetishism of commodities, the supermarkets become the temples of the new religion and the cash till the gateway to heaven.

Green consumerism enables people to feel that if they buy 'environmentally friendly' goods when they go shopping in the supermarket, they are somehow helping the planet. It gives them a sense of power, the power of consumer choice. You can indulge yourself and still do good. You can have imported caviar and champagne as long as it is organic. But there is a slight hitch. Consumer choices are invariably private and uninformed and are easily manipulated by the big companies' advertising campaigns.

The constant flow of 'new' and 'improved' goods promises more satisfaction, but they invariably make people feel dissatisfied with what they already have. People work harder and longer in order to buy 'labour-saving' gadgets. More 'freedom of choice' for the consumer inevitably means enslavement and exploitation down the line for the producers, animals, fish, plants, land and sea.

Above all, so-called consumer power ignores the more fundamental questions. You can buy 'dolphin-friendly' tuna in the supermarket, but what about 'tuna-friendly' dolphin? Do you need to eat fish in the first place? What about the *level* of consumption and waste? Unlimited consumption and production, however 'environmentally friendly', is impossible to sustain in a limited system like the planet. The true message of sustainability is not simply to wield one's purchasing power responsibly, but to reduce it and to wield it less often.

Again, 'ethical investor groups' offer a service to increase your money without effort on your part. They often quote the seventeenth-century divine John Wesley: 'Earn all you can, but not at the expense of conscience, not at the expense of our neighbours' wealth, not at the expense of our neighbours' health'. So-called 'ethical investments' based on such principles are still aimed at making a 'healthy profit'. Yet any profit is *always* based on injustice and exploitation, on appropriating the surplus labour of someone in the world who does not receive the full fruits of his or her labour.

Clearly it is better not to invest in companies which experiment with animals or harm the environment, but the problem is not just the kind of consumerism, but the level of consumption; not just the way you make your profit, but the profit motive itself. If anything, the greening of consumerism and capitalism has entrenched an economic system wedded to growth and exploitation of people, animals and the planet, and a social philosophy which affirms that possession and consumption will bring happiness and fulfilment.

You can be greedy, the business gurus say, and still feel good about yourself. But can you? There are unavoidable ecological and social limits to growth. It is not enough to switch to different goods; the level of consumption itself needs to be challenged. We return to the question of vital needs and artificial wants. It is better to have lead-free than regular petrol in your car, but do you need the car in the first place? The finite nature of the earth restricts not only the amount of energy and resources available, but also its capacity to absorb the waste and pollution which are inevitably generated by the very process of production and consumption.

There is a limit to the wear and tear of Gaia, however well she manages to heal herself. In the long run, to bring about a free and sustainable society, it will be necessary to reject those lifestyles, goods and services which exploit people and the planet. It will involve creating eco-communities of humans, animals and plants which honour the diversity of life and meet the vital needs of all. Above all, it will mean creating a way of life which is materially simpler but socially and spiritually richer.

What is real poverty? It is not just the lack of bread but also the poverty of spirit. It is the daily grind of trying to survive which exhausts and alienates, which reduces life to a constant hassle to make ends meet. It is to wake up with a sinking feeling and to go to bed with a heavy heart. It is to make agonizing choices about giving food to the old or the young members of your family. It is abandoning thinking for oneself and bowing to the powers that be. It is to remain in a culture of silence. It is fearing life and welcoming death.

What is real wealth? It is not money or possessions. It is knowing when you have enough. It is having the opportunity to expand the treasures of the mind, body and spirit and to develop one's full potential. It is to stand full square on the earth. It is to feel grounded and centred. It is to watch the rising of the sun with hope and see it set with contentment. It is to joke with friends and family. It is to see a child's smile. It is to know that life has meaning and purpose. It is to see a ripening field of corn waving in the breeze and salmon leaping in a clean, tumbling torrent. It is to look up at the heavens and to know that the universe is creative and good.

Living well on earth requires a degree of humility, a move away from dominion over all beings and things and a move towards fellowship. It means accepting that for all our knowledge, we know little of the long-term consequences of our actions. We have only just begun to understand some of the mysteries of the universe. The world is so complex and our ignorance is so vast, that we should think three times before we interfere with natural processes. The onus is on those who intervene to prove any definite benefit rather than on those who point out the potential dangers. If in doubt, we should leave nature alone. We do not have to forever push back the frontiers of science and we can decline to do the things we know how to do.

The humanist faith in the power of reason to bring about progress through technology and science, which promised so much in the eighteenth and nineteenth centuries, has faltered. Scientific and industrial revolutions produced the steam engine and penicillin but also the guillotine and the atomic bomb. The heady dream of a world of peace and plenty through the application of science and technology has evaporated in the shadows on the walls in Hiroshima, the silence of the concentration camp at Auschwitz and the deformed plants around Chernobyl. All were highly efficient, all were triumphs of modern technology, but all are now symbols of power out of control and emblems of death.

Prometheus stole fire from the gods and was chained to a rock for his arrogance and had his liver devoured by eagles. We have stolen fire from the atom and we may yet be consumed in its conflagration. We can equally fade away in the darkness of a nuclear winter. But there is another way. If we proceed more carefully and more humbly, if we learn when to stop, we can avoid the looming social and ecological crisis of the new millennium.

Humility above all means recognizing the kinship we share with other creatures on this fragile and finite earth. It means considering the possibility that trees feel when we cut them down and that when we crush a rock, it might hurt. It means rejecting the arrogance of thinking ourselves the lords of creation and becoming shepherds of being. It means singing: 'Hands off Gaia! Let the Tao be!'

Real wealth is to live a simple and natural life, in harmony with each other and the rest of the creation. It involves understanding the way of nature and working with the grain. It is travelling light and leaving few tracks behind. It is above all becoming buoyant and cultivating a certain lightness of being as we journey through life. The boatman, if he misjudges the tide, is obliged to drag his boat with great effort across the mud flats, leaving behind a long and ugly furrow. But if he waits with patience and skill for the flood tide, he sails effortlessly to the haven of his choice and leaves nothing in his wake. Abandoning gravity, he rides the wind!

# 17

# Doing Nothing, Nothing Undone

*One day a woodcarver got an important commission for a statue for the main square of his village. When the figure of the woman and child was revealed everybody was astounded. They said it must be the work of angels. 'What is your secret?', they asked him.*

*'I am only a workman', he replied. 'I have no secret. This is what happened. When I received the commission and began to think about the work, I focused my attention and did not bother with trifles. I meditated in order to set my mind at rest. After three days, I had forgotten gain and success. After five days I had forgotten praise and criticism. After seven days, I had forgotten my hands and body. All that might distract me from the work disappeared and I was collected in the single thought of the statue.*

*When I went into the forest, the right tree stood out. I could clearly see the statue within it. All I had to do was to pick up my tools and reveal it. The carving happened of itself, with effortless ease. My own mind simply saw the hidden potential of the wood and from this encounter came the work you ascribe to the angels.'*

After Chuang Tzu

Most people, if they could, would avoid work like the plague. They are fed up to the teeth with work, with the daily grind. In the present state of affairs all equilibrium is upset: we either work in order to live, or worse still live just to work. The rhythm of most people's lives in the West is as the French say: *metro,*

201

*boulot, dodo*: underground, work, kip and so on for evermore until they drop or are dropped. That is the great tragedy of modern living.

People either have to work too much, constantly fearful of losing their jobs, stressed out by the increasing pressure, or they do not have enough work, worried about making ends meet, ashamed of their low status. Too much or not enough, fear of work or fear of unemployment; fear of not having enough, fear of losing all: where is the balance in that? If people have a house, they are worried that they will lose their job and it will be taken away; if they are homeless, all they dream of is a warm and dry house. At work, all one can talk about is 'time off'; in 'free time' all one can talk about is work. People say they have no time for things they want to do, but when they become unemployed or retire, time weighs heavily and they do not know what to do.

Work in its most general sense means doing something. It is the sign of the times that it has come to mean paid employment. A person who is not paid a wage is unemployed, although he may be working very hard. The phrase 'She is a woman who works' usually refers to a woman who goes out to work for a wage and not one who runs a house and brings up children from dawn to dusk and beyond. Work has come to mean not only productive effort but a form of social relations: one is 'in work', or 'out of work', or in the case of actors, resting, or of aristocrats, enjoying life. For many work means labour and is associated with pain. Those who work with their hands are generally called labourers. Labour has become a name for a class, a commodity, as well as a political party, although the latter in Britain remembers the commodity but forgets the class.

Work for most means toil, something they would rather not do. That is because of the conditions and nature of most work. 'Toil' comes from the Latin word for 'stirring' or 'crushing': toil and trouble have long been linked. It is usually associated with manual labour which is repetitive and exhausting. In the present division of labour, those who labour with their hands more than their heads usually have less status and more repetitive work for a low wage. Why should this be so? If anything, intellectuals who usually get more intrinsic satisfaction from their work deserve less financial reward. At the same time, there can be great dignity and real satisfaction in physical labour if it is undertaken voluntarily and in a meaningful setting. Unfortunately, under present arrangements both intellectuals and labourers are equally alienated, one from their minds and the other from their bodies and both from their spirits. They become lop-sided creatures, overdeveloped in some areas and underdeveloped in others, fragmented by overspecialization, and cut off from each other as well as from their true selves.

The ideal would be to develop both physical and mental skills and to celebrate the whole of one's being: mind, body and spirit. I have always been drawn to this ideal, and that is why I left the academic world to set up a community in which I hoped to live by my pen and my spade. At times, I have written more with my spade and dug with my pen but I have nevertheless tried to achieve a balance. One of the main reasons why I like sailing a yacht is that it calls on many different mental and physical skills: you have to be a mathematician to work out the navigation, a mechanic to understand the auxiliary engine, a sailor to work the ropes, an artisan to do the maintenance, a meteorologist to understand the weather, an artist to admire the beauty of the billowing sails, a philosopher to appreciate the solitude, and a mystic to be at one with the sea. The Buddha is in the bilges, the cylinder head, and at the top of the mast. Above all, sailing brings its own intrinsic satisfaction, regardless of any material reward. It is the ultimate happening.

In our present society, the market dominates all. The value of a person is his or her price. If people are employable and can command large salaries in the market-place, they are valuable; if they have no job and are not needed, they are considered worthless. Such is the language of the market. The tragedy is that most people are beginning to think and talk in the same way. Having become wedded to the idea that their worth is their work and salary, when they lose both in retirement they feel they have no value. The continuous flow of a person's life is split into the artificial categories of work and leisure, toil and play, and above all into work, unemployment and retirement. In the past, aristocrats had no problem with being unemployed and redundant, but the genuinely redundant and unemployed now feel that they are on the scrap heap and a burden to the rest of society. Yet in one way or other they continue to work, even if it is not for paid employment.

Work at its simplest level is the expenditure of energy. An engine works. For the most part, work falls into two kinds: rearranging atoms on the earth's surface, or telling other people to rearrange them. Thus we have workers and bosses, ruled and rulers. In our present society, it is entirely regimented. From the time we get up in the morning and go to the office or factory, to the time we return home, the clock ticks inexorably away, measuring out our days. We clock on, we clock off, forlorn slaves to the tyranny of the clock. We no longer measure our lives by the natural rhythms of light, the rising and setting of the sun, the coming and going of the seasons. On winter evenings in the city, we cannot see the stars in the night sky because it is an orange glow; on summer days of glorious sunshine, we sit in the dark in front of our flickering screens.

In work, we mix our labour with the rest of nature in order to satisfy our needs. Digging or ploughing is the most obvious example, but the same process, however disguised, is going on in the fields, in the mines, in the factories or in the offices. Most workers today are alienated from their fellow workers and from the product of their labour. In the towns and cities where the vast majority subsist behind concrete and glass, people are cut off from nature which is the source of all value and offers physical and spiritual renewal. Nature appears as a hostile force in the artificial human world, a force to be held at bay, conquered or exploited. The result is that things seem to be in the saddle and they hold our imagination on a tight rein. The relations of production weigh like heavy chains. Work has become the curse of the thinking as well as the drinking classes.

In the drive to increase profit and therefore production and consumption, the division of labour leads to overspecialization in one small area, so the worker is divided within and without. Mind is separated from body, eye from hand. Indeed, as a member of the 'workforce', the worker is reduced to 'a hand'. Having been turned into an efficient mechanic, the next step is to turn the worker into a cog in the machine. The final insult is to replace him or her with a robot. As the machines take over, skills learned over a lifetime become redundant, and unless a person 'retools', he or she is done for. In an earlier generation, if the poor fell on harder times, they ended up in the 'workhouse' for correction; now the 'work shy' are forced to perform some unengaging task if they are to get any dole.

In the West, many have become slaves of the Protestant work ethic which claims that success in business is a sign of God's grace, not of ruthless exploitation or inherited wealth. If you want to be successful, we are told, then you must work with whatever you have and grab whatever you can regardless of others. And everyone works, everyone scrambles over each other to get on to the throne of success, elbowing, pushing, punching, leap-frogging to the top.

The Protestant ethic sanctifies all: work not only brings material wealth, but it is virtuous. Does not the Devil find mischief for idle hands? Is not sloth a deadly sin? But if that is so, why was there no work in the Garden of Eden? Work came after the Fall. It was only after eating from the Tree of Knowledge that humans were condemned to live by the sweat of their brow. If that is the case, then work must be a reminder of our original sin. If we were in a state of grace, we would not have to work. But, alas, we have forgotten what it is like to be the lilies of the valley, which neither reap nor sow. We have forgotten that it is harder for a rich man to enter heaven than a camel to pass through the eye of a needle. We have forgotten that the love of money is at the root of all evil.

Under the present system, everyone works if they can for a wage; they are driven by material incentives. It is the peculiar nature of capitalism that those with capital – who own property and control the means of production, distribution and exchange – can get others to work for them. Since labour is what creates wealth, they live off the surplus labour of the workers who only have themselves to sell on the job market. They cream off the profit after paying the production and labour costs. They justify their reward for the alleged risk they take with their capital, but it is the workers who create the wealth and live a life of unending drudgery and anxiety. They do not receive the fruits of their labour; for the most part it goes to others.

A few from the ranks of the poor can join the rich – and that is the carrot along with the stick of unemployment and poverty which make the many put up with the present arrangements. But in general those that inherit money make more, while those who do not are condemned to work all their life to make ends meet or are obliged to live in ignominy on welfare benefits. The capitalist seems to possess magic, for the value of his property and shares increases without any apparent work or effort. But ultimately any increase in wealth is the product of people mixing their labour with nature somewhere in the world.

It is an economic see-saw: as some get richer, others get poorer, and the process is directly related. The increasing wealth of a third of the nations in the world is based on the growing impoverishment of the rest. The same is true within Western societies. Rich individuals and nations appropriate most of the good things for themselves: the common treasury of the earth is not shared. That is why property is theft. But in the process both rich and poor are condemned to unhappiness and anxiety: the former cannot resist craving for more and are fearful of losing what they already have, while the latter are constantly harassed about earning a living. Both are wedded to the notion of work for reward; both are slaves of the market.

There have been attempts to motivate people without financial reward. During the Stalinist era in the Soviet Union workers under the Stakhanovite scheme were made proletarian heroes of the Revolution for their self-denying labour for the good of the state. In reality, it became another way of making them work even harder for less while those who urged them on lived in ease and comfort. Under the influence of Che Guevara, there was also a genuine and inspiring attempt in the early days of the Cuban Revolution to motivate people through moral rather than material incentives, for the satisfaction of helping others and contributing to the general good. It still lives on in some brigades of volunteers who practise mutual aid, but the experiment has largely been swamped by the re-emergence of the dollar as the primary measure of worth and the primary reward for work.

Capitalism gets people to work hard by the lure of consumerism and the fear of unemployment in an uncertain world. The contagion is spreading to the East where, given their philosophical heritage, they ought to know better. Tokyo is now worse than New York. Rushing to and from work, people can no longer breathe – literally. In a country where breath was long considered as a symbol of life and easy breathing as essential for calm meditation and a tranquil mind, workers now interrupt their headlong rush amongst the traffic jams to get a quick fix of oxygen from a roadside booth. Rip-roaring capitalism has also come to the new business zones in China, where people sell their bodies and their souls for the privilege of buying consumer goods with their sweat and loneliness.

Permanently harassed and worried, people around the world and around the clock just work and work and work. The hard work never ceases. Consuming the goods they buy with their labour is hard work. Dealing with the heart attacks and cancers is hard work. No wonder at the end of the day you are tired, irritable and deflated. The more driven you are, the less you achieve. If you struggle against the grain, you are struggling against the universe.

Even leisure has become regimented, costly and hard work. 'Leisure' comes from the Latin word for 'permit' (*licere*) and has long meant 'free time'. But now leisure is 'leisure time' and we have to work hard to use it up. We fly off to camps and on tours, herded by couriers and touts. Because it is so uniform, we try to spice it with the exotic but the further afield we travel, the harder it becomes. Travel increasingly confirms prejudices rather than broadens the mind.

The organized consumption of leisure even reaches children. My son recently told me about a collection at his local school for a girl of 8 who was dying of leukaemia. Her last wish was to go to Disneyland. What about the beauty of the mountains, lakes and sea at her doorstep? What about the warmth and support of her local community? Instead, she had become another victim of the American Dream which defines the ultimate experience as a trip to a foreign land to see mock-ups of mock-ups, cardboard façades of celluloid images. Signs no longer correspond to reality; the theme park, the museum experience and television have become the reality. May she now be in paradise, where Disneyland is not.

But we do not have to be constantly straining in work or leisure. I sing the praises of idleness, the song of an idle day, of a day when people can be themselves, have time to stop and stare, can live in the present, without regretting the past or worrying about the future. I sing the song of real work.

In nearly all cases, the so-called work-shy are square pegs in round holes. Given a meaningful activity which fulfils their natures rather than degrades them, which is undertaken voluntarily rather than forced upon them, which unites them with their fellows rather than divides them, which enhances nature rather than destroys it, then I believe virtually everyone would be pleased to do real work. They would then work not for the sake of money, not for the sake of reward, not for the sake of status, but for the intrinsic value of the work itself.

Nature works with effortless ease. It works in a non-linear, holistic way, without friction or effort. Like flowing water or a growing plant, it follows the path of least resistance. It is the nature of the sun to shine and of the tides to come in and out without striving. A tree does not try to grow, it just grows. A horse does not try to gallop, it just gallops. The wind does not try to blow, it just blows, without ever tiring.

The ancient sages of China and India recognized the law of least effort, the law which states that the less you do, the more you accomplish. If you reach a state of self-harmony, an idea translates itself into action with carefree spontaneity. This is what some might call a 'miracle'.

A baby cries without getting hoarse. Unfortunately we forget this carefree spontaneity as we grow up and begin to strive and force ourselves to do things which we do not want to do or for which we are ill intended. We become driven. We find that the more we force the situation, the greater the resistance. The more we try, the less we succeed.

But we can be like the new-born babe again. We can mirror the effortless processes of nature. We can cease to be driven. We can unlearn our bad habits of striving. We can do less and accomplish more. All problems contain the seeds of their solution. If we are in harmony with nature, if we go with the grain, then we can attain our goal with ease.

When we channel skilfully the harmonious forces of nature, we expend the least effort. But if we seek power over others, it is a waste of energy. If we seek personal gain and the aggrandizement of our ego, it is a waste of energy. If we regret the past or worry about the future, it is a waste of energy. But if we act spontaneously without any calculation for ourselves, we attain our end. If we let go, things will happen of themselves.

If you live in the present, accept responsibility for what is, there can be no end to change. If you are centred and fearless, acting without thought of reward or punishment, then you can harness the power of love. If you give up resentment, striving and defensiveness, then you become light-hearted and full of joy. If you go with the flow of universal energy, you begin to ride the wind!

The ancient Chinese Taoists had a word for this: *wu-wei*. It is usually translated as 'non-action' or 'non-doing'. But it does not mean idleness or inactivity. It is work without effort and striving, work which gets things done without any hassle. It is creating yet not possessing, working yet not taking credit. In this sense, *wu-wei* might be best translated as 'non-striving'. I call it real work.

Real work is joy.
Real work is having control over what you do.
Real work is receiving the fruits of your labour.
Real work is beautiful, releasing the harmony within.
Real work involves the whole person, mind, body and spirit.
Real work is voluntary, undertaken freely with an open heart.
Real work is creative, mixing labour with the rest of nature to enhance both.
Real work is knowing the material and going with the grain.
Real work is satisfying in itself, with no thought of reward.
Real work transforms *homo faber* into *homo ludens*.
Real work is unfurling and realizing your potential.
Real work is attention to the whole and the detail.
Real work is beneficial for all.
Real work is meaningful play.
Real work is joy.

*Wu-wei* is real work which goes with and not against the grain. It does not divide, separate and alienate. It is work which is a creative affirmation of the worker, which is a process of self-realization, which respects and enhances nature, and which brings deep satisfaction and joy. In short, *wu-wei* transforms work into meaningful play. The factory or officer worker who returns exhausted and irritable, but who then works another few hours in an allotment and comes home invigorated and satisfied has experienced *wu-wei*. The pace of their work is not set by the tyranny of the clock but follows natural rhythms. The allotment holder is not being forced to work but undertakes it voluntarily, co-operating and not competing with fellow diggers. They all see a direct relationship between their labour and the fruits of their labour. They reap what they sow. I know because I have experienced this myself in my own allotments. And I feel it now whilst writing this book.

*Wu wei* does not mean inactivity. There is a need for preparation: if we do not sow, there is no harvest. It may take years to achieve a state of *wu wei*. Like the Zen gardener, it involves a long training, a honing of mind, body and spirit in unison. Every blossom comes from a seed in the earth and is the result of a long period of gestation and growth. Every artist needs time to come to fruition. But in the process, nothing is forced, nothing wasted, nothing polluted. Although careful preparation went before, when things happen, they happen as if spontaneously.

Having gone beyond the stage of hunting and gathering, which might only take a few hours a day, we have to produce things – food, shelter, clothing – in order to satisfy our vital needs. In order to thrive as well as survive, we may decide to produce more than the bare necessities and create objects which are both beautiful and useless. But we do not have to be in the ridiculous situation where some have too much work and others not enough, where a few tell the many what to do, where those who work are divided within, from each other, and from nature. We also do not have to produce and consume so much, sucking up all the world's resources, in order to live well. Real work would involve the whole person and reinforce the organic threads of the community. It would be effortless and life-enhancing, something to look forward to and not avoid like the plague. The person who practises *wu-wei*, who undertakes real work without effort or striving, will do nothing but leaves nothing undone.

# 18

# Learning to Live

*When he first began to study mountains, mountains were mountains; when he went further, mountains were not mountains; but when he came to full knowledge, mountains were mountains again.*

Zen saying

Children are born free and come into the world trailing clouds of glory. They have innate knowledge of the essential things in life, like eating, sleeping, learning, playing and laughing. They exude natural exuberance and vitality. Their bodies and minds are supple. Their imagination is rich and creative. They see things clearly. Unfortunately, at an early age in our society the shades of the prison house fall across them. It is called school. They begin to lose their joy and their vision. They become pupils.

There is no such thing as a dunce. All children are bright. All shine. If they appear dull it is because they are round pegs in a square hole. It is simply that their real skills have not been discovered or awakened. Students with so-called learning difficulties are invariably being taught the wrong thing in the wrong way at the wrong time. Left-handed children forced to write with their right hand begin to stutter and stumble; allowed to choose their own hand, they grow confident and sure.

No one deliberately wills ill. Vice is a form of ignorance and a lack of skill. Vicious people, like so-called vicious horses, have had their original good natures depraved. If they grow up in light and air, with love and affection, they grow straight and strong and supple. If crushed, distorted, their impulses repressed, they grow nasty and stunted. A bully is ignorant and lacks skill and is to be helped.

Vicious people do wrong, because they know no better. They have been brought up and taught in the wrong way. They lose their instinctive skill of dealing with their feelings. A good person is enlightened and skilful. Children are naturally so, until they are twisted by their upbringing and schooling. They already know what they need to know to fulfil their natures. Parents and teachers and neighbours can help or hinder the process, can crush or release their spirit, force them into another mould or let them be.

Children learn not so much from what they are told but from what they see around them. At present, they see a society largely based on hypocrisy. They are told about truth, generosity and love, and all around them they observe lies, selfishness and violence. They are taught that might is right and evil is everywhere ('I'll hit you if you don't do what I say, you little devil!'). No wonder they learn rapidly to dissemble their true feelings and to appear what they are not. They distrust what grown ups say because their actions belie their words. Not being trusted, they become themselves untrustworthy and end up trusting no one. They grow up bewildered and are schooled into an absurd world.

School has great prestige and receives so many resources from the state because it is one of the chief ways of preserving and strengthening the existing order and passing it down from one generation to another. Today, schooling is primarily concerned with forcibly training young people for a rapidly disappearing 'work force'. Its ultimate aim is to make people pliable, docile, regimented, competitive and unquestioning subjects of capital and the state. The more it fails, the more funds are poured into it. It is profoundly divisive, yet it receives universal support. Faced with such contradictions and failures, it would seem that the answer is not more formal schooling but less.

The original Latin word for school – *skhole* – meant leisure in the pursuit of knowledge. Nothing could be farther from the modern school, which is a total institution in which children spend most of their waking time undergoing a compulsory system of education. It is often little more than a process of socialization and indoctrination into the virtues of work and the glories of the status quo. By distorting their natural emotional, intellectual and physical development most pupils become hostile to the very idea of education, certainly as a continuous lifelong process. Yet having hated school, most adults end up imposing the painful process on their children, as if it were some necessary rite of passage to adult suffering: 'It was good enough for me', they say, 'so it's good enough for you.'

It is a widespread delusion to think that education can only be achieved through institutions like school and university. We have been schooled to think them essential, yet most people learn more out of educational institutions than within them. I too suffered from the delusion for a while. Having left school young to go to sea, I became convinced that there was some special truth and enlightenment to be discovered at university. I came back as an older student. After three degrees and ten years, it finally became clear to me that I probably would have been more creative if I had continued my own studies outside the institution.

Modern universities hardly live up to their original name. The word comes from the original Latin for universe, and from medieval Latin – *universitas* – for a group of scholars. Although scholarly work goes on and many lecturers are dedicated scholars, most students seem primarily interested in obtaining a degree so that they can get more money, status and power in life rather than to pursue truth or to extend the frontiers of knowledge. Nevertheless, the original idea of the university remains an inspiration and free and genuine learning can occasionally take place within its walls despite its bureaucracy and close links with industry and government.

Although school is now an almost universal demand for young people, it has only been with us for a short time. A child and school boy or school girl have now become virtually synonymous. A child in the street or wood during school hours is either ill or playing truant. Yet the idea of childhood as distinct from infancy, adolescence or youth is a recent development, and the notion of a teenager even more so. Artists in the eighteenth century depicted infants as miniature adults. It was only with industrial society that childhood was invented and a new market created. Children are now segregated from the rest of society in school.

A school is often defined as an institution or building in which young people receive a compulsory education. The operative words are 'receive' and 'compulsory'. They are given a pre-packed programme in school to digest. It is not something that they make for themselves, or participate in making. Since it is compulsory, truancy is considered a major crime and paradoxically offers grounds for expulsion. The Educational Welfare

Officer in England was formerly called the School Attendance Officer, whose job was to make sure that all pupils received their wadge of information, whether they liked it or not. Fortunately, children are highly resilient and imaginative, especially in escaping the rod of authority.

It is not surprising that school begins and ends with the ringing of a bell. Each lesson has an allotted amount of time. There is no flexibility to relate the length of a study session to the rhythm of the children or the teacher. The first important lesson is the tyranny of the clock which eventually culminates in the stifling discipline of work.

In a conventional school, children are taught how to regurgitate what the teachers say, how to adapt their thoughts and feelings to win their approval, and how to curb their natural exuberance. If they look out of the window at the trees swaying in the breeze, they lack concentration and need to be chastized. To be dreamy is a special sin. It means that you do not force yourself to listen to a teacher droning on about something which is completely pointless, dead and above all boring. It means you have thoughts and images and desires of your own. Forcibly sitting behind a desk, elbows in, eyes forward towards the blackboard, the mind of the ideal pupil is blinkered, so that nothing is seen in his or her peripheral vision and lateral thinking is impossible.

It is the dream of every Minister of Education to look at his watch and to know what every child in the education system is doing at that time. That is the purpose of imposing a national curriculum and of having the same timetable in all schools. Nothing could be worse. Nothing could be more regimented. It marks the ultimate triumph of the centralized state and its control over the minds and bodies of its citizens. It perfectly demonstrates that national education is aimed not so much at the individual needs of children, or even the needs of their community, but at the needs of employers, capital and the state.

A school is to a large extent a penal institution. A child is registered, assessed, examined, taught, corrected, detained, punished, expelled. These common verbs reflect the school as an institution of coercion. It is not surprising that their architecture and organization resemble barracks, with the play-ground as parade ground behind high wire. They are run like prisons, with the head teacher as governor, and like mental

214

asylums, where staff try to make the inmates function 'normally' in an unnatural situation. The hierarchy not only extends to the different grades of teachers, but to the rigid distinction between 'years' and the creation of prefects and, at boarding schools, 'dormitory captains'.

Teachers cannot escape the general contagion. It is not enough for teachers just to teach their subject. They are expected to be custodians, inculcating elaborate rituals, rules, and drills and enforcing discipline; moralists, indoctrinating what is right and wrong and the established religion; and increasingly therapists, delving into the emotional life of their pupils to make them adjust to school and wider society.

Since most children do not want to sit still and silent in school, teachers spend much of the time trying to keep order. If they do win the pupils' attention, they then often teach them irrelevant subjects, such as the names and dates of kings and battles rather than the struggles of the people; to criticize a poem rather than to write one; to dissect a frog rather than to understand nature's web. No wonder children go to school like snails and run home like hares. No wonder so many play truant ('play' not 'work' being the operative word). No wonder at the end of term, they shout joyously 'School's Out', throw their bags in the air, leap about, and rush for the school gates. I can remember only too well the wonderful exhilaration of packing my trunk at the end of term at my dismal boarding school.

While there was an attempt in the 1960s to make school more amenable to the individual needs of children, to relax the oppressive discipline, and to encourage imagination and creativity, in recent times there have been deeply reactionary developments in education. The school itself has been turned into a business with the head teacher as managing director and the other teachers as executives. Administrative skills have become more important than teaching abilities; making the books balance more central than making children flourish. The state has decreed that their schools must not only inculcate the three 'R's, but also morality, religion, patriotism, and respect for authority.

School as a limited company now limits the horizons of all who come under its sway. The supreme end of education is to prepare the young for work in the organized system. The new emphasis is on economic performance and work discipline. Before leaving school, pupils are obliged to see a careers officer, often paid by local industry, to be told what few options await them in factory or office. They are obliged to undergo 'work' experience which usually means training in how to keep time and to accept the most soul-destroying repetitive task without complaining. Rather than developing their whole person, education now schools children into becoming cogs in the machine.

The present system of education represses the personality and crushes the spirit. The process is not dissimilar to 'breaking in' a horse for the harness. The aim is not to channel its natural exuberance and energy, to understand its mind, but to dominate it completely by superior force so that its spirit is literally broken. The horse eventually gives in to the rein and the bit, and when whipped it will plod on, harnessed, blinkered, unable to break out and kick up its heels. If it tries to, it is called vicious, and is viciously beaten. If it continues to rebel, it ends up in the knacker's yard.

In the same way, many children are broken in their youth and carry on in life doing what they are told, never questioning authority, never kicking up their heels and making a run for it. They become tame, sad, plodding, unfulfilled creatures. They take the bit in their mouth and keep their heads down. They have forgotten the freedom and dreams of early childhood, the joy and the vision, when their imaginations roamed freely through the streets, the parks, the fields, the woods and the sky.

At present, the education system is chiefly geared towards production and consumption, taking on different local forms according to the region, culture and class. In North Wales where I live, the state schools are seen as the principal means of keeping the Welsh language alive and of preventing the young from leaving the area. The private schools are usually for the children of wealthy English immigrants who want them to follow in their footsteps and tell others what to do. In the old mining valleys of South Wales, the schools are geared towards getting jobs in an area of high unemployment and low expectations. In all cases, education is intended to make them good producers and consumers.

It also trains children into conformity. The experience does not nurture free spirits and enquiring minds but docile, pliable and loyal workers and subjects. They are still expected to give way to someone in a more expensive suit, and, if ordered by their 'betters', to sacrifice themselves for their religion or government.

216

Their duty is not to question why, but to do and die. It is not surprising that when they leave school, so many young people find it difficult to act and think for themselves. School enslaves more profoundly than the hidden curriculum of family, health care, or the media since it is involved in the well-orchestrated manipulation of the world through its demands, language and vision. We cannot escape its hand; it is everywhere.

The system of competition and examinations early encourages pupils to see their fellows as opponents rather than partners. On the playing field or in the school room, pupils are not trying to help their fellows to realize their best by doing their best, as in the original Olympics, but to beat them. To do well is to come in the top ten; to excel is to come first. By definition, school turns out generations of losers. The experience only fosters a sense of fear and failure. For some, it takes years to recover a sense of self-worth and the courage to make demands for themselves. Vast amounts of time, energy and money are spent so that adults can at last say to themselves: 'I'm OK. You're OK. We're OK.' School taught them otherwise. Therapy can help, but it can also encourage the old pattern of dependency which is transferred from teacher to therapist.

Most private schools are even worse than state schools, expensive tools for the elite to transfer their power and privilege from generation to generation. Their offspring are taught the same exploded errors and reactionary prejudices that they inherited. Organized along military lines, they take children at a young age from their homes and families and make them adjust to a total institution in which every moment of their lives is surveyed. It is usually single-sex, which means they lose the ease and familiarity that growing up with the opposite sex brings. They are forced to repress their natural feelings of compassion, and many become cold, calculating, cruel, competitive and self-sufficient individuals.

Later on in life, they find it difficult to express their emotions but very easy to be ruthless and cunning. The system was ideal to forge the rulers of empire who would never question their orders and find no disquiet in massacring rebellious natives. Without their ruthlessness and righteousness, thousands would not have been able to subject millions in the colonies. The times have changed, the empire has gone, but the system of education and its values live on.

217

To be well-educated in certain circles means to have attended a certain school with a certain accent and with certain manners. It means being informed of arcane rituals and obscure traditions. It means regurgitating what you have been taught and performing well in examinations for which you have been crammed. It does not mean having an original turn of mind, an independent spirit and a creative imagination.

Fortunately, not everyone in state and private schools is brainwashed. Some teachers rise above the regimentation and commercialization of the system and manage to inspire a genuine love of learning. In spite of the system, they are able to foster enquiring minds, lively imaginations and open hearts. There are also some village and neighbourhood schools which manage to link home and community and provide a caring and inventive atmosphere. And in every generation there arise young people who can question authority, think for themselves, and imagine a different future. They demystify what they have been taught and refuse to be docile subjects and forlorn slaves.

Not all schools are bad. To be forced to go to work at a very young age can be worse. As the son of an Italian peasant once said: 'School is better than cowshit'. In reality, most countries in the world can only give the barest minimum of education. The majority of children in the so-called 'developing world' are out of school and those in school drop out as soon as possible.

Education can be used to brainwash and manipulate, or it can be a means of enlightenment and liberation. An illiterate person today can be confused and easily duped in a society which places so much emphasis on the written word. To be illiterate in the modern world is to live in a culture of silence. To learn how to read and write can be a liberation, since it enables you to understand the world you live in and oppose the forces which oppress you. It is significant that the first Sunday schools in Britain taught children of the poor to read the Bible but not to write. Their teachers were concerned that their charges might end up writing tracts on the rights of men and women and on the iniquities of church, state and capital. They knew that language interprets reality. To write the word 'boss' or 'government' is the first step to understand them and realize that you do not need them. You are no longer imprisoned in a Bastille of words you do not understand. Being able to use language sets you free. To write and read a true word is to change the world.

In highly industrialized countries, the image is becoming as important as the written word. After five hundred years of printing we are moving from a literary to a visual culture with the development of computers and television. But this does not mean that we should abandon the written word as it remains the main means of communication. All the more reason to make the media and the new information technology instruments of change rather than tools of control, to keep the Internet free for all its users rather than the vehicle for governments and corporations.

It is difficult to overestimate the value of true learning. It enables individuals to shape their own lives and realize their full potential. It prevents them from becoming the dupes of charlatans, leaders, bosses, experts, and of all those who have the arrogance to claim that they know better. It enables them to think and act for themselves. It liberates them from a culture of darkness and silence. It sets people free. Learning enables people to understand their situation and thereby change it, to be active participants in the making of history rather than bemused victims or bystanders. It helps them to deal creatively with reality. It is something positive and hazardous, creative and spontaneous. It is open-ended and never ends. It is a continuous process throughout our lives, unless we wish to live by inherited prejudices and fixed ideas and refuse to question how we have been taught to judge, imagine and feel. A wise person thinks against herself.

If the learning is not compulsory and there are no examinations, classes can also be an enriching experience, helping people to make sense of themselves, their society and the world at large. For many years, I was a tutor in a small group of adults who attended freely to study philosophy. We eventually formed an affinity group, a voluntary association of enquiring and sympathetic individuals. The meetings were organized around the discussion of a chosen subject; the intention was to draw out wisdom, not pack in information. Although I often had more to say than most, the meetings took the form of mutual explorations. I learned as much as anyone else. After our deliberations, we would often retire to a pub, long the university of the working man and woman, a warm and friendly place where they could discuss their lives in a convivial and unrestricted atmosphere outside the daily grind of work and home.

The key point of these learning groups for me was that they were voluntary, without examinations or obligatory written work. One came only for the pleasure and enlightenment, for the pursuit of knowledge in good company for its own sake. In my view, all education should be like this, a voluntary process in which people come together out of common interest and pursue their studies at their own pace. It is the very opposite of mainstream education today, including adult education, which is increasingly geared towards competition, examination, qualification, control and standardization.

All is not lost. Not only can some teachers and pupils rise above the general decay, but it is possible to deschool oneself and society. There is an urgent need to separate the school from the state and learning from control. School is an institution based on the maxim that learning is the result of teaching, yet there is overwhelming evidence to the contrary. It is a liberating experience to realize that most learning requires no teaching and that we can learn more outside the walls of school and university than within.

A good education system serves several purposes. Firstly, it gives access to the available resources to all those who want to learn at any time in their lives. Secondly, it enables all those who want to share their knowledge and skills to find those who want to learn from them. Thirdly, it is based on free enquiry, free speech and free assembly. Above all, it remains voluntary, so that they who learn do so from their own desire and free will. Only in this way will teaching by rote be transformed into genuine learning for oneself and one's community. A good education system is therefore open, continuous, democratic, voluntary and libertarian.

To educate otherwise than in the existing system is difficult. To educate your children at home presumes you know best for them and denies them the important company of other children. There are few alternative schools, and many of those are inflexible, following one fixed method or outlook. The ideal is to create a free school with like-minded families within the community. Failing that, one can search for the least pernicious school in the neighbourhood and try and make it more amenable to the individual needs of children and more accountable to their parents and communities. It is always possible to counter the indoctrination of school with one's own inspiration and experience. The influence of family background is still more influential than that of school. Despite the attempt to make schools more comprehensive and egalitarian, the pupils who do well tend to be the children of parents who previously did well in the system since they speak the same language and share the same concepts and beliefs.

Libertarian education should be concerned with the all-round development of the young, so that they can understand who they are, the kind of society they are growing up in, and the nature of the world around them. There would be no rigid distinction between subjects, so that science would become art, and art would become science, and the poetry of mathematics would be appreciated as much as the alchemy of love. It would be concerned not with inculcating particular information but in developing the mind, body and spirit as a harmonious whole.

The two fundamental principles of libertarian education are freedom and flexibility. It is based on the voluntary principle. Individuals only learn through desire, and study best if they want to do so. There is no compulsion or coercion. The maximum degree of autonomy is allowed in their learning so that they can grow in freedom and responsibility and have confidence in their own individual judgement. Freedom is central because it is not the goal but a necessary condition of emancipation. The young should be free from the tyranny of teachers and parents, and free to express themselves and be fully themselves. Only through self-rule and participation will a young person become a responsible member of the community as an adult. By experiencing themselves as creative subjects rather than as passive objects, they are then able to understand their situation and change it if they so wish. People cannot be educated to be free, for freedom is the condition of true learning.

Rather than imposing a set curriculum at a particular age, the teacher should be attentive to the particular differences, needs, desires and interests of individual children. A libertarian approach is child-orientated, not orientated towards the demands of work, production and consumption or the requirements of the state.

Clearly children are not just blank sheets, noble savages, or repressed geniuses. They are shaped by their wider society, culture and upbringing. But in general it would seem that throughout the world children learn well when they want to and when they are allowed to proceed at their own pace. If they are free to develop their own rhythm and style, they often learn quicker and are more capable of grasping difficult ideas. The most important thing is to excite their interest. All else follows. They then begin to learn and discover for themselves. Whatever their culture, they have their own ways of understanding and of thinking things out. It is invariably a fresh, original and inventive style of thinking compared to that of the adults who surround them.

There are broad stages in the development of the minds and bodies of children, but these should not be rigidly adhered to. A free school would develop the mental and physical skills of children, but there would be no need to have a rigid curriculum or fixed stages of development. To fit a growing child into an inflexible framework is to place them on a Procrustes' bed which stretches or cuts off the limbs of whoever lies on it to make them fit.

To begin with, the emphasis should be more on the body than the mind, on physical action than on thinking, but the two always go hand in hand. At present, children are encouraged to read and write very early but it often cramps their style. Better to learn at first orally, through stories and discussions, visually through drawing and painting, and physically, through singing, dancing and playing music, than through the written word. When children are ready they will pick up a book and read if there are interesting books available. Once they can read and write, and they enjoy both, there is no stopping them.

Learning is not a matter of memorizing and repeating given words and concepts, but of reflecting critically and imagining creatively. Acquiring the tools of learning are therefore more important than the content of any particular subject. In the early years, what is important is all-round, harmonious development of children's ability to feel, think, imagine and create.

The goal of libertarian education is to develop imaginative, enquiring, compassionate and creative people, who are confident in themselves as individuals, and yet who see themselves as an organic part of society and nature. It aims to develop in a harmonious way the whole person, unfurling and realizing their potential. It develops all their faculties, their mind, body and spirit, their mind and imagination, their reason and feeling, their judgement and empathy, their logic and intuition. It transcends the present artificial division of subjects and adopts an interdisciplinary approach, combining arts and sciences, philosophy and poetry, dance and art, music and mathematics.

222

Again, it does not separate teachers and pupils, old and young, but develops a community of learners who meet voluntarily to pursue their studies and common interests. There should be room for group learning as well as solitary study. And it need not always take place indoors. Even philosophy, as in Aristotle's lyceum, can be peripatetic with teacher and pupils strolling together in the open air. As with Socrates, the mode of discourse need not be the lecture but conversation. Truth emerges dialectically through the free exchange of opinions and intuitions.

A free school would take down the barriers – the barriers between teacher and taught, young and old, male and female, school and family, school and community, work and play. Young people could acquire skills working alongside adults in the community, field, factory and workshop, while adults could come to share their skills, experience and knowledge in the learning centre. In turn, the adults themselves would learn. The topics would address the real issues of the community and the wider world. In order to match learners and teachers within the community, learning webs could be developed, especially through the use of computers and other directories.

The organization would be based on direct and participatory democracy, with all involved in running the school, teachers and students, parents and anyone else interested in the community. They would make decisions in open meetings based on consensus as far as possible. They would not slavishly follow a national or regional curriculum, but follow their own agenda. As for size, small is beautiful for education as well as for production. It enables the students to know each other and to be in touch with their local community, to be rooted in their neighbourhood, to know its language, culture and traditions.

In the process, students would become familiar with the contours, moods and rhythms of their bioregion, and get to know its history, geography and ecology. They would acquire an intimate knowledge of the natural world around them. Since the soil at their feet is a microcosm of the universe, they would know the very small and the very large, the earth and the heavens. They would become aware that they are part of the web of relationships in society and nature and that everything is interconnected and interdependent: whatever they do affects everything else. At the same time, while acting locally, they would think globally, aware of how other people live and do things. They would appreciate the universal values of tolerance, minimum harm, and compassion for all beings.

The libertarian teacher's role is to act like a catalyst, releasing the children's creativity. The Latin root of the word 'educate' is *ducere*, which means 'to draw out' or 'to lead forth' something which is potentially there. In its best and purest sense, it means to help someone realize his or her potential. A teacher should act as a spark to trigger off a love of learning and a concern for truth; someone who has gone before, who might know a little more, but is not necessarily the wiser.

What is important is not the content of the subjects, but the process of developing the mind and imagination, not *what* to think and feel, but *how* to think and feel. The process involves play, creativity, self-expression, free enquiry and even remembering what we knew when we were very young but have forgotten. By thinking and acting for themselves, students become shapers of their own destiny and puppets and fools of none.

If education is to change and to bring about change in society, we are left with the question, 'Who educates the educators?' The answer is simple. They educate themselves, and are educated by their fellows, their students, their community and their wider society. Education for all is a lifelong and continuous process, and there is no telling exactly when real learning takes place. It is not a question of the chicken before the egg, but of two birds soaring together.

The best students leave their teachers behind: they have been stepping-stones and ladders. Eventually, there would no longer be teachers and taught, leaders and led, but a group of learners, each helping the other to discover truth, understand reality and to make sense of themselves and the world around them.

The best a teacher can do is to excite the interest of a child, to engage the mind, to fire the imagination. Children learn best if they want to. Excite the desire for learning and the main work is done. If there is no interest excited, then the whole process is merely a question of forcing children to behave like unconscious automata. Learning by rote is called learning parrot-fashion, but a parrot does at least have a mind of itself and can choose the moments when to clean its beak and to make rude noises.

A child's body and mind are supple and flexible; it is tragic to make them prematurely stiff and rigid. Fitting them into a fixed framework, binding them in a tight harness, is like placing a large stone on a growing daffodil. The young need good soil, light and air to grow at their own pace, to develop and stretch according to their own individual natures and particular rates of development. They should be allowed to study subjects in their own way and order. To say that a child must not learn to read, for instance, before age 7, is as bad as to say that they must read at 5. All children have a time when they want to learn to read and write.

In general, I would say that it is better at first to learn through direct experience of nature than in the books of humanity. Theory is best learned by experiment and doing. If they have access to beaches, woods and streams, virtually all children love to make castles, dens and dams. They experience the spontaneous play of creation, the freedom and space of nature, the deep calm of trees, and the irresistible force of water. They learn that living is a relationship which involves balance, give and take, and no excess. They know that if they are to succeed they must go with the flow and work with the grain. What is contrary to nature does not last long. That is the greatest lesson of all.

Naturally, such a system based on learning through desire would encourage co-operation rather than competition between learners, each helping the other to develop their talents and abilities and to realize their best. They would not be judged, examined, assessed, passed or failed. They would not be classified as excellent, very good, good, satisfactory or poor. At the same time, individuals could seek sensitive advice from their teachers of their own progress and development, if they so wished.

If we are to create a free and sustainable society in harmony with nature, it is essential to deschool society, to separate learning from control, to open up schools, and to break down the barriers with the rest of society. We can start here and now. Life is a continuous learning experience. The first step to deschooling society is to deschool oneself, to question what one has been taught and to discard all the useless information and distorted values acquired in youth. To get rid of all the rubbish which parents, teachers, leaders and the media have packed into your head can be a long and painful process, or it can happen suddenly overnight. Eureka, you have a clean slate. The mind is pure and clear as a mountain stream.

I have found after a lifetime of deschooling myself that the process gets easier as you grow older. One can acquire a new craft which requires little effort. Some people find it disconcerting, and many strain against it, but it is an important stage on the path to wisdom. I call it creative forgetfulness. You forget the immediate, the pressing, the unimportant, but the essential remains. You discard superficial cleverness. Going beyond fixed ideas and surface fads and fashions, you dive to deeper and calmer waters. You reconnect with the uncarved block which you knew intimately as a child. You splice rope rather than weave sophistries.

There are important differences between information, knowledge and wisdom. We are bombarded with superficial information everywhere. If we fill our memories with such rubbish we clog ourselves up. Knowledge is deeper and lasts longer; it shows how an engine works, how the weather changes, how the garden grows. Wisdom on the other hand is distilled experience and the essence of knowledge. It is the end result of the alchemy of living. It changes little over the centuries and can be found in all societies, especially in those without the written word. In our great cities, we think we are very grand, but a pygmy in a rainforest knows more about where he lives, and may have a great deal more wisdom about the fundamentals of life.

The original meaning of 'philosophy' in Greek is 'love of wisdom'. I have learned in a lifelong study of philosophy that we know very little about the ultimate mysteries of the universe. With all our gadgets and information, we have not yet learned how to live well on earth. I know that I know very little, and much of what I have been taught I want to forget. The wise person never tries to store things up. It is a very liberating experience to just let go of the useless information which has settled in your mind and to feel the waters of lucidity wash away the accumulated silt of a lifetime. True wisdom brings a clear and tranquil mind and makes you calm and free. And it comes without effort.

# 19

# The Enigma of Joy

*One day two friends were crossing a river, when one of them said: 'See how free the fishes leap and dart: that is happiness!'*

*'Since you are not a fish how do you know what makes fishes happy?', said the other.*

*'Since you are not I how can you possibly know that I do not know what makes fishes happy?', said the first friend.*

*'If I, not being you, cannot know what you know, it follows that you, not being a fish, cannot know what they know', said the second.*

*'Wait a minute!', said the first. 'Let us get back to the original question. What you asked me was "How do you know what makes fishes happy?" From the terms of your question you evidently know I know what makes fishes happy. I know the joy of fishes in the river through my own joy, as I go walking along the same river!'*

Chuang Tzu

It seems almost universal that human beings seek happiness. And it seems almost universal that they suffer. Perhaps they seek happiness so ardently because the everyday experience of most people is sorrow. Unable to find happiness, many people give up the search altogether and make no attempt to escape their misery. Others insist that because there is unhappiness in the world, one has no right to be happy: 'You selfish bastard', they say, 'how can you be so happy when everyone is so wretched!'

From as far back as I can remember, whenever I thought of the end or purpose of life, I was for some reason more interested in the pursuit of 'truth' than the search for happiness, even if it might be painful and make me unhappy. By truth I understood not so much what is logically coherent but what corresponds to reality. It involved going beyond the veil of appearances to see things as they really are. It meant being able to distinguish between truth and falsehood, appearance and reality, integrity and deception. It meant understanding the way of nature, being authentic and aiming straight.

It was an attitude which was not appreciated by my partner at the time, who thought we should be pursuing happiness together. I felt that to pursue personal happiness as the main goal in this world was egotistical and neglected the problems of the rest of the world. How could I fiddle while Rome burned? Besides it seemed grossly insensitive to be happy in such a troubled world. I had been early impressed by the question that John Stuart Mill posed to his utilitarian father who had defined happiness in terms of pleasure: 'Is it better to be Socrates dissatisfied or a pig contented?'

The romantic implication that all sensitive souls must inevitably suffer in this absurd world no doubt appealed to my youthful existential angst and possibly to an unconscious elitism. Not for me the fight in the trough after the swill of consumerism. We might all be in the gutter, but I liked to gaze at the stars. I preferred the disinterested pursuit of truth to the ledgers of profit and loss, pain and pleasure.

At the same time, I dismissed early on the Christian belief that we are born in a state of sin, that this world is a vale of tears, and that only a minority of the elect are predestined, regardless of their works, to escape eternal damnation. My own experience denied it. Life after all was worth living: I enjoyed rowing in a little boat on a sparkling bay, climbing a mountain at dawn, sharing chestnuts with my grandfather around the fire, kissing a girl on the seashore under the moon.

After having enjoyed my fair share of youthful pleasures, when I came across Buddhism in my twenties it struck a deep chord in me. Buddha taught that the cause of suffering is to be found in wrongly directed desire, in the ignorant craving for material things – possessions, wealth, power or status. As long as a person remained ignorant and attached to such artificial desires, he would be chained by a great burden. 'Work out your own salvation with diligence', Buddha said. I agreed with his four noble truths on the origin and cause of suffering but it took some time to work out exactly what he meant by the eight-fold path which leads to the end of suffering. I still had to find out the meaning of right action and right mindfulness.

As a young man, I sailed around the world as a cadet on a luxury liner and saw how many of the richest and most powerful people in the West were poor in spirit, anxious and troubled, indifferent to the peoples and cultures of the countries they visited. Wherever they went, they carried with them their own worries and narrow concerns. Wealth had not liberated them, but seemed like a ball and chain, preventing their mental and spiritual development. Their idea of fun was to gorge themselves with sensory pleasures which usually left them in sorrow the next day. Pain followed them like a shadow.

Most people I encountered seemed to be carried away with the pursuit of happiness: grim, obsessed and anxious, unable to stop themselves or change direction. Just one more effort, just one more project, just one more deal, and everything would be transformed and they would be happy. They were always on the point of attaining happiness, yet it always escaped them. In their headlong rush, they exhausted themselves and were only halted by illness or an early death. They did not seem very happy to me.

My experience only confirmed for me that the pursuit of truth is more important than the search for happiness. I recognized that truth could be painful, especially the recognition that suffering is inevitable in this world, that we are born to die, and that everything passes away. At the same time, it occurred to me that just as truth and beauty are inextricably entwined, so joy inevitably accompanies the discovery of truth. If I discover truth, I am joyful although that is not the reason for pursuing it. It is not the end, but a by-product of the process of discovery.

Perhaps I was a 'selfish bastard' pursuing truth for myself and trying to change the world while neglecting to a degree the happiness of those around me. Yet I realize now that perhaps the reason I was not looking for happiness was that in a sense I was *already* happy searching for the truth. I now conclude that the more you search for happiness, the less you will find it. You will never find happiness until you stop looking for it. Perhaps the greatest happiness is precisely in doing nothing whatever that is calculated to attain happiness. If I cease to strive for happiness, the 'right' and 'wrong' actions become obvious without any calculation or judgement. In this way I obtain contentment and well-being.

I am not a pessimist. Despite the terrors of the twentieth century, after living on earth for more than fifty years, I am convinced more than ever that ultimately truth is not only victorious over error, but a mind filled with truth aims straight and attains its goal. To discover the truth brings joy and peace which pass all understanding.

Most people regard happiness as the beginning and end of a good life. But what is happiness? It is usually defined in terms of pleasure. The chief means to pleasure are said to be wealth, fame, material comfort, long life, sex, good food, fine clothes, beautiful things to look at and pleasant music to hear. Those who are deprived of these things often panic or become depressed. Even when they have the things they think they want, they are so anxious about losing them that their lives become intolerable.

The rich drive themselves to make more money which they really cannot use, exhausting and enslaving themselves in the process. The ambitious are wracked by every detail of their plans and obsessed with success and failure. They live for what is always out of reach, and their thirst for the future makes them incapable of living in and enjoying the present. The powerful are caught in the whirring machine of power, crushed down by external forces, victims of fashion, the market, events, and public opinion. Their lives thus become unbearable, however rich, successful and powerful they may become. Prisoners in the world of objects, what a pity they do not know when to stop.

For the Greek philosopher Epicurus, writing over 2000 years ago, happiness was an absence of bodily pain and a tranquil mind. Intense pain does not last long – it ends in death. Even low-level pain can be mixed with pleasure, so much so that you can bear the pain. Indeed, for all the suffering in the world, it seems that we quickly forget pain and yet can easily remember the moments of pleasure. Indeed, one of the pleasures of old age, despite the aches and pains, is the ability to recall the good times in life.

The British utilitarian philosophers in the early nineteenth century defined the end of morality as the general good, by which they meant the greatest happiness of the greatest number. Fine democratic sentiments. But what is the greatest happiness? What makes people happy? Their answer was simple: pleasure. And what brings about suffering? Pain, of course.

But how do you measure pleasure? The utilitarians tried to work out a 'felicific calculus', calculating the different degrees of felicity. But they very quickly got themselves into painful knots. Is short intense pleasure better than long shallow pleasure? Is it true that the pleasure of the flesh does not increase once the pain of want has been removed? Are the pleasures of the mind superior to the pleasures of the body? Are the pleasures of virtue better than both? Is the good life necessarily the longest or the most pleasant? Is pleasure just the absence of pain?

The utilitarian philosopher James Mill argued that in the scale of pleasures skittles are of equal importance as poetry, but his son John Stuart Mill suggested that intellectual pleasures are greater than physical ones. The unlettered ploughman can have a pleasant life, but the artist and philosopher may have more sources of pleasure, intellectual and aesthetic as well as physical ones, available to them. On the other hand, it may be that the plough-man's instinctive virtue is far greater than the cool calculations of the philosopher or the wild imaginings of the artist.

Entering this fray, I would say that the best form of happiness in terms of pleasure results from the uninterrupted enjoyment of the pleasures of the mind and the body, but the greatest pleasure of all is to be had from the satisfaction of living a good life, a life which causes no harm. This involves a certain knowledge of the consequences of our actions and an awareness of reasonable limits.

In my view, the greatest problem with utilitarian ethics is that it neglects motives of an action in favour of consequences. What about the benevolent error of a person who means well but causes great harm or the malevolent benefit of a person who intends harm but inadvertently brings about great good? For an action to be good it should be based on good intentions as well as have beneficial consequences, but for a person to be good it is enough that he or she is well motivated.

However knowledgeable and aware we may be, it is difficult to calculate the long-term consequences of your actions. What is intended to contribute to the general good can often have the reverse effect. By busily helping others you may be fleeing from yourself and preventing them from helping themselves.

In my experience, you can never be sure in the long run what is

231

success or failure. Stumbling-blocks have an uncanny habit of turning into stepping-stones. The young man who loses a leg thinks it is a disaster until a war breaks out, then he is pleased because he is not enlisted. When the enemy reaches his village it is a disaster because he cannot run away. Then he is fortunate because only the able-bodied are put to forced labour. He may well end up with a pension so that he has the leisure to become a great artist or thinker, or better still, decide to become a simple ferryman.

Who knows what is good or bad, success or failure in the long term? It may be that there is no success like failure and no failure like success. The break-up of a relationship can seem like a disaster at the time, but a few years later one can look back and see it as a liberation, the beginning of a new way of life with unimagined possibilities of fulfilment.

The utilitarians are always concerned with the use of things, with how things will contribute to the general good or bring happiness. But some of the best things have no use. What practical use have clouds scudding across a wintry sky or bird song in spring? What practical use is the beauty of a dawn or a pool of light sparkling on the sea? On occasion, it is a definite advantage to have no use. The disabled person is not sent to the front line in times of war. The gnarled tree is not cut down because it is of no use to the carpenter. The powerless are not noticed.

Worse of all, the utilitarian ethic implies that we should always be rational calculators of our actions, constantly weighing the advantages and disadvantages of their consequences in terms of pleasure. Such an approach to life not only encourages self-interest but denies all spontaneity. It fails to see that a good person does not calculate with the mind but acts spontaneously from the heart. Indeed, as soon as you worry about what is right and wrong, confusion ensues and clarity of mind is lost.

Unfortunately for those addicted to pleasure, it seems that it is the way of the world that pain inevitably follows pleasure and that craving leads to sorrow and fear. You cannot have pleasure without pain. This is because of the fundamental nature of desire. A neurotic attachment to pleasure is never satisfied. The greater the pleasure, the more you want it. Yet the frustration increases when you do not have it and the dissatisfaction is more acute when it is attained. Not to have pleasure is sorrow, while to have it inevitably ends in sorrow when it ceases, as it always will. At all times, there remains the fear that the pleasure you have may be taken away or that one day you will be unable to enjoy it.

Craving leads to suffering as night follows day. The hunger of the passions leads to disharmony which is the greatest sorrow. A person who lives only for pleasure, and who consequently has no self-harmony is like a weather cock, constantly moved by temptations, this way and that, without any conscious sense of direction. By having too much pleasure and too much pain, you are thrown off balance. Thoughts run wild: you start everything, finish nothing. You rush here and there, forever running after your own tail.

In the eternal web of cause and effect, in the web of karma, you reap what you sow. People who do evil will suffer sooner or later; their evil will return to them like dust thrown against the wind. The more cruel individuals seem to prosper outwardly, the more they harm themselves within. By doing evil, by hurting others, they are lighting a fire in which they will eventually burn. It is in the nature of life that any person who for the sake of happiness seeks to hurt others will never find it.

On the other hand, the person who loves and does not intentionally hurt any living being can be joyful in this world. It is the way of things that love is not only the highest good but also its own reward. In the long run, truth overcomes error, peacefulness overcomes anger, the generous overcome the mean, the yielding overcomes the hard, and love overcomes hatred. In a storm, it is the supple willow which survives, not the rigid oak. Water divides at the headland but it will eventually wear it away. A wise person who acts with truth, peacefulness and love will obtain self-harmony. The alchemy of well-being is to cultivate the three treasures of vitality, energy and spirit and to harmonize instinct, emotion and reason. By doing so, one will realize one's full potential and reach one's full stature.

Happiness and sorrow, pleasure and pain, success and failure, life and death are as inevitable as night and day. You cannot have one without the other; indeed, one defines the other. But there is a way beyond all calculations of pleasure and pain, beyond good and evil. When people become watchful and awake, when they can direct their desires like a sailor his boat, they become free of craving and grasping, they can discover peace and joy. There are no fetters beyond the demands of pleasure and pain. If people are free from craving and grasping, they are free from sorrow and fear.

Day after day, there are a thousand reasons for worry, but the sensible person does not think about them. Ninety-eight per cent of worries never happen. Better to concentrate on the two per cent only when they do occur and then deal with them with clear seeing and calm abiding. There is a Hindu saying that if you do not worry about a misfortune for three years, it will become a blessing. The sunken moon returns: a wise person who ponders this is not troubled in adversity.

The fearful calculate the odds, see the obstacles, and shy away. Unexpected difficulties lead them to give up at the first hurdle. The wise, on the other hand, welcome difficulties calmly and see the obstacles as a challenge and as an adventure. By overcoming them, they develop themselves and complete their tasks. They transform adversity into benefit. They accept that there will be the rough and the smooth in life; indeed, both are necessary for development in the dialectic of growth. Without conflict, there can be no progression. When the going gets rough, you often develop faster than when it is smooth. A sailor travels further with rising waves and wind than in a flat calm.

Tranquillity is perhaps the greatest good. A tranquil heart is not disturbed by anxiety or stress, fear of failure or longing for success, artificial desires or uncontrollable passions. A tranquil mind experiences lasting contentment. Like a still pond, it is the mirror of heaven and earth. If a person speaks or acts with a pure and tranquil heart and mind, joy inevitably follows. Joy goes beyond good and evil, pleasure and pain. Joy is free of care and brings long life. Joy does all things without concern but leaves nothing undone. Joy comes when you cease to act with it in view. Joy is the fullness of life which makes it worth living. This joyous contentment is not a state of passive repose nor is it a passionless ideal. Tranquillity does not seek to eradicate or suppress passion but it recognizes its disruptive power and knows the dangers of craving and grasping. Tranquillity is an emotion, not a denial of emotion. It is a skill which knows how to direct powerful energy creatively and not be destroyed by it.

Despite the suffering of the world, it is possible to make a joyous affirmation of life; it is possible to throw off the fetters of gravity and seriousness. If you can attain self-harmony and a tranquil heart and mind, you can become free like the sea which no net can catch, fearless like a bear which no sound frightens, calm like a whale meditating in the deep. With

234

energy and vision, you can become a laughing lion and a dancing wolf. You can ride the wind!

The good and joyful life involves considerations of truth, justice and beauty. A spontaneous act of generosity – a gift of a flower or a compliment – is worth more than the cold analysis of benefit. It is better to be unfortunate while acting well – that is to say, justly and honestly – than to prosper acting foolishly. The just attain the greatest peace of mind and contentment, although ultimately the wise transcend good and evil and are spontaneously good. They are good like a young tree is good, like a mountain stream is good, like a shooting star is good. They cause minimum harm to other beings by their actions yet they do not know that they are being kind or gentle. They make no virtue of poverty nor do they struggle to make money. They do not bother with their own interests. They follow their own paths without relying on others but are not proud to be solitary walkers. They do not make calculations of right and wrong, good and bad, profit and loss, yes and no. They are self-reliant, yet not alone; independent, yet not isolated. The wise individual simply is.

The good life is only possible within certain limits of justice so that all, both human and non-human, can share and enjoy the good things of the earth. While happiness for many has come to mean ownership and consumption and the greatest possible stimulation of the senses, there are simply not enough resources to go round for all to have the kind of consumerist lifestyle endured by a small elite and dreamed of by the majority in the West.

But apart from being unjust, such a life is also unwise. Excess undermines the health and cloys the senses. The endless pursuit of power and wealth leaves one anxious and worried, fearful that one will lose one's position or possessions. A continuous round of sex, drinking and eating only leads to ill health and unease. A continual feast ceases to be a feast.

A moderate life of independence and simplicity close to the earth is most likely to bring a tranquil heart and mind and therefore contentment and joy. If you are independent, you are not concerned about the whims of the powerful or the vagaries of fortune. You are secure and not anxious about the future. If you live a simple life and never feel 'this is mine' and crave for things that are not, then you will never be poor. For those whose palates are not jaded, wholesome food gives as much pleasure as an extravagant diet. The wise will thus live simply within the limits of nature, content with what little they have and knowing when they have had enough. And if you have discovered the riches of independence and simplicity, you will know better how to give than to receive.

Having less materially does not mean a poorer life. A sustainable society in harmony with nature is not puritanically miserly, pinched or retentive. On the contrary, it is generously convivial, life-affirming and imaginative, encouraging art as well as craft, inventiveness as well as efficiency. Its goods would be sumptuously frugal. They would consume few resources and cause minimum harm in their production, but they would be rich in meaning, beauty and use.

It will be up to the people living in their regions to decide their own level of production and consumption, but once the basic minimum is guaranteed for all, there would no doubt be room for some luxuries and occasional excess. Many celebrations and rituals are enhanced because they are lapses from frugality and simple living. It need not be a fatted calf or a thousand larks' tongues (especially if you are vegetarian), but a feast with a few friends or a wild party on the seashore are all the more enjoyable because they are a break in everyday living. Fireworks are resources going up in smoke, but they are a great occasion for a communal celebration and remind us that we too can make stars.

For those who live in destitution and misery, it is absurd to call for frugality. But for those living in affluence, those who have become poor in spirit through excessive wealth, it can be a virtue. Excess in one area of the world is directly related to want in another. Two-thirds of the world is getting poorer while one-third in the remaining third grows richer. Excessive property is indeed a form of theft: what you have and don't need is stolen from those who need it and don't have it. Since everything is interconnected and interdependent in nature's web, by consuming less we release more to satisfy the vital needs of others. Frugality has nothing to do with real poverty; it is part of the joy of living simply in harmony with nature.

But what are vital needs? We all need to satisfy our vital needs in order to survive. Vital needs are those which threaten life when not satisfied; in other words, they are necessities of life. For individuals to survive, they need food, water and shelter. That is clear. For our species to survive, some of us need to reproduce. That is clear. The most natural desires of humans are therefore for food and sex. When they are not met we feel discomfort and when they are we feel satisfied. But if they get out of hand and come to dominate our lives, then we feel discomfort again and lose self-harmony. If we end up craving for them, then suffering follows as surely as a ripe apple falls to the ground.

As potentially reasonable creatures we do not have to respond to the urgings of hunger and sexual desire. We need not be slaves of our passions. A person may choose to be celibate, to fast or even to starve to death. In this case the power of the mind is greater than the power of appetite. If we have the power to override natural desires in this way, why should the artificial, interdependent and complex desires created by modern civilization prove so strong?

Modern civilization has distorted the natural desires of humans and corrupted their minds to such an extent that most people live in a state of permanent frustration and anxiety, swinging violently between the extremes of boredom and fear. All over the world more and more people are being won over to the philosophy that happiness means consumption and ownership. Without flashy possessions, they feel their lives have no meaning and they have no self-worth. People are brainwashed into thinking they need the latest car, washing machine, television or computer and it hurts when they do not have them. Enough is always too little. Artificial desires become wants and wants are experienced as needs. The result is that they live in a state of constant agitation. There is no bait like illusion and no rushing torrent like craving, yet they cannot see through their folly and are caught like salmon leaping for imaginary flies.

The craving for unlimited wealth is the greatest poverty. For most, the acquisition of riches does not put an end to their troubles, but merely changes them. On the other hand, simplicity and independence are the greatest of all riches. Better to be a hungry fox and running wild than a chained mastiff at its master's gate. Better to be free of fear in a small hut than full of anxiety in a grand house. Individuals are free to the degree they can leave their possessions alone.

The greatest enjoyment is to be had from a tranquil heart and mind which are undisturbed by thoughts of wealth and power or fear of the future. A calm temperament makes light of physical pain. Even in the hour of death, in a moment of agony, the mind can enjoy good memories and the delights of love and friendship. Having shaped their own lives, the wise enjoy the present, recall the good things of life, laugh at destiny, and have no fear of death. Death cannot be escaped but it is not worth a worry. If a person considers this world as a bubble of froth on the ocean of being then death has no sting. There is nothing to fear in God or an afterlife. We come into this world without strain, and so we should leave, without resistance. Easy come and easy go!

It is best to live in the here and now, not in a mythical future when all will be well or in the past when things were different. They live badly who are always beginning to live or regret what has been. What we are today comes from our thoughts and actions in the past, and our present thoughts and actions build the dwelling of our life in the future. And they who are content today and least need tomorrow will most gladly go to meet their destinies.

The wise can find joy in this life. They dive down below the surface confusion and go with the deeper flow. They are calm and easy. They meet obstacles without care, hardly knowing that they are there. They are grounded and centred. They hold their being secure and quiet. They are not concerned with success or failure, pleasure or pain, happiness or sorrow. They wake without worries and sleep when they are tired.

They are content with what they have. They do nothing and leave nothing undone. They work without striving. They create without taking credit. They are spontaneous like a new-born babe and supple like a young willow. They value love and friendship but do not seek to possess others and are dependent on no one. They are not afraid of standing alone with their views. They are collected in their own centres and yet form part of the whole. They feel at home anywhere in the universe. They seek no power over others and their steps leave no trace. Their boats are empty as they sail on the ocean of being. They are content with what they have. They are joyful to be alive but meet death calmly. They come and go like the four seasons. And, yes, they ride the wind! Such people amongst mortals are rare, but all of us can become like them.

# 20

# The Alchemy of Love

*When brothers love each other, they will be peaceful and harmonious. When all the people in the world love each other, the strong will not overcome the weak, the many will not oppress the few, the rich will not insult the poor, the honoured will not despise the humble, and the cunning will not deceive the ignorant. Because of universal love, all the calamities, usurpations, hatred, and animosity in the world would be prevented from arising. Therefore the person of humanity praises it.*

Mo Tzu

What is love? Is love an instantaneous falling in love, an overwhelming intuition that the person you have met is the right one for ever? Is love a blending of common interests and characteristics, a harmonious combination of personality traits? Is it a fusion of two individuals who were made for each other, like two pieces of jigsaw? Is it an *égoïsme à deux*, an exclusive union of two individuals for whom the rest of the world no longer exists? Is it a process of transformation in which the soul grows wings and takes flight to a higher reality? Or is it none of these experiences but something deeper and more enduring?

There are many different ways in which people use the word 'love'. Children love sweets, teenage girls love clothes, businessmen love money, artists love beauty, philosophers love wisdom. There is love for parents, for children, for ancestors, for the homeland. When I say 'I love you', I mean something rather different. I say it to one other person and my love takes on an emotional, a physical and a spiritual dimension.

For most of my life I found it difficult to say these three words because I felt that they had become debased from overuse or were used by people to reassure each other while feeling the very opposite of love. An authentic person did not say them, I felt. If love were true, it need not be said; it was simply manifest. But I also know that they have deep meaning and can be said from the bottom of the soul.

Although love is a universal and permanent characteristic of human life, it does have different expressions in different societies and its meaning has changed over the centuries. In the West, love between the sexes has developed according to the evolving attitudes and relationships between men and women. The ancient Greeks, for instance, personified passionate love as Eros, the god of love, but they felt true love could only exist between men. Love between the sexes was largely seen as sexual, appealing to one's lower instincts.

In the Judaeo-Christian tradition, the expression of love has been channelled through monogamous marriage, no doubt because ancient Hebrew society was a patriarchy with a strong sense of private property. Women were seen as the property of men; hence the ten commandments making adultery a deadly sin. In a traditionally chauvinistic society, women are not only the chattels of men but are often depicted as temptresses, under-mining with their sensual attractions the nobler and loftier ideals of men. Was it not Eve who offered Adam the apple from the Tree of Knowledge, bringing about his downfall and introducing sex, work and pain into the Garden of Eden?

By contrast, in the tradition of courtly love, which first developed in Europe during the early Middle Ages, women were put on a pedestal to be adored and revered. As in the myth of Tristan and Iseult, the brave knight worships a fair lady as a symbol of beauty and perfection; she is his ideal and inspiration to noble and refined actions. The travelling troubadours passing from court to court knew what the women of the powerful men wanted to hear, and celebrated their grace and beauty in their ballads and poems. At the same time, women who did not fit neatly into society as wives or whores, women who were masterless and women who developed special powers, were seen as a threat to social stability, that is, to male superiority and rule. Other women consulted them for their wisdom, and some men became their equal companions, but for the most part they were ostracized and persecuted as witches.

240

Although there were voices of dissent, the education of women continued until well into the twentieth century to be geared towards making her attractive to man, a pleasing handmaiden, a brightly coloured singing bird in a gilded cage. Both men and women suffered from this unequal and demeaning relationship. Many women resented being condemned to the domestic sphere, while many men felt overburdened by having to be the sole provider and protector in the wider society. While women's work at home was undervalued, a man without work was considered worthless. Both sexes would therefore benefit from becoming intelligent and imaginative companions, equally at ease at home or in society, partners in sharing life's tasks.

Today in the West it is still widespread to consider women as angels, witches or whores, or a combination of all three. But the most powerful version of love is the one which emerged from the courtly tradition. Romantic love, which is peculiar to the West, creates a vast source of energy. Indeed, it has almost replaced religion as the arena in which men and women seek meaning, wholeness and ecstasy in their lives. To find the intensity of being *in love* has for many, especially for women, become the ultimate aim.

Real love is the union of physical, emotional, intellectual and spiritual aspects of men and women. It is a coming together of the whole person, of body, mind and spirit. Historically, men and women have cultivated different qualities and been associated with different values – the one courageous, active and bold, and the other caring, sympathetic and receptive. Yet these qualities are not innate; both sexes can develop them in equal measure if they so wish. *Yin* and *yang* – 'feminine' and 'masculine' elements – are in us all. Women are not condemned to feel any more than men are condemned to think: both can be rational *and* feeling beings. It is our conditioning and upbringing, not our sexual identity, which make us so. Many men unconsciously search for their lost feminine side in women and many women idealize masculine values in their men, but they can find them in themselves.

Sex as a physical act brings pleasure in the sense of release from pressure and tension. But it can be much more than that; humans are not just steam engines. Sexuality is a source of vitality, an essential element in the harmony of our being. Combined with energy and spirit, it can bring health and long life. In the privacy of sex, everything is permissible if it is uncoerced, unexploitative

241

and based on voluntary consent. Between two loving individuals sex brings the ecstasy of being. It takes one completely out of the everyday and offers a glimpse of eternity, a window on the infinite. Erotic love is not just confined to the genitals but involves the complete union of two individuals who become temporarily one while maintaining their separate selves.

Unfortunately, it is only too common in our society of shifting relationships and great expectations for romantic love to be short-lived. People become infatuated with each other, 'fall in' love with love, and have wild hopes. They project what they most desire on to the loved one. They then 'fall out' of love and if locked in marriage lead a lifetime of antagonism, boredom or quiet despair. Experiencing the heart-breaking disillusion that romantic love invariably brings, they often spend much of the rest of their lives with a deep sense of loneliness, alienation and frustration.

Marriage in the West has proved no bulwark to this disappointment. It was long the custom for a woman to be 'given' in marriage or to give herself in exchange for security and status. A masterless woman was considered worse than a masterless man. She needed to find herself a protector and to avoid the stigma of being an 'old maid' or 'mistress'. She needed to be safely allocated a place in society. At the same time, men were expected to be the providers and protectors and without women were incapable of looking after themselves, let alone children.

Marriage may now no longer be a form of legalized prostitution, where a woman sells herself for security and becomes a permanent servant, but it is still a possessive monopoly. If a couple remain in an unhappy marriage they end up feeling unfulfilled, unloved and unlovable; if they divorce, they feel they have failed and are often condemned to loneliness. The children usually suffer either way, if their parents stay together or if they part, because of the prevailing pressures to conform to the norm of marriage.

At present, many relations between men and women seem to turn on the master–slave relationship and degenerate into a form of masochism or sadism. The cause seems to be the almost universal desire to possess the loved one, a desire which is only part of the wider possessive individualism fostered by Western society. This leads to a fundamental contradiction at the heart of modern love.

242

I can only love someone freely, yet my love also wants to possess the person I love, to bind her to me. I want to think, 'She is mine'. At the same time, she can only love me freely, yet she too wants to enslave me to her. The more she wants to possess and enslave me, the less I am free to love her. The greater the desire for possession, the greater the feeling of jealousy when her attention is directed towards someone else. If this type of possessive love continues, it is doomed to fail. The desire to possess usually comes from a sense of insecurity, a fear of betrayal, a lack of confidence. It is also linked to an egoistic desire to get as much as possible from a relationship – what is good for me. In this way, love becomes a distorted form of self-love.

Although jealousy is a very strong and understandable passion, it is nearly always negative. It comes from a desire to possess, to turn the beloved into a property of one's own. It usually has the opposite effect to the one intended, only alienating the person it seeks to hold. Jealousy sows the seeds of hatred and revenge. In the long run, jealousy poisons and kills love.

In possessive love, the beloved becomes an object to own; it becomes an 'I–it' relation. I treat the other as an object, an object which I command, control, manipulate. I am free and she is possessed. I am master, she is slave. If she acquiesces, she becomes a masochist; if I continue, I become a sadist. I try to turn her into a stone, without her own volition, to play with as I wish. It is no way to be, whether in the field, factory, office, home or bed. If the beloved accepts this kind of situation, and is submissive, obedient and sacrificing, she enters an 'it–thou' relation. She turns herself into an object for her man. If the relationship is purely sexual and is based on the coming together of two bodies as objects, it degenerates into an 'it–it' relation.

If love is to succeed, it should not seek to possess the other: I can only love freely and you can only love freely. Freedom is therefore the basis of all true love. For that reason, it does not need the chains of law or the sanction of social approval to protect it. A lasting relationship needs to be based on trust and not law, on a voluntary union, not a binding contract of marriage.

There is a difference between free love and loving freely, just as there is between freedom and licence. To be genuinely free involves responsibility for the consequences of one's actions. To follow any whim or passing desire is to be a slave of one's passions; it is a frittering away of one's freedom. The licentious person, who flits from one relationship to another like a butterfly, is not necessarily free. Ideally, free love means loving freely, although the uplifting notion of 'free love' has become debased to mean promiscuity or serial relationships. Genuine free love is as free as the wind, but it is also responsible and involves trust and commitment. For love to develop between two individuals on many different levels it needs to be deep and long and lasting.

The art of loving cannot be taken for granted. It requires care, respect, responsibility and trust. Like any art, it needs concentration, patience and skill. It is something to nurture if it is to grow, in the same way that a plant needs good soil, fresh water and sunlight to blossom. For love to stretch and grow, it needs to be like a tree with its roots firmly in the ground as its branches reach for the heavens.

Love involves growing in awareness, listening, and being listened to, touching and being touched. It involves an open heart and an engaged mind. It is non-judgemental, providing a sheltered space for a person to be truly him or herself. It helps lovers realize their best and reach their full stature.

Although love is a union, it is not a complete fusion. There should be space in the togetherness, space to be oneself and space to grow independently. Love is a power within us – a power of the soul – which affirms and values and celebrates the beloved as she or he is, not as some ideal or projection of what we would like them to be. It means being clear and sensitive about his or her needs. It values the other person as an individual self who has the potential of becoming a complete and independent person. It is giving not taking; it is accepting not judging. In the sacred space of love, there is no fear of insecurity, no dependence but a trusting and creative opening.

True love develops into an 'I–thou' relation. It does not seek to have, but allows to be. It is a caring space for two individuals to be themselves together. It recognizes the beloved as a developing, growing, opening self. The ash cannot grow in the shade of an oak, so neither one dominates nor overshadows the other. Each person remains a person in the sunlight of love. But together they form a greater whole, like the branches of two trees forming an arch over the river of life.

Loving offers shelter and accepts. If I say, 'You should not do that' or, 'Don't be so silly', I begin to judge. If I judge, I begin to see the other person as an object with certain traits, as an 'it'. I may feel pleased that she shares my values and ideas, and disappointed that she does not, but these feelings should not harden into approval or disapproval. A person is always an evolving, unique self, and to judge her for what she is at any given moment is to deny her potential and her openness to creative change. To be with a loved one is to experience the deep relaxation of being oneself and the trust and security of mutual acceptance.

True love has no desire to possess the other. Neither dominating nor submitting, each person nourishes the freedom of the other to be him or herself. Avoiding dependence, each person stands whole, enhanced but not completed by the other. What emerges is a trust that no marriage contract can create, a trust which lays down no conditions. It brings about a greater intimacy which is sensitive to each other's needs and desires, and open to each other's evolving being.

Love is not one person fleeing into the arms of another, but a mutual unfurling of individuality. It involves the paradox of two people becoming one yet remaining two. It is better to stand alone complete than to feel only complete with another. The loved one comes and goes but your self will always remain. The death of your beloved does not mean your death. No one can die your death for you. Coming together and forming a larger whole, you can still feel complete on your own. There is no need to feel lonely in solitude, or homeless when apart. Although they make music together, the strings of the guitar are separate and drums are beaten by different hands.

Love, especially romantic love, can often appear like madness. It can often start like a *coup de foudre*, as if you are hit by lightning, and excite a storm of emotion in which all rational self-control is lost. You are overwhelmed by a flood of longing. All normal concerns slip away, work is neglected, other relationships forgotten. It is like being on a horse which has bolted and which careers headlong down a steep track, not knowing what is around the corner. And then you are unseated, falling out of love and out of the saddle, and falling into the mire.

On the other hand, love can be a divine madness, a gift from heaven, which inspires the greatest works of art and action. When this happens, your relationship grows in harmony and joy. Your souls grow wings which enable you to ride the wind, and go where you will with ease.

Love does not say, 'What can I get from the relationship' or, 'How can I satisfy my needs, my dreams, my desires?' It wishes the other person to live fully and find joy in life. By its very nature, it is the opposite of egoism. It encourages giving rather than taking. It means taking responsibility for your actions and not blaming others. It sees the sacred in the midst of the humble and everyday, baking bread, making love, sowing seeds, walking in the woods, sharing a bath. It is hearing the breath of the universe in the steady breathing of the person asleep next to you. It is warming your hands by the fire of her self. It is not swinging wildly from falling in love or out of love, from adoration to disillusionment, but involves a steady, warm, growing affection. It is an art which can improve with age and has different joys in different seasons. This is the condition of 'standing in love', or better still of 'dwelling in love'.

Friendship can melt into love, and love can melt into friendship. All true lovers are friends, although not all friends are lovers. Friendship is a sheltering tree in a sacred space: it provides rest and shelter on the journey of life and gives you energy and enlightenment. Friendship, like love, accepts and does not judge. It understands and forgives. You may know your friend's weaknesses, but you do not have to find fault constantly.

At the same time, while friendship accepts it does not always condone, and to help your friend to realize his best you may sometimes be a hard rather than a soft bed for him. It is better to be a spark which lights the lantern of change, than a prop which keeps him in one place. Although it is always good to offer a helping hand to enable your friend to reach higher ground, it is not wise to have him always climb behind you. A good friend does not always lead or follow but walks at your side.

As with a rose, love has it thorns and can hurt. But that is no reason for failing to appreciate its beauty. It is better to risk pain for the joy of love than to hold back out of fear of being hurt. It is better to experience the tears of tenderness than the cold sneer of indifference. The exuberance of the coming together of two mountain streams is preferable to the stagnant stillness of an isolated pool. The creative fire of love is better than the cool darkness of holding back.

Love transforms individuals and the world around them. Something deep and subterranean takes places in the psyche of lovers. It is like a branch which after being left in a dark cavern

246

for a while emerges covered with glittering crystals, flashing in the iridescent rays of the sun.

Love is a phoenix rising from the ashes of despair. In the alchemy of love, *sol* (sun) and *luna* (moon) come together in an alchemical wedding: leaden life is transformed into a golden state. Not only does the man link up with the woman, but the woman's energy suffuses through the man's body. The complementary forces unite in bliss as we go beyond separation to become part of the whole.

Sexual craving is undoubtedly a problem, whether we try to repress it or seek satisfaction for it. But sexual desire is not like the desire for possession, wealth or fame. If we are not addicted to it, it can expand the mind and bring lasting joy and wholeness. The sacred temple of the body is organized spirit, and sexuality is an expression of spiritual energy. It can be a way of transforming ourselves in the here and now, a way of going beyond duality to experience reality as a whole. It can express the essential clarity of our deepest being. If skilfully woven, it can lead to increased vitality, health and long life. It can bring about feelings of serenity, buoyancy and compassion. It can make you feel calm, centred and free. Above all, it can give a sense of intense aliveness, a deep love for life in all its myriad forms.

As in life, the journey in love-making is more important than the arrival. There comes a stage, when you are deeply relaxed in the expanding space of your being, that you are no longer making love, but love is making you. You are no longer confined to two bodies, but in touch with the essence of things, the Being of beings. And the experience is bliss and lingers on long after you have become your own separate selves again. It goes beyond mere satisfaction to fulfilment. It is a glimpse of eternity.

In our present society, it is often difficult to nurture a loving relationship. With the emancipation of women, the roles of men and women have become more confused. It is not always easy to decide who should go out to work and who should look after the household and care for the children, if there are any. The pressures of status take their toll, with more women competing with men for fewer jobs. Many have unreasonable expectations of their partners and do not give them space to be themselves and grow. Yet for all these difficulties in a changing world, people do achieve deep, lasting and fulfilling relationships.

True love is infinite; it can embrace the world. Although we love particular individuals as lovers, friends and family, it need not stop there. If I love you, I love the whole world in you. Love can go beyond the distinction between friend and stranger, and even between friend and enemy, to appreciate every being as of equal intrinsic value. Love is not a limited quantity, like perfume in a bottle. It is an activity, the highest activity of the soul. The more we love, the more love there is to give. Love grows on love. Ultimately, all we need is love. And the greatest love is unconditional love, love which expects nothing in return.

There are of course many different types of love – love for a mother, father, brother, sister, son, daughter and friend. Brotherly and sisterly love is the most fundamental; it is love among equals and is the basis of a good society. The principle, 'Love they neighbour as thyself' extends love for the family to love for friends, and beyond. Motherly and fatherly love is between unequals, is unconditional love for children and seeks to unfurl their best potential. While being protective and offering shelter, to be effective it must allow the young to grow up and to grow away, to become separate loving individuals. But whatever their nature, the more loving relations we have, the more we thrive.

Tragically, while most people in the West are worn out searching for romantic love, loving relations grow less. Our society has reduced love primarily to a relationship between a couple, and if children are involved, to a nuclear family. While this might be good for those who provide profitable services and goods, it is not good for those involved. The traditional extended family living in one neighbourhood, in which many different loving relationships are possible between young and old, is largely a thing of the past. Even the nuclear family is breaking down, and an increasing number of children are growing up moving between the households of their separated parents or growing up with only one of them. And more and more people are living alone.

The family is dying in the West as society is being turned into a lonely crowd. It need not be like this. The family may now be the last bulwark against a disintegrating society, but in a free and sustainable society it might be only one of many different convivial social forms. In a renewed community of caring neighbours, there could be families of close-knit relations based not only on the blood tie but on common affections and aspirations. Affinity groups of many different kinds would spring up in which loving individuals could live together as long as they wanted, without fear of loneliness and insecurity.

Children would be able to grow up in stable homes, although the home itself could be made up of a single parent, a couple, an extended family, or a larger affinity group. Even the stable home does not have to be in one place, as nomads know. It is good for children to grow up with two loving parents close by, but the most important thing is a loving and secure space which they can use as a springboard to their future life.

People say 'my' children, but no one strictly speaking can own children any more than they can own the sea or the sky. Although they might live with you, children do not belong to you. You are their protectors and guides when they are young but not their owners. You can help their bodies grow strong, supple and straight, but they do the growing. You can help them to think and imagine, but it is not good to impose your thoughts and images for they have their own. You can help them question authority, including your own authority, for they are free spirits as they set off on the varied paths of life and must find their own way to the mountain top.

Perhaps the greatest challenge for parents is to overcome their possessive love of their children. With children, there is a time for nurturing and a time for letting go, a time for giving guidance and a time to retire. You guide them so that they can become guides themselves. A good parent is like a lighthouse, pointing out the rocks and shallows of life, but allowing children to sail their own boats in their own way on the ocean of Being.

When all is said and done, the call of liberation ecology for universal friendliness, compassion for all beings, and Reverence for Being may be summed up by the word 'love'. Love is the most fundamental passion. It holds society and the world together. Relationships based on love are concerned about the well-being of others. Work based on love fulfils the whole personality and leads to a form of voluntary communism based on the gift relation. A morality of love has affection for all. A metaphysics of love leads to communion with and concern for the whole cosmos.

Ultimately, liberation ecology is an ecology of love which recognizes the interwoven nature of all beings and the universal need to care for each other. Love drives the green fuse and makes the planets go round. Love is complete liberation. If you love, it requires no laws or rules; if you love, there is no analysis or calculation. If you love, you act spontaneously well. Love gives nothing but itself and expects nothing in return. Love does not seek to possess nor to be possessed. Love is of itself and for itself. Living simply, loving freely, the world is full of hope and joy. Love, and do what you will!

# 21

# Riding the Wind

*Riding the wind is singing a deep song.*
*Riding the wind is being like a new-born babe.*
*Riding the wind is the exhilaration of the moment.*
*Riding the wind is returning to the uncarved block.*
*Riding the wind is going with the flow of the natural.*
*Riding the wind is being the stream of the universe.*
*Riding the wind is touching the primordial.*
*Riding the wind is settling in the Tao.*
*Riding the wind is riding the wind.*

As the third millennium dawns, we are at a fork in our evolution and history. We can continue as we have done for the last 300 years and seek fulfilment in material goods and coercive power, applying naked reason to achieve our narrow ends, travelling down the path of grasping and craving, to the cave of melancholy. Alternatively, we can branch out to take the broader, sunnier path of deep feeling and high thinking, uniting mind, body and spirit as we walk along, in rhythm with each other and the rest of nature. We can work with or against the grain, go with the deeper flow or swim against it. We can continue in our artificial life or settle into a more natural way. We can remain lords of creation or become lovers of being.

In this work, I have sought to establish fundamental principles rather than consider their specific application, outlining an organic philosophy of nature as the basis of our moral and social actions. I have challenged the dominant mechanical and materialist world view and developed a new holistic and life-affirming philosophy for a new era. I have presented a vision of a free and sustainable society in harmony with nature. But how do we get from here to there, from things as they are to things as they might be? How do we awaken from our present slumber as our ship steams towards the iceberg?

Whatever the strategies for change one thing is certain: means are ends-in-the-making. You cannot use destructive and violent means to achieve creative and peaceful ends. Fighting for peace is like trying to hew a passage through a river; it cannot be done. In order to bring about a free and sustainable society, we must use ecological and libertarian means. You cannot end authority with authority, coercive power with coercive power. Violence breeds violence and those who live by the sword die by the sword. The only way to enlighten and awaken people is through persuasion, whether by careful reasoning, sudden illumination or inspiring example.

The best way to overcome the hard is by yielding. Water wears away the hardest stone. In a storm, it is the supple willow, not the rigid oak, which survives. The strong and mighty fall from a great height while the soft and yielding rise above them all. It takes courage to know when to yield and when to withdraw. But it is effective. A man is born gentle and weak; at his death he is hard and stiff. The stiff and unbending are the disciples of death. The supple and yielding are the creators of life.

If we are to survive and live well in the new millennium, there needs to be a radical shift in consciousness and a thorough overhaul of our social arrangements. Without changing the fundamental premises of Western civilization in this way we are just changing the seating on the *Titanic*. It is our good fortune, and the good fortune of the planet, that the necessary changes are already under way. Everywhere fresh shoots are pushing through the cracking concrete slabs of mechanical thinking. New light is shining through the darkness of materialism. People are awakening from the fitful sleep of consumerism. Life is beginning to stretch its wings. A new consciousness, a new awareness, a new sen-sibility, and a new spirituality are emerging.

This sea-change is well under way as the old mechanical and reductionist paradigm in science, philosophy and religion crumbles. The new consciousness is based on relationship rather than analysis, sees the whole rather than the parts, is earth-centred rather than man-centred, and is concerned with the general well-being rather than private interest. This emerging world-view sees humans as whole beings made of mind, body and spirit, the human species as part of a wider community of life, and the earth as a living organism. It knows that the universe is a caring and reassuring place; that in solitude, there is no need to feel lonely; and that the wilderness is our home.

This growing understanding is only a recent phenomenon. In the late 1960s, when I was a young man, the main concern was with aggressive war abroad and inequality and injustice at home. These issues combined to make me increasingly aware of the unjust and unequal relationships between nations, especially between the North and the South. I travelled to Tanzania and Cuba to witness at first hand the social experiments to build an independent and just society in the developing world. But the principal aim was still the conquest of bread through the conquest of nature; there was little awareness of the wider ecological context. All that has changed. My children still live in an unequal and unjust world, but they and their friends have a vivid notion of the earth as a fragile and finite planet spinning in space. They are aware of what we are doing to the earth. They know Gaia is suffering. My social conscience has become their cosmic consciousness.

Many people feel overwhelmed by the thought of the looming ecological crisis. Many feel powerless in the face of the megamachine of capital and state. Many feel anxious about the present and fearful of the future. Many are paralysed. But there is no reason to be. If you *feel* you can change things, you already have. If you take a few small steps to change your life, you soon find that you already are striding out. Every long journey has to begin somewhere and it begins with the first step. Every adversity is a challenge, and every difficulty an opportunity to grow. You cannot climb a mountain cliff without rough places on the smooth rock to pull yourself up. A wise person always confronts difficulties and therefore never experiences them as insuperable.

It has been a long complaint that philosophers only interpret the world, while the point is to change it. But by changing our consciousness, we change our being in the world, for our being and consciousness are inextricably connected. To interpret the world *is* to change it. Thought is act and feeling is conduct. If our heart changes, it changes our whole body. If chaos theory is right and everything is connected, the flap of a butterfly's wings in Japan can affect the weather in New York. If quantum mechanics is right, every change in the field of energy affects that field. If the

253

doctrine of karma is right, and every action has a consequence, then every thought or feeling will have a result. If the idea of morphic resonance is true, then a flock of birds, a migrating herd of deer, and a group of human beings can experience sudden change in the collective field of consciousness and energy instantaneously. A person therefore meditating in a cave may well affect the world. If I silently wish something to happen, then in some way I help to bring it about. Hence the power of prayer and meditation.

But what is to be done and where to begin? There are many things to be done, from developing new ideas and values, creating new lifestyles, regenerating our communities, transforming our relationships to liberating society from the state. Now is the time for the re-enchantment of everyday life, the re-enchantment of humanity and the re-enchantment of the planet, recognizing that they are all interwoven in nature's wondrous web.

The important thing is *praxis*, that we practise what we preach and that we begin here and now. There is no point nostalgically looking to the past for a mythical golden age, or dreaming of some future Utopia, although both can inspire our imagination. We can begin here and now, with ourselves, our neighbourhood, our district, our region, our nation, our planet, in ever widening circles so that the rings join up to create a network of thoughts, feelings and actions which will inaugurate the new era. By thinking and feeling differently, by forming fresh relationships, by acting anew, we are already making it real. By creating a new society within the shell of the old, when it collapses new life will be there, already in place, already prepared, stretching its wings. In the alchemy of change, when the moment of coagulation is reached, the transformation will take place of itself.

Every slight change towards a freer and more sustainable society is going in the right direction. The thoughts, feelings and actions of individuals, groups and movements committed to these ends all make their contribution. But certain ways are more effective than others, and some well-intentioned means can be counter-productive. There are many paths on the side of a mountain, but they do not necessarily all reach the summit: some may take you downhill, others may lead you into an impasse. Having reached the summit, you might realize, as in the Alps, that it is only one of many higher peaks which stretch out before you. But whatever path you take, it is important to remember that the journey is more important than the arrival, and how you travel will intimately affect what you discover and attain.

What is clear is that as a strategy for radical change, representative government is an impasse. A change of government, with a slightly more benign face, changes little. All existing governments in the West are wedded to economic growth, full paid employment, hard technologies, armed forces, and the centralized state. There is no parliamentary road to a genuinely free and sustainable society. If voting for a government really changed anything, it would be made illegal. The problem is not the *choice* of government, but the *principle* of government itself. To try and bring about real change through the passing of laws is trying to get a hornet to fly away with a mountain. It is largely the fault of government in all its forms that the conditions of life grow worse, that the trees crash down in the forest, that poison spreads across the land, that animals cry out in pain, that the springs become more silent.

All of us can change the economic and social conditions of society as well as our consciousness, the nature of work as well as the spirit of life. No particular group is central to bring about change, no one class has a world-historic mission. We have had enough of leaders and vanguards who claim to know the right direction but only lead us into bogs and thickets.

In the past, different groups have expanded human freedom. The so-called peasantry, working class, and middle-class reformers have all tried in their separate ways to pick up the baton of freedom. But the agents of change in the new millennium are most likely to come from those on the margins of economic life, whether by choice or necessity. They are the ones who have the least to lose and the most to gain – women, ethnic minorities, the unemployed, the drop-outs, the young, the old, the imaginative and the wise. They are united more by cultural affinity than economic ties, more by a wish to develop a new relationship with each other and the earth than to get a larger cut of the rapidly disappearing cake.

Even some of the wealthy and privileged are beginning to have their doubts. Those trundling on the gravy train are increasingly finding it a thick sauce to swallow. Individuals who have experienced material comfort know that its pleasures soon wane. The more one consumes, the weaker the pleasure and the worse the after-effects. Even for the elite, the quality of life is becoming more important than the size of their bank balance. A growing number realize that the more possessions they have, the more they want, and the more anxious they are about losing them. In the long run, a materialistic way of life does not bring deep contentment or a tranquil mind; on the contrary, it makes people frustrated, agitated, anxious and unfulfilled. A person is free to the extent that he or she is not attached to possessions.

It is not one class in existing society which suffers, but all. No one class will bring about the necessary changes, but sections from all of them. Until recently, most people were concerned with family and work and the problems and struggles of everyday living. Few were concerned about the fate of the nation and even less about the fate of the earth. But the growing awareness of the looming ecological crisis is changing all that. The desire to save the world now transcends class, sex and race and involves the whole of humanity.

Certainly there is a struggle between rich and poor, capital and labour, North and South, but the old exclusive categories no longer apply. We are now living in a radically different situation and it is in the interests of all to create a free and sustainable society in the new millennium. It will only happen when enough people want it. Rulers disappear when people refuse to be ruled. Nature will begin to breathe freely again when the human species decides to get off its back. A free society will only emerge if enough people want to be free.

Although the parliamentary road is a road to nowhere and no one group has a special mission, there is plenty that one can do to bring about change. Each individual counts. Every thought, feeling and action has a ripple effect which reverberates throughout the world. The personal is the social.

If you are concerned with the Earth Household and how to live well within it, then it makes sense to begin with your self and to put your own dwelling in order. If you want to create a free society without hierarchy and domination, then it is not a good idea to dominate others. If you seek an enlightened form of anarchy – the absence of rule – then you should refuse to become a patriarch or a matriarch. By changing our relationships with each other, we begin to change society. By loving and giving, we create a society of love and abundance.

If we want a sustainable society, we can live more simply, use the minimum of resources and energy, recycle waste, keep a

256

compost bucket, and turn off the light in an empty room. If we want a compassionate society, we can reduce our consumption of meat, look after our neighbours, and pick the spider out of the bath. If we want a healthier life, we can eat whole food and walk to the local shops. If we want an equal society, we can share voluntarily the household tasks, clean the toilet, cook the evening meal and look after the children. If we want a more balanced ecology, we can develop organic gardens and welcome in the wildlife, whether snails or birds, aphids or bees. If we want to cause minimum harm to the planet, we can reduce our consumption as well as buy environmentally-friendly goods.

Changing one's lifestyle is a first step, but it is also important to link up with others to revitalize the community in order to shape a convivial and caring society. Since the state is a condition as well as a set of institutions, by forming new relationships based on solidarity, sharing and self-reliance, we make its rule superfluous. By developing new ways of living for ourselves, we make it obsolete.

Beginning with our family, friends and neighbours, we can extend our web of relationships to form affinity groups, voluntary associations, clubs and unions based on common interests and values. We can create communal households, whether in city flats or village dwellings, which share resources and bring out the best in each other. We can set up rural communities which live lightly on the earth outside the modern, technological and centralized state and which can become sources of inspiration. We can create temporary autonomous zones in which to celebrate companionship, freedom and creativity.

This is not all. We can opt out of the mainstream and with a quiet dignity refuse to drive in the fast lane of success and failure, fashions and fads. We can form new families and allegiances in loose tribes. We can join schemes which exchange skills through a local currency, thereby bypassing the formal economy based on profit and interest. We can try and make existing schools more amenable to our children's individual needs or help set up alternative schools which develop their minds and imaginations rather than prepare them to become cogs in the 'workforce'. We can do things for ourselves.

In the wider social sphere, we can work in the trade union movement increasing self-management, participation and control. We can become part of the co-operative movement, whether in production or distribution. We can participate in local affairs, challenging the emergence of hierarchy and domination and questioning the antics of would-be leaders. We can seek to make democracy as direct and participatory as possible.

There is a whole range of activities, movements and campaigns which have emerged which challenge the status quo, question centralized authority, and try to create a peaceful, just and sharing society. All such activities which celebrate life, mutual aid, communal responsibility and voluntary work are positive. Every action counts just as every drop contributes to a tidal wave.

The old dream of the post-industrial future was one of continuous growth, high technology, expanding services, greater leisure and material comfort. It is not only impossible in the long run because of the biophysical limits of the planet, but the dream increasingly appears like a nightmare. The new vision of liberation ecology offers on the other hand a materially simpler but a socially and spiritually richer life. It offers a life with meaning and purpose, with a real sense of belonging to a vital community, with a harmonious and joyful relationship with the earth. The vision is both humbling and uplifting. It rejects the idea that humans are the measure of all things and sees humanity as only one species among others in the odyssey of evolution. Above all, it proposes a new and caring relationship with the rest of nature, rediscovers our rootedness in the earth, and presents the genuine possibility of creating a free and sustainable society.

The new vision of liberation ecology is radically libertarian. It celebrates the happy connection and the inspiring convergence between the spontaneous order of nature and the freedom of a sustainable society. All life forms are interdependent in nature's web. No one organism is superior to another: soil bacteria are as important as mammals to the health of an ecosystem. Indeed, the more diverse the life forms, the greater the overall stability and vitality. Modern ecology not only depicts nature as self-organizing but confirms the ancient view of the Taoists that whatever is contrary to nature will not last long.

We do not have to follow nature. In some cases, such as in the humane treatment of animals, we might act differently from other species. But if we want to live long and well it makes sense to work with nature rather than against it, and to organize society so that it reflects the creative and spontaneous order of nature.

Nature thus not only offers lessons for us if we want to learn them, but provides a rich ground for our moral values and social actions.

Nature is fundamentally libertarian. It lets things be and lets beings grow. To be natural is to be tolerant. The wild *is* free. Translated into social terms, this implies the values of freedom and toleration. A sustainable and ecological society would therefore be a tolerant and free society. To follow nature's example is to allow human species and other species to unfold in their own ways and to realize their full potential within the grand adventure of evolution.

There are many prophecies, from the Mayan to the Hopi, the Book of Revelation to Nostradamus, which warn that we are entering a very difficult period. If we do not cause a global disaster ourselves, through nuclear war or ecological folly, then a natural catastrophe such as a shift in the earth's crust or a collision of giant asteroids might finish us off. This has happened before and could happen again.

These prophets of gloom might well be too hasty. They offer trends and possibilities, not certainties. We can avoid disaster. It is not too late to create a future in harmony with each other and the earth. New ideas and values are springing up everywhere, and often in the most unexpected places. They were always there, like seeds beneath the snow, but now the thaw is rapidly setting in. There may be some cracking of ice, some floods of anger, some storms of reaction, but the seeds have already taken root. After a long period of winter darkness, spring is returning with new light, growth and song. It is the time of a new dawn and a new beginning.

It is up to us whether we want to help or hinder this new growth. We could carry on as we did in the last millennium, despoiling the land, polluting the water, fouling the air, releasing the dragon from the heart of matter. Or we can try a new, largely untried way, drawing on ancient wisdom and modern insights, learning from the ways of people still close to the earth and the heavens. We can continue to slumber in the darkness, or we can awaken to the new dawn and learn to live lightly and well and in harmony with Gaia.

More and more people are beginning to realize that they are not like stones, limited by their conditioning and fixed in their situation until moved by an external force. They are realizing that a free and sustainable society is not a fantasy and that their actions, thoughts and feelings can bring it about in a new world in the new millennium.

How we act in the present creates the future just as our past actions created the present. Finding ourselves in a particular situation, if we accept our responsibility for it, we can take up our past and begin to shape our future. In a sense the future comes before the present, since it is a vision of what might be which motivates us in the here and now. If we wish to bring about future well-being, it is therefore essential to act well now.

If we can liberate the self from craving and grasping, from coercing and causing harm, all will be well. If we can liberate society from hierarchy and domination, from government and the state, all will be well. If we can liberate nature from the burden of humanity and society, limiting our numbers, minimizing waste, and dwelling lightly on the earth, all will be well.

Therefore the wise and skilful dwell on what is real and dive below the surface turmoil to deeper and calmer waters. They abandon all pretence at ruling like an old shoe. They live in harmony with nature. They know the strength of man, but keep a woman's care. Becoming supple and creative like a child once more, they live long and well. They settle quietly in the stream of the universe. In this way, all things are at peace again.

We are in nature and nature is in us. We are nature becoming conscious of itself. We experience nature and nature experiences us. If we damage the web of life, we damage ourselves. We should have the courage to trust in nature. Although we have on occasion harmed nature, the whole of creation, including humanity, is fundamentally good.

Nature pursues its own beneficent course, when least interfered with. It knows best how to manage itself: it is self-regulating, self-organizing and self-sustaining. It is of itself. A tree does not have to be told how to grow any more than a lion to hunt or a mouse to hide. The more we humans intervene in the natural process, the more trouble there is. We have learned how to control, manipulate and conquer. Now is the time for letting go. Let the Tao be!

By being receptive and open, the ancient Taoists in China observed the Way of Nature and became very wise. By observing the flight of birds and the currents of the wind, they were the first to invent kites. In their sacred mountain retreats, in their high and windy dwellings, some went even further. They invented manned kite flying, the first hang gliders, and flew to the region known as the Purest of Empty Space. Minds focused and bodies relaxed, they did not notice where they ended and the surrounding air began. They were borne this way and that on the wind, like dry chaff or leaves falling from a tree. They did not know whether they were riding the wind or the wind was riding them!

Riding the wind is a symbol for the state of self-harmony in which mind and body, the internal and external, subject and object, are blended into unity. Following the way of nature, settling into the stream, it gives the experience of absolute freedom.

Riding the wind is like walking on air. It is a state of heightened perception and keen responsiveness and gives an intense feeling of being alive. The ability comes to the enlightened and awakened, to those who have found their rightful place in the scheme of things, who are centred, who welcome change, who sleep without dreams and wake without worry, who no longer discriminate between right and wrong, who do not cling to life or are fearful of death.

For me, sailing on the sea is the closest I have experienced to riding the wind. The sails of a yacht operate in the same way as the wings of a bird. Riding the wind in this way offers an ecological parable for living well and lightly on the earth. By understanding the way of nature, we can temporarily channel its energy to achieve our ends. We can go with and not against the tides and currents and winds. We can cause minimum harm and leave nothing in our wake.

We are living in dangerous times. The winds of change are beginning to blow and the waves are picking up. White horses of the Apocalypse are galloping across the sea. But if we keep a steady hand on the helm of ourselves, follow the compass of our inner voice, we will ride the wind and arrive in the land of our dreams. If we falter, we will be shipwrecked on the rocks of ignorance and the reefs of history.

It is a time of danger and opportunity. In every difficulty, there are seeds of growth; in every adversity, a challenge. We are now deep in a period of ecological and social crisis and the very survival of our life on earth is at stake. We can choose to create or destroy. We can sink or swim. We can stumble or fly. The choice is ours.

It is not too late. There is nothing to prevent us from developing a new philosophy for a new era. We can create a new society in harmony with each other and the earth. We can, above all, learn how to ride the wind of the new millennium and to sail well together on the vast ocean of being – exhilarated, joyful and free!